Remarkable People!

Ready-to-Use Biography Activities for Grades 4–8

Marguerite Lewis
Pamela J. Kudla

**THE CENTER FOR APPLIED
RESEARCH IN EDUCATION**
West Nyack, New York 10995

© 1991

THE CENTER FOR APPLIED
RESEARCH IN EDUCATION
West Nyack, N.Y.

10 9 8 7 6 5 4 3 2 1

Library of Congress Cataloging-in-Publication Data

Lewis, Marguerite
    Remarkable people! : ready-to-use biography activities for grades
4-8 / Marguerite Lewis, Pamela J. Kudla.
        p.   cm.
    Includes index.
    ISBN 0-87628-792-5
    1. Biography—Juvenile literature. 2. United States—Biogra-
phy—
    Juvenile literature. 3. Elementary school libraries—Activity
    programs. I. Kudla, Pamela J. II. Title.
    CT104.L36 1991
    920.076—dc20   90-25770
                                                        CIP

ISBN 0-87628-792-5

**THE CENTER FOR APPLIED
RESEARCH IN EDUCATION**
BUSINESS & PROFESSIONAL DIVISION
A division of Simon & Schuster
West Nyack, New York 10995

Printed in the United States of America

About the Author and Illustrator

MARGUERITE LEWIS was a library media specialist in the Bethlehem Central School District, Delmar, New York, for twenty years. She received her Bachelor of Science degree from Boston University and her master's in educational communication from the State University of New York at Albany. Mrs. Lewis has published articles, stories, puzzles, and activities in professional and children's magazines. She teamed up with Pamela J. Kudla to write *Hooked on Research! Ready-to-Use Projects and Crosswords for Practice in Basic Library Skills* (1984), *Hooked on Reading! 114 Wordsearch and Crossword Puzzles Based on the Newbery and Caldecott Award Winners* (1986), *Hooked on Library Skills! A Sequential Activities Program for Grades K-6* (1988), and *Hooked on Independent Study! A Programmed Approach to Library Skills for Grades 3-8* (1990), all published by The Center for Applied Research in Education, Inc. Mrs. Lewis is currently working on freelance projects.

PAMELA J. KUDLA received her bachelor's degree in graphic design from Rochester Institute of Technology, Rochester, New York. She was a design consultant for *New York Alive* magazine, as well as assistant art director for Communication and Design, Latham, New York, and an art director for B. Sterling Benkhart, Ltd., Newport, Rhode Island. Mrs. Kudla is currently pursuing a master's degree in art education.

Dedicated to my mother, Marguerite I. Bickerstaffe, who, had she been given the opportunity, could very well have become a fine writer.

Marguerite Lewis

About This Book

Biography can inspire us not only by adulation, but also by realism. It helps us to see not only the qualities in others that we hope to emulate, but also the weaknesses that made them "human." By helping us to identify with the subject on a more personal level, they help us to feel that we, too, can achieve such goals.

Matina Horner
Former President of Radcliffe College

All significant ideas and events are born out of the dreams, ideals, goals, and desires of *people*. REMARKABLE PEOPLE! is designed to introduce your students to over one hundred inspirational individuals who have in some way shaped and changed our world. Reading, writing, research, and critical-thinking skills will be reinforced as your students complete the over two-hundred activities and worksheets in this resource.

The content areas come alive as your students are given the opportunity to discover and experience the disappointments, heartaches, dilemmas, and joys of a broad range of interesting and important people. For your convenience, REMARKABLE PEOPLE! is divided into five content-related sections:

- U.S. Leaders
- Literature and the Arts
- Science and Discovery
- Sports
- World Leaders

Provided for each person covered within these sections you will find:

- a short biography, including a few unusual facts and tidbits of information
- a bibliography of books for further reading to encourage students who take a special interest in a particular person to read more about that person
- suggested activities, with an emphasis on research skills, that can be used with individual students, small groups, or the whole class
- a reproducible student worksheet

REMARKABLE PEOPLE! is indexed alphabetically to assist you with curriculum development and lesson planning.

The reading selections and activities provided in this resource may be used in a variety of ways and for many purposes, including:

- as a springboard to whole-language learning
- as a social studies extender to give students a deeper understanding of and connection with the people who have shaped particular events and times in history
- as an introduction to the genre of biography and as an alternative to fiction
- to provide role models of people who have risen above adversity to achieve their goals
- to encourage students who may have similar cultural or ethnic backgrounds, talents, abilities, problems, or interests

I carefully selected the people included in this book based on the following criteria:

1. Are books about the person readily available?
2. Would the person be of interest to students in grades 4–8?
3. Will knowledge of the person help students in their everyday lives and in their quest for knowledge?
4. Is the person generally considered to have had a positive effect on society?
5. Is the person a suitable role model?

Knowledge of what, how, when, and where is not complete without the *who*. I hope this resource will be helpful to you as you try to interest, educate, and inspire your students with the achievements of the special people featured in these pages.

Marguerite Lewis

Contents

About This Book v

U.S. LEADERS 1

Abigail Adams: Equal Partner 2

Jane Addams: Hull House, the First Community Center 4

Susan B. Anthony: Crusader for Women's Rights 6

Benjamin Banneker: Self-Taught Genius 8

Clara Barton: "The Angel of the Battlefield" 10

Mary McLeod Bethune: First Lady of the Struggle 12

Cesar Chavez: Viva La Huelga! 15

Amelia Earhart: The Pilot Who Disappeared 16

Benjamin Franklin: Master of Many Trades 18

Thomas Gallaudet: "What Might Be" 20

Rebecca Gratz: Founder of the First Jewish Sunday School in America 22

Barbara Jordan: Governor for a Day 24

Lydia Kamekeha: Queen Liliuokalani of Hawaii 26

Helen Keller: "Knowledge Is Happiness" 28

Martin Luther King, Jr.: "I Have a Dream" 30

Ray Kroc: "Mr. Big Mac" 32

Juliette Low: "Be Prepared" 34

Mary Lyon: Founder of Mount Holyoke College 36

Horace Mann: Father of Public Education 38

Sandra Day O'Connor: Supreme Court Justice 40

Alice Freeman Palmer: College President 42

Rosa Parks: The Spark That Ignited 44

Frances Perkins: The First Madame Secretary 46

The Ringling Brothers: The Greatest Show on Earth 48

Anna Eleanor Roosevelt: Extraordinary First Lady 50

Sequoyah: The Cadmus of America 52

Sojourner Truth: Traveler for Freedom 54

Harriet Tubman: A Woman Called "Moses" 56

Booker T. Washington: All Men Are Brothers 58
Noah Webster: Collector of Words 60

LITERATURE AND THE ARTS 63

Marian Anderson: World-Renowned Contralto 64
John James Audubon: Painter of Birds 66
Mikhail Baryshnikov: Ballet Superstar 68
Leonard Bernstein: American Maestro 70
Judy Blume: "She Writes About Me" 72
George Catlin: Mission with a Paintbrush 74
William Henry Cosby, Jr.: Entertainer and Teacher 76
Emily Dickinson: A Major American Poet 78
Walt Disney: Creator of Mickey Mouse 80
Anne Frank: Het Achterhuis (The Diary) 82
Theodor Seuss Geisel: The Cat in the Hat Himself 84
Johannes Gutenberg: The Father of Printing 86
Winslow Homer: Yankee Painter 88
Langston Hughes: "Minstrel Man" 90
Joseph Rudyard Kipling: Storyteller 92
Emma Lazarus: Sweet Singer of Israel 94
Anna Mary Robertson Moses: Grandma Moses 96
Georgia O'Keeffe: Poet of Art 98
Steven Spielberg: Mr. Movies 100
Robert Louis Stevenson: Novelist and Poet 102
Maria Tallchief: First Internationally Recognized American Indian Ballerina 104
Laura Ingalls Wilder: A True Pioneer 106
Frank Lloyd Wright: Master of Light and Shadow 108

SCIENCE AND DISCOVERY 111

Frederick Banting: The Mysterious Hormone X 112
Alexander Graham Bell: Scientist and Educator 114
Louis Braille: Real Books for the Blind 116
Rachel Carson: Protector of Our Resources 118
George Washington Carver: Agricultural Scientist 120
Captain James Cook: Explorer of the Pacific Ocean 122
Jacques Cousteau: Skipper of the Calypso 124
Marie Curie: Discover of Radium 126
Thomas Alva Edison: The Wizard of Menlo Park 128
Albert Einstein: An Artist of Science 130

Sigmund Freud: Explorer of the Subconscious Mind   132
Robert Goddard: Rocket Pioneer   134
Samuel F.B. Morse: Instant Communication   136
John Muir: Protector of the Wilderness   138
Alfred Nobel: Construction and Destruction   140
Louis Pasteur: "Slow Learner" or Genius?   142
Sacagawea: Interpreter for Lewis and Clark   144
Albert Schweitzer: Missionary Doctor   146
Eli Whitney: Mechanical Genius   148
Daniel Hale Williams: Pioneer of Heart Surgery   150
Wilbur and Orville Wright: American Aviation Pioneers   152

SPORTS   155

Henry Aaron: Baseball's Quiet Hero   156
Kareem Abdul-Jabbar: "My Biggest Resource Is My Mind"   158
Muhammad Ali: "Worthy of All Praise"   159
Paul "Bear" Bryant: Winningest Coach in History   162
Rod Carew: A Dream and a Goal   164
Roberto Clemente: Prince of the Pittsburgh Pirates   166
Mary Decker: Fast and Feminine   168
Janet Guthrie: "Racing Is My Passion"   170
Dorothy Hamill: World-Champion Figure Skater   172
Billie Jean King: Seventeen Wimbledon Wins   174
Jack Nicklaus: Golfer of the Century   176
Bobby Orr: Spark Plug of the Bruins   178
Jesse Owens: Ambassador of Sports   180
Pelé: Brazil's "National Treasure"   182
Mary Lou Retton: "Hard Work Pays Off"   184
Jackie Robinson: Courage Not to Strike Back   186
Babe Ruth: Baseball's Immortal Giant   188
Jim Thorpe: The Wonder of Sports   190
Mildred Didrikson Zaharias: All-Time Champion Athlete   192

WORLD LEADERS   195

Corazon Aquino: The Hope of the Philippines   196
Robert Baden-Powell: World Scout   198
David Ben-Gurion: Mandate for Peace   200
Elizabeth Blackwell: The First Woman M.D.   202
Winston Churchill: Statesman of the Hour   204

Indira Gandhi: Star of India 206
Mahatma Gandhi: "The Great Soul" 208
Dag Hammarskjöld: A Man for Peace 210
Winnie Mandela: The Struggle Is My Life 212
Margaret Mead: World-Famous Anthropologist 214
Golda Meir: Daughter of Isreal 216
Dr. Maria Montessori: Champion of Children's Rights 218
Florence Nightingale: Mother of Nursing 220
Anwar el-Sadat: Negotiator for Peace 222
Levi Strauss: The King of Blue Jeans 224
Mother Teresa: Sister to Those in Need 226
Margaret Thatcher: "Iron Lady" Prime Minister 228
Bishop Desmond Tutu: The Conscience of His Nation 230

Answer Keys for Worksheet Puzzles 232
Alphabetical Index 237

The Measure of a Man

Not—"How did he die?"
But—"How did he live?"
  Not—"What did he gain?"
But—"What did he give?"
  These are the units
To measure the worth
  Of a man, as a man,
  Regardless of birth.

  Not—"What was his station?"
But—"Had he a heart?"
  And—"How did he play
His God-fearing part?"
  Was he ever ready
With words o'cheer
  To bring back a smile
To banish a tear?

  Not—"What was his church?"
Nor—"What was his creed?"
  But—"Had he befriended
Those really in need?"
  Not—"What did the sketch
In the newpaper say?"
  But—"How many were sorry
When he passed away?"

—Author Unknown

Braude, *Braude's Sourcebook for Speakers and Writers.* Prentice-Hall, 1968. Selection 1071, p. 169.

U.S. Leaders

Through our scientific genius we have made this world a neighborhood; and now we are challenged, through our moral genius, to make it a brotherhood.

—*Martin Luther King, Jr.*

Life was meant to be lived and curiosity must be kept alive. One must never, for any reason, turn his back on life.

—*Eleanor Roosevelt*

1

Name _____ Date _____

Meet Abigail Adams: Equal Partner

When Abigail was growing up, girls did not go to school. They were expected only to marry, raise children, manage a household, and please a husband.

Abigail Smith was born on November 11, 1744, in Weymouth, Massachusetts. Her mother taught her the needed household skills. Her father taught her to read and write. He gave her free access to his library and encouraged her to think for herself and form opinions. Abigail was determined to marry a man who would value her intelligence and knowledge. In John Adams, a lawyer and graduate of Harvard College, she found such a man, and they were married on October 25, 1764. As John began moving up the political ladder, Abigail became his confidante. Abigail managed their home and four children when political duties kept John away from home for long periods. She wrote John long letters, keeping him informed of political matters in Boston. After the Revolutionary War, John was elected vice-president for two terms. When George Washington declined a third term, John was elected president. John discussed all matters with Abigail; it was said that he would not make a decision without her approval. In 1800, when John lost the election to Thomas Jefferson, John and Abigail retired to Quincy, Massachusetts. Abigail remained active in family and world affairs until her death on October 28, 1818. When their son, John Quincy Adams, was elected president in 1826, Abigail became the only woman ever to have been both the wife and mother of a president.

In the days when a woman had no rights, when everything belonged to her husband, when a man had complete control of wife and children, Abigail and John were equal partners in home, family, finances, and opinions.

READ MORE ABOUT ABIGAIL ADAMS

- Fradin, *Abigail Adams: Advisor to a President.* Enslow Publications, 1989.
- Osborne, *Abigail Adams: Women's Rights Advocate.* Chelsea House, 1989.
- Peterson, *Abigail Adams: "Dear Partner."* Garrard, 1967.

DISCOVERY ACTIVITIES

- Using reference sources, discover the political offices held by John Adams.
- When John Adams was elected vice-president in 1789, the nation's capital was New York City. Using reference sources, discover when and how Washington, D.C., became the nation's capital.
- Using reference sources, discover Abigail Adams's famous quote, beginning "Remember the ladies . . ." What was the entire quote?

Name _____   Date _____

Abigail Adams: Equal Partner

Parents today provide the basic necessities for their children, as did the parents in the 1700s. However, the manner in which they provide for their children is different. Below is a list of the basic necessities.

DIRECTIONS In the proper space, write how parents provided that necessity in the 1700s and how they provide that necessity today.

	1700s	**TODAY**
SHELTER		
FOOD		
CLOTHING		
EDUCATION		
ENTERTAINMENT		

Meet Jane Addams: Hull House, the First Community Center

When Jane saw the tiny, crowded houses in the city of Freeport, Illinois, she thought of her own large, comfortable home in the country. "When I grow up," she told her father, "I shall buy a big house with a big yard in the city and invite all the children to come and visit me."

Jane Addams was born on September 6, 1860, outside Freeport, in Cedarville, Illinois. Her father was a respected state senator. Jane loved to read, and her father encouraged her by paying her five cents for every book she read and discussed with him. Jane wanted to study medicine, but a back problem requiring an operation changed her plans. She became restless and unhappy. She wanted to help people. On a trip to England she visited Toynbee Hall, a settlement house in London. Inspired, Jane leased a large house in Chicago. On September 18, 1889, she opened Hull House, a neighborhood center, and began providing services for the neighborhood. She started child day care for working mothers and added after-school activities for the children. She organized evening classes and social clubs for the adults. She talked city leaders into financial support. She worked successfully for the eight-hour day for working women, child labor laws, housing reform, and juvenile courts. In 1931, Jane received the Nobel Peace Price. Hull House continued to expand until, at the time of Jane's death on May 21, 1935, it had grown to a whole city block of buildings and grounds.

Jane spent forty-five years as the head of Hull House. Her goal of buying a large house and inviting the children to visit her had evolved into inviting people of all ages to come visit her and providing many activities for them to engage in.

READ MORE ABOUT JANE ADDAMS

- Gilbert, *Jane Addams: World Neighbor.* Abingdon Press, 1960.
- Keller, *Jane Addams.* Thomas Y. Crowell, 1971.
- Klingel, *Jane Addams.* Creative Education, 1989.

DISCOVERY ACTIVITIES

- A settlement house was organized to improve living conditions in a city. Using reference sources, discover why a settlement house was needed in the city of Chicago in the early 1900s.
- Jane worked for child labor laws. Using reference sources, discover the conditions that existed for working children in the early 1900s.
- Settlement houses are often called neighborhood or community centers today. Compare the activities offered at a neighborhood or community center with the activities offered at the settlement house in the early 1900s.

Jane Addams: Hull House, The First Community Center

The settlement house, an institution organized to improve the lives of the people living in the city, has evolved into the community center, an institution that provides services for members of a neighborhood, community, town, or city.

DIRECTIONS If your neighborhood, community, town, or city organized and built such a center, what facilities do you believe would be needed to serve the people? On the lines below, plan the activities that you feel should be offered by the center.

Meet Susan B. Anthony: Crusader for Women's Rights

"You're going to be an old maid," Susan's sisters teased her. Susan retorted, "As a single, employed woman, I can afford elegant dresses and luxuries. I can be my own person. I am not subjected to complete control by a husband."

Susan Brownell Anthony was born near Adams, Massachusetts, on February 15, 1820. Her Quaker parents believed in equal opportunities and education for both boys and girls. As a young woman, Susan was disturbed by the attitude of men who felt they had to protect women from all decision making because women did not have the ability to think for themselves. Women were completely subordinate to their husbands, who controlled all that a woman owned or earned. Susan believed that women should have the right to control their own lives.

Although Susan was deeply involved with the temperance and antislavery movements, her goal was to secure for women the right to vote. She traveled throughout the country, lecturing on the rights of women. She was a cool and calm speaker and always had her facts correct. With flashing eyes, speaking in clear, precise sentences, she compelled audiences to listen.

In 1876, a women's suffrage (right to vote) amendment petition was presented to Congress. It was rejected. Each year thereafter, the petition was again presented. It was ignored or defeated. Susan continued to travel and lecture. After speaking at a suffrage convention in Baltimore, at the age of eighty-six, Susan became ill with pneumonia. She returned to her home in Rochester, New York, where she died on March 13, 1906.

On May 21, 1919, Congress passed the Nineteenth Amendment, giving women the right to vote. It was quickly ratified by the states. In November of 1920, one hundred years after the birth of Susan B. Anthony, the women of America cast their vote.

READ MORE ABOUT SUSAN B. ANTHONY

- Cooper, *Susan B. Anthony*. Franklin Watts, 1984.
- Noble, *Susan B. Anthony*. Julian Messner, 1975.
- Weisberg, *Susan B. Anthony: Woman Suffragist*. Chelsea House, 1988.

DISCOVERY ACTIVITIES

- Using reference sources, discover the exact wording of the Nineteenth Amendment.
- Susan B. Anthony believed she could vote because of the Fifteenth Amendment. Using reference sources, discover why she believed this.
- Using reference sources, discover how many state votes are needed to ratify an amendment to the Constitution.

Susan B. Anthony: Crusader for Women's Rights

Many changes in the opportunities for women have occurred since Susan B. Anthony crusaded for the right of women to vote.

DIRECTIONS In the symbols below, write as many of these changes as you can.

Meet Benjamin Banneker: Self-Taught Genius

Benjamin was a property owner at age six. His father, a black freeman, bought 120 acres in Maryland and added Benjamin's name to the deed.

Benjamin Banneker was born on November 9, 1731, on a farm along the Patapsco River in Maryland. Benjamin was so quick and so bright that he taught himself to read. His mother arranged for him to attend a Quaker school for a few years. Benjamin loved learning and became more interested in reading, writing, and thinking than in farming. At the age of thirty, he saw his first watch, which he took apart and put back together perfectly. He became a clock and watch repairman, riding circuit to plantations to repair timepieces. When Benjamin received a gift of some crude astrological instruments, and three books on astronomy, and lunar and tide tables, he taught himself how to use them. He discovered errors in the books. In 1792, he published *Benjamin Banneker's Almanack*. Later he helped to survey and plan out the city of Washington, D.C.

Benjamin continued to publish his almanac through 1803. It became the most popular book in America, second only to the Bible, and it was nicknamed "the poor man's encyclopedia." In his later years Benjamin lived on his farm, reading, writing letters, and thinking out problems until he died, sitting in his yard, leaning against a tree, on October 19, 1806.

Benjamin Benneker was a man ahead of his time. His accomplishments rested for many years. It was not until scholars reading his almanacs, letters, and journals realized his true contributions and published them for the world to read.

READ MORE ABOUT BENJAMIN BANNEKER

- Conley, *Benjamin Banneker*. Chelsea House, 1989.
- Ferris, *What Are You Figuring Now? A Story About Benjamin Banneker*. Carolrhoda Books, 1988.
- Patterson, *Benjamin Banneker: Genius of Early America*. Abingdon, 1978.

DISCOVERY ACTIVITIES

- Benjamin Banneker had a rich heritage. Using reference sources, discover the history of Benjamin's grandmother and grandfather.
- Benjamin Banneker is given credit for "saving" Washington D.C. Using reference sources, discover how Benjamin accomplished this deed.
- Benjamin Banneker's almanac was called "the poor man's encyclopedia." Using reference sources, discover why and how his almanac earned this nickname.

Benjamin Banneker: Self-Taught Genius

Benjamin's grandmother, Molly Welsh, was accused of stealing milk in England. She was shipped to America to serve seven years bondage. On gaining her freedom, Molly purchased several acres on the Patapsco River in Maryland, where for generations afterward, the family owned farms.

DIRECTIONS   Below is a map of the state of Maryland. Using reference sources, locate and draw the Patapsco River on the map.

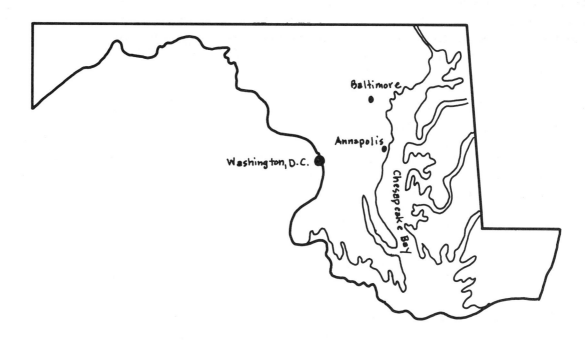

Meet Clara Barton: "The Angel of the Battlefield"

Clara's four brothers and sisters were so much older, she felt she grew up having three fathers and three mothers. They enjoyed helping and teaching their little "Christmas present."

Clarissa Harlow Barton, called Clara, was born on December 25, 1821, in North Oxford, Massachusetts. She began teaching school at age fifteen. She was such a good teacher that she was offered a bigger and better school each year. At the age of thirty, Clara began teaching at Bordentown, New Jersey. A state law requiring free education for all children was not enforced. Clara shamed the School Committee into providing a building and supplies. She invited all the children to come to school. By 1854, the school had more than two hundred students. The school needed a superintendent but the School Committee would not consider Clara because she was a woman.

During the Civil War, Clara worked as a volunteer, bringing supplies and giving care to the wounded on the battlefield. After the war, she organized a service that provided information to families of missing prisoners of war. In 1869, Clara went to Europe and joined the International Red Cross. When Congress ratified the Geneva Treaty, she returned to the United States and established the American Red Cross. She served as president of the American Red Cross for twenty-two years. She founded the National First Aid Association and served as chaplain of the Women's Relief Corp until her death on April 12, 1912.

Clara Barton's name is synonymous with the American Red Cross's tradition of serving victims of peacetime disasters as well as those wounded in the service of their country.

READ MORE ABOUT CLARA BARTON

- Bains, *Clara Barton: Angel of the Battlefield.* Troll Associates, 1982.
- Hamilton, *Clara Barton.* Chelsea House, 1988.
- Stevenson, *Clara Barton: Founder of the American Red Cross.* Macmillan, 1983.

DISCOVERY ACTIVITIES

- Using reference sources, discover the history of the International Red Cross. Who was its founder? When, where, and why was it founded?
- Using reference sources, discover the name of the president who signed the Geneva Treaty after it was ratified by Congress.
- Using reference sources, discover the aims and objectives of the International and American Red Cross.

Clara Barton: "The Angel of the Battlefield"

The Red Cross Water Safety Program was organized in 1914 by Wilbert E. Longfellow, whose ambition was to "waterproof America."

DIRECTIONS   Using reference sources, discover the Red Cross Water Safety Program. Write the services within the "red cross" below.

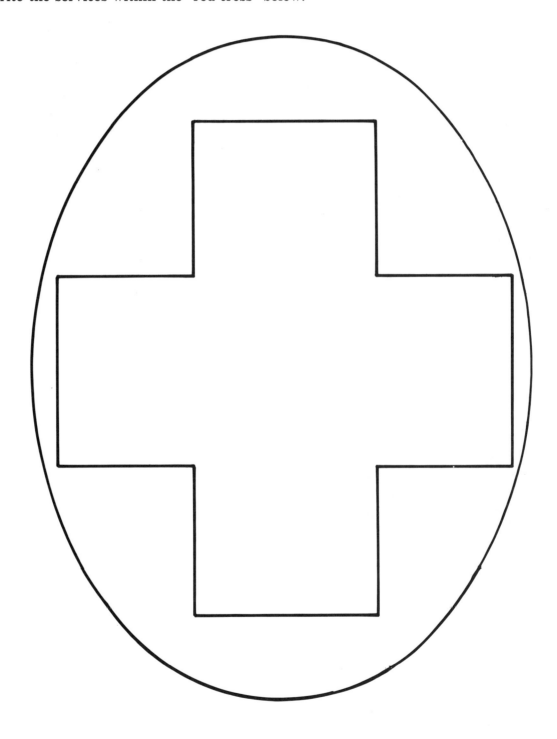

Meet Mary McLeod Bethune: First Lady of the Struggle

"Why can white folks read, but we black folks cannot? Why is there a school for white kids, but no school for us?" Mary asked.

Mary McLeod Bethune was born July 20, 1875, in Manesville, North Carolina. She was the first free child born in her family. She longed to be able to read and write. When a mission school opened in town, Mary walked five miles each way to attend school for four months of the year. School was only in session in between the cotton seasons, for all black children had to work in the fields. Everything Mary learned at school she taught to her family.

Mary won a scholarship to Scotia Academy. She studied to become a missionary. She wanted to go to Africa, but there were no openings for black missionaries in black Africa. She married Albertus Bethune and instead became head of a mission school in Florida.

On October 3, 1903, Mary opened her own school with five girl students. She added evening classes for adults and Sunday afternoon classes for the community. Two years later, the school had 250 students. She combined the school with Cookman Institute for Boys. Today the school is called Bethune-Cookman College.

Mary organized the National Council of Negro Women. She worked for black freedom and rights for all women. Mary did not bully people. Blessed with a quick wit, she told homespun stories to drive home a point. During the Roosevelt Administration, Mary spent ten years in Washington as head of the National Youth Administration.

Mary retired to a cottage at Bethune-Cookman College, where she continued to work for equality for all people until her death in May of 1955.

READ MORE ABOUT MARY MCLEOD BETHUNE

- Holt, *Mary McLeod Bethune: A Biography.* Doubleday, 1964.
- Meltzer, *Mary McLeod Bethune: A Voice of Black Hope.* Viking Kestral, 1987.
- Stern, *Mary McLeod Bethune.* Knopf, 1957.

DISCOVERY ACTIVITIES

- Using reference sources, discover where Bethune-Cookman College is located. What types of studies and degrees are offered at the college?
- The motto for Mary's first school was "Enter to learn, depart to serve." What do you feel was the meaning of that motto?
- Mary McLeod Bethune won the Spingarn Medal. Using reference sources, discover by whom, when, and why the award was initiated.

Mary McLeod Bethune: First Lady of the Struggle

Mary McLeod Bethune won the Spingarn Medal in 1935 for her work in education.

DIRECTIONS Within the outline below, design a medal that could be used to honor the person in your school who has done the most to help students in their quest for knowledge. Include a design and an inscription.

  If such an award were to be used in your school, to whom would you award the medal this year, and why? You may use the back of this sheet for your answer.

Meet Cesar Chavez: Viva La Huelga!

Cesar strongly believed in a person's right to a fair wage for a day's work. He admired the teachings of Ghandi and Martin Luther King and followed their principles of non violent protest to gain this right for Mexican Americans.

Cesar Chavez was born March 31, 1927, on his grandparents farm in Arizona. His family lost the farm in 1937 because they could not pay the taxes. They joined the thousands of people moving to California to become migrant farm workers. They traveled the state, picking the crops as they ripened. Cesar went to more than three dozen schools, attending each only a few days at a time.

Cesar became a member of the Community Service Organization, a group dedicated to helping Mexican Americans help themselves. As their representative, he traveled through the southwest organizing local units. He saw hunger and despair everywhere. He returned to Delano, California and organized a union for farm workers. In 1965, when the Filipino workers struck against the growers, Cesar's National Farm Workers Association joined in the strike which continued for five years. On July 29, 1970, Cesar signed contracts with the growers.

Today, the NFWA has its headquarters at *Forty Acres* in Delano. A heavy iron bell was donated by the Transport Workers of England and the Whitehall Bell Foundry, makers of the original Liberty Bell. The clapper is chained. It will not ring clear until there is a union for all farm workers in the United States.

READ MORE ABOUT CESAR CHAVEZ

- Franchere, *Cesar Chavez.* Harper Junior, 1988.
- Roberts, *Cesar Chavez & La Causa.* Childrens Press, 1986.
- White, *Cesar Chavez: Man of Courage.* Garrard, 1973.

DISCOVERY ACTIVITIES

- Labor Day is celebrated throughout the United States. Using reference sources, discover the significance of Labor Day.
- Using reference sources, discover the history of the labor movement in the United States. Design a time line, showing when particular unions were organized.
- The symbol of the NFWA is the Aztec eagle. In your opinion, why was that symbol chosen?
- Using reference sources, discover whether or not the bell at Forty Acres is ringing clear. If it is, when did this event occur?

Cesar Chavez: Viva La Huelga!

DIRECTIONS The symbol of the National Farm Workers Association is the Aztec eagle, reproduced below. Color the symbol, using colors you feel best represent the characteristics of the eagle.

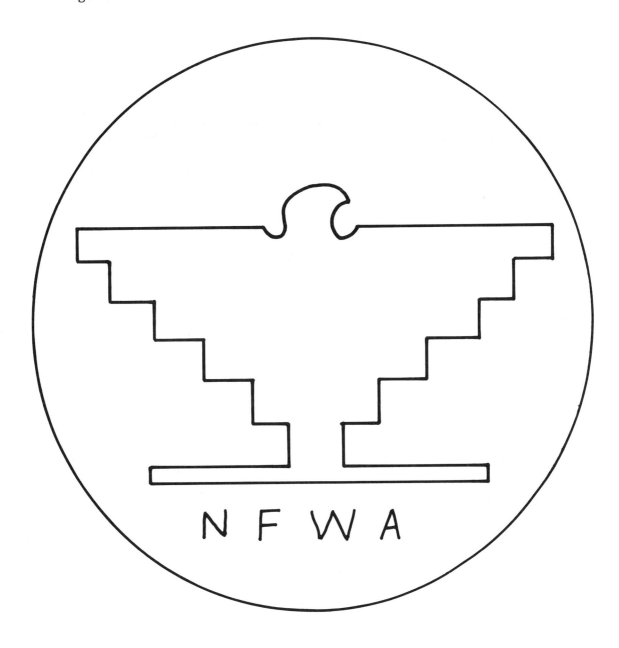

Meet Amelia Earhart: The Pilot Who Disappeared

There was an old horse carriage in Grandma's barn. The young Amelia and her cousins invented a game called "bogie." They studied maps then sat in the carriage and took imaginary trips around the world. The grown up Amelia said, "Our childhood game of map traveling was like ground flying an airplane."

Amelia Earhart was born July 24, 1897, in Atchison, Kansas. The family moved many times and Amelia grew up a loner, preferring her imagination and books as company. She had her first airplane ride in 1920. The experience was exhilarating; she felt happy and free. Amelia took flying lessons, spending every spare minute at the airport. On her twenty-fifth birthday, Amelia bought her first airplane. After Lindbergh flew the Atlantic in 1927, Amelia was determined to be the first woman to fly the Atlantic. In 1928, she was invited to fly the Atlantic as a passenger. This was second best, but she accepted. The trip was successful and Amelia became famous. She continued to fly and broke many records. In 1932, she became the first woman to solo the Atlantic. In 1935, she soloed the Pacific from Honolulu to California. On June 1, 1937, Amelia flew out of Miami, with Fred Noonan as navigator, on a trip around the world. She was in radio contact until the last leg of the journey, from Lai, New Zealand, to Howeland Island, a speck of land in 250,000 miles of Pacific Ocean. During radio contact with the Coast Guard cutter *Itasca*, Amelia's voice abruptly stopped. No word from her was ever heard again.

The official statement was that the plane had crashed into the ocean. Although rumors still persist, the mystery of what actually happened to Amelia Earhart, Fred Noonan, and the *Electra* has never been solved.

READ MORE ABOUT AMELIA EARHART

- Brown, *Amelia Earhart Takes Off.* Albert Whitman, 1985.
- Chadwick, *Amelia Earhart: Aviation Pioneer.* Lerner Publications, 1987.
- Lauber, *Lost Star: The Story of Amelia Earhart.* Scholastic, 1988.

DISCOVERY ACTIVITIES

- Using reference sources, compare the qualifications for being a pilot in Amelia Earhart's day and today.
- Using reference sources, trace Amelia Earhart's final flight. How far had she traveled?
- Using reference sources, discover how Amelia Earhart's final flight might have had a different ending if her plane contained many of the technologies available to aircraft today. What do you think happened to Amelia Earhart?

Amelia Earhart: The Pilot Who Disappeared

Although Amelia Earhart's *Electra* was very different from today's modern aircraft, the basic parts of an airplane remain the same.

DIRECTIONS   Below is a picture of a typical airplane. The major parts of the airplane are listed below. Match up the part on the plane by writing the correct number at the line leading to the part.

1. Antenna
2. Cabin
3. Engine
4. Fin
5. Fuselage
6. Landing gear
7. Left aileron
8. Left flap
9. Main spar
10. Propeller
11. Ribs
12. Right aileron
13. Right flap
14. Rudder
15. Tail assembly
16. Trim tab
17. Wing
18. Wing tab

Meet Benjamin Franklin: Master of Many Trades

Young Ben's head was chock-full of ideas. "Some of your ideas are crazy," his friends laughed. "But most of them are great."

Benjamin Franklin was born in Boston, Massachusetts, on January 17, 1706. At the age of twelve, Ben was apprenticed to his brother James to learn the printing trade. Ben learned quickly and soon became a skilled printer. He wanted to write articles for the paper but his brother was jealous of his ability to write and refused to print anything Ben wrote. When Ben was seventeen, he ran away to Philadelphia, Pennsylvania. He set up his own printing business to publish the Pennsylvania Gazette and *Poor Richard's Almanac.* He became interested in public affairs and worked to make Philadelphia a model city. He proved that lightning is electricity by flying a kite during a thunderstorm. He loved to invent things. Some of his inventions included lightning rods, a stove that fit into the fireplace, and bifocal eyeglasses.

Ben helped write the Declaration of Independence. During the Revolutionary War, Ben lived in France, enlisting French support for the colonies. After the war, he served as a delegate at the first constitutional convention. Ben was opposed to slavery and served as president of the first anti-slavery society in America . . . His last official act was to sign an appeal to Congress requesting the abolition of slavery. Ben died April 17, 1790, and was buried in the cemetery at Christ Church in Philadelphia.

READ MORE ABOUT BENJAMIN FRANKLIN

- Donovan, *The Many Worlds of Benjamin Franklin.* American Heritage, 1964.
- Fritz, *What's the Big Idea, Ben Franklin?* Putnam, 1982.
- Graves, *Benjamin Franklin: Man of Ideas.* Garrard, 1960.
- Sandak, *Benjamin Franklin.* Watts, 1986.

DISCOVERY ACTIVITIES

- Ben Franklin wanted to be remembered because "he lived usefully" rather than because he died rich. Using reference sources, discover the useful things Ben did for the people of Philadelphia.
- Benjamin Franklin was involved in the *Plan of Union* and *The Treaty of Paris.* Using reference sources, discover the purpose of these documents, including when and where they were signed.
- Ben Franklin refused to patent his many inventions. He wanted everyone to be able to use his ideas. Using reference sources, discover how lightning rods, the Franklin stove, and bifocal eyeglasses helped people.

Benjamin Franklin: Master of Many Trades

Benjamin Franklin published *Poor Richard's Almanac,* a collection of weather reports, recipes, poetry, and wise sayings, from 1733 to 1758. Some of the sayings are still used today.

DIRECTIONS Below are some of the still-popular sayings from *Poor Richard's Almanac.* On the lines, explain what the sayings mean to you.

"God helps them that help themselves"

_____
_____
_____
_____
_____
_____

"A stitch in time saves nine"

_____
_____
_____
_____
_____

"Early to bed
Early to rise
Makes a man
healthy,
wealthy
and wise"

_____
_____
_____
_____
_____
_____
_____

"Little strokes
fell
great oaks"

_____
_____
_____
_____
_____
_____

Name ——— Date ———

Meet Thomas Gallaudet: "What Might Be"

Thomas kept a secret journal. He wrote over and over again that he wished he could climb a tree. His weak lungs and poor eyesight kept him from participating in any type of physical activity.

Thomas Gallaudet was born in Philadelphia, Pennsylvania, on December 10, 1787. He earned the right to be valedictorian of his class at Yale University, but the second-best student was chosen because he was tall and robust. Thomas became a lawyer and a tutor, but ill health forced his retirement. To live an outdoor life, he worked as a peddler.

Thomas became interested in a young child named Alice Cogswell, who became deaf at the age of two. He was sure her intelligence could be unlocked through sign language. After successfully teaching Alice, Thomas studied the two methods of teaching the deaf: sign language and lip reading. It was his opinion that sign language was the better method, but he developed a program using both methods.

Thomas convinced some wealthy Philadelphia citizens to sponsor a school for the deaf. As the school's first principal, the gray-eyed, quiet man calmed the fears of children, locked into silence and separated from home and family. The first signs the children learned were tears and smiles. Later, when his health forced him to retire, he wrote books on the deaf, with the help of his deaf wife.

After his death on September 10, 1851, the National Deaf–Mute College in Washington, D.C., was renamed Gallaudet College. Today, a bronze statue of Thomas teaching Alice greets students from all over the world. They come to study in preparation for taking their rightful place in all walks of life.

READ MORE ABOUT THOMAS GALLAUDET

- Benderly, *Dancing Without Music.* Doubleday, 1980.
- Niemark, *A Deaf Child Listened: Thomas Gallaudet, Pioneer in American Education.* William Morrow, 1983.
- Spradley, *Deaf Like Me.* Random House, 1980.

DISCOVERY ACTIVITIES

- Read about Louis Braille, who helped the blind, and discover the ways in which Thomas Gallaudet and he were alike and different.
- Using reference sources, discover what opportunities are available for educating hearing-impaired students in your state.
- Using reference sources, discover the philosophy and purpose of Gallaudet College today.

© 1991 by The Center for Applied Research in Education

20

Thomas Gallaudet: "What Might Be"

The American Sign Language (ASL) is based on ideas rather than words. When deaf people communicate with each other, they usually use ASL. When deaf people communicate with hearing people, they usually use the manual alphabet, which consists of a different sign for each letter of the English alphabet.

DIRECTIONS Below are words in American Sign Language expressing emotions. Practice this type of signing with a friend.

Meet Rebecca Gratz:
Founder of the First Jewish Sunday School in America

"I thought I grew up in a large family," Becky laughed. "But today, I have the largest family anyone ever had." Every child Becky had contact with became one of "my children" as she lovingly referred to them.

Rebecca was born in Philadelphia, Pennsylvania, in March of 1791. There were ten children in the Gratz family. She grew up secure and happy in her Jewish faith. With her best friend, Maria, she attended parties and exchanged confidences. She fell in love with Samuel Ewing, but as he was not of her faith, she did not marry him. She enjoyed helping to care for her numerous nieces and nephews, and after the death of her parents kept house for her brothers.

Becky was concerned over the lack of religious training for Jewish children. Boys of wealthy families had cheder, but poor boys and all girls had no instruction except what could be taught at home. She wished to set up a Hebrew class in her home that would meet on Sunday. It would be called a Sunday school. Rabbi Isaac Leeser was opposed to her plan. He had dreams of a Hebrew day school. Becky convinced him that the children needed a Sunday school now.

The first Hebrew Sunday school in America for both boys and girls opened on March 4, 1838. Becky supervised a staff of six volunteer teachers and fifty students. As news of the school spread, more schools were organized and opened by women in Philadelphia and throughout America. Becky acted as president of the school for more than twenty years. At age seventy-seven, she organized a Jewish foster home and orphanage. She worked happily with and for children until her death in 1879, after eighty-eight years of loving and being loved in return.

READ MORE ABOUT REBECCA GRATZ

- Biskin, *Pattern for a Heroine: The Life Story of Rebecca Gratz.* Union of American Hebrew Congregation, 1967.

DISCOVERY ACTIVITIES

- Rebecca convinced Rabbi Isaac to support her Sunday school by reminding him that the Talmud stated, "The children are the builders of tomorrow." What does that statement mean to you?

- Rebecca's mother taught her that "In doing good works, there is happiness." What does that statement mean to you?

- Using reference sources, trace the history of religious instruction for Jewish children from Rebecca's Sunday school to today.

Rebecca Gratz:
Founder of the First Jewish Sunday School in America

Rebecca's children would be familiar with the terms listed below.

DIRECTIONS The terms defined below are hidden in the puzzle. Locate and circle all the terms. They can be found forward, backward, horizontally, vertically, and diagonally. How many terms are you familiar with? _____

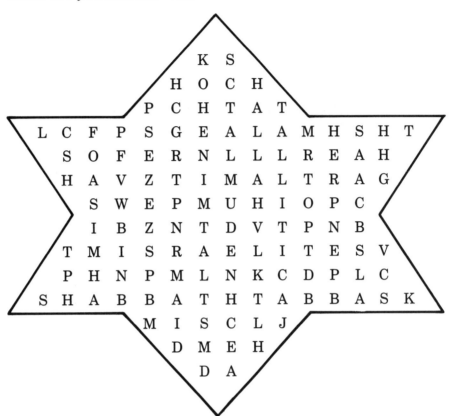

```
                    K S
                  H O C H
                P C H T A T
  L C F P S G E A L A M H S H T
    S O F E R N L L L R E A H
    H A V Z T I M A L T R A G
      S W E P M U H I O P C
      I B Z N T D V T P N B
    T M I S R A E L I T E S V
    P H N P M L N K C D P L C
  S H A B B A T H T A B B A S K
        M I S C L J
        D M E H
        D A
```

BIMA	The raised platform of a synagogue
COVENANT	A promise or agreement
DALED	A letter of the Hebrew alphabet
HALLAH	A braided egg bread
KIPPAH	A head covering worn when praying or studying
ISRAELITES	One of the three families to whom Jews belong
KOHENIM	One of the three families to whom Jews belong
LEVITES	One of the three families to whom Jews belong
MITZVAH	A good deed
SABBATH	The seventh day of the week
SHABBAT	Hebrew for *Sabbath*
SH'MA	The most important Jewish prayer
SIMHA	A joyous event
SOFER	A scribe
TALLIT	A prayer shawl
TALMUD	Commentaries on the Torah
TORAH	The five books of Moses

Meet Barbara Jordan: Governor for a Day

"My father taught us that we could be anything we wanted to be if we were willing to work hard enough," said Barbara. "Today, I am governor of Texas, even if it is only for today."

Barbara Charline Jordan was born February 21, 1936, in Houston, Texas. Her father, a stern disciplinarian, believed in respect, dignity, and self-worth. "Develop your brain power," he taught his three daughters. "No one can take away your brain." Barbara, an A student, graduated *magna cum laude* from Texas Southern University in 1956. She earned her law degree from Boston University in 1959. She began her own law practice, using the family dining room as an office. Barbara ran for the Texas State Senate in 1962 and lost. She ran again in 1964 and lost again. In 1966 she ran again and won. She was elected temporary president of the State Senate. When on June 10 both the governor and the lieutenant governor had to be out of the state for a day, Barbara was sworn in as governor in their absence. She was the first black woman in the United States to be a governor, even for a day.

In 1972, Barbara was elected to Congress. After serving three terms, she retired to become a professor at the University of Texas. Barbara is a fine speaker. She has an immense vocabulary and speaks in clear, ringing tones. When she spoke at the 1976 Democratic National Convention in New York City, she received a standing ovation. At the 1988 Democratic National Convention, she delivered a nomination speech for vice-presidential candidate Lloyd Bentsen.

Today, Barbara is confined to a wheelchair due to her multiple sclerosis. Although her physical future is uncertain, she still has plenty of brain power.

READ MORE ABOUT BARBARA JORDAN

- Haskins, *Barbara Jordan.* Dial Press, 1977.
- Roberts, *Barbara Jordan: The Great Lady from Texas.* Childrens Press, 1984.

DISCOVERY ACTIVITIES

- Using reference sources, discover the requirements for running for the United States House of Representatives.
- Using reference sources, discover the length of term for a member of the United States House of Representatives. Discover the length of term for a member of the United States Senate.
- Using reference sources, discover how many United States representatives Texas is allowed. How many United States senators are elected from Texas?

Barbara Jordan: Governor for a Day

DIRECTIONS Complete the following activities.

1. Barbara Jordan was born in Texas. Locate Texas on the map below. Color it red.
2. Barbara Jordan earned her law degree at Boston University in Massachusetts. Locate Massachusetts on the map below. Color it blue.
3. When Barbara Jordan was elected to Congress, she moved to Washington, D.C. Locate Washington, D.C., on the map below. Color it green.
4. When Barbara Jordan traveled to Boston University, in what direction did she travel? _____
5. When she traveled from Boston University to Texas, in what direction did she travel? _____
6. Locate the state in which you attend school. Color it orange.
7. If you were traveling from your state to Texas, in what direction would you travel? (If you live in Texas, in what direction would you travel from your school to Houston? If you live in Houston, in what direction would you travel to the State House?) _____

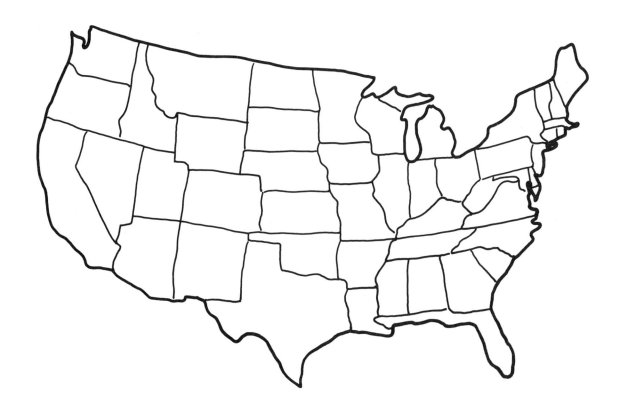

Meet Lydia Kamekeha: Queen Liliuokalani of Hawaii

Lydia was four years old when she discovered that Chief Paki and Konia were not her real parents. She had been adopted at birth. It was the custom in Hawaii in the 1800s for chiefs of royal blood to give their children to other chiefs. They believed it was better not to bring up their own children.

Lydia Kamekeha was born in 1838. Her Hawaiian name was Liliuokalani. She attended the Royal School, a small boarding school run by missionaries. Her childhood was filled with happy times with family and friends, and sad events affecting the Hawaiian people. She married John Dominis, an American who had been appointed governor of Oahu. In October of 1877, King David Kalekema named his blood sister, Lydia, heir to the throne. Lydia became Queen Liliuokalani when he died in January of 1891.

A fierce legal battle followed in 1893 between the wealthy, powerful American land owners and Queen Liliuokalani. They wanted Hawaii to become part of the United States. She wanted to restore power to the throne and to the Hawaiian people. Queen Liliuokalani lost the battle. Hawaii was annexed to the United States in 1898.

To help overcome her sorrow of the changing Hawaii, Lydia wrote the song *Aloha Oe,* which became the traditional farewell song of Hawaii. Lydia died in 1917, a queen without a crown, but a queen in the hearts of her people.

READ MORE ABOUT LYDIA KAMEKEHA

- Allen, *The Betrayal of Liliuokalani: Last Queen of Hawaii.* A. H. Clark, 1983.
- Malone, *Liliuokalani: Queen of Hawaii.* Garrard, 1975.
- Wilson, *Last Queen of Hawaii: Liliuokalani.* Knopf, 1963.

DISCOVERY ACTIVITIES

- Using reference sources, discover who is given the credit of being the first white person to begin the change of Hawaii.
- Using reference sources, discover why the American settlers and land owners wanted Hawaii to become part of the United States.
- Using reference sources, discover the date that Hawaii became the fiftieth state of the United States.

Lydia Kamekeha: Queen Liliuokalani of Hawaii

The *lei*, a necklace of flowers, is the traditional personal decoration worn by Hawaiians.

DIRECTIONS Color the *lei* to provide a suitable frame for the chorus of Lydia's song, printed below.

Farewell to thee, farewell to thee,

Thou charming one who dwells in shaded bowers.

A fond embrace 'ere I depart,

Until we meet again.

Meet Helen Keller: "Knowledge Is Happiness"

Helen was a bright, lively baby. She was beginning to talk and toddle about on unsteady legs. Suddenly, her world became dark and silent.

Helen Keller was born in Tuscumbia, Alabama, on June 27, 1880. During February of her second year, she developed a high fever. The fever passed, leaving her deaf and blind. She became a very difficult child. Locked in her solitary world, she was filled with anger and frustration. Anne Sullivan, a teacher of the blind, came to live with Helen. She won Helen's love and communicated with her through touch and spelling: She had Helen feel an object, then spelled the word into Helen's palm. Anne and Helen became a life-long team. Helen mastered Braille and learned to speak. In 1899, they went to Radcliffe College. Anne attended all classes with Helen. She spelled the lectures into Helen's palm and read her textbooks to her. After graduation, Helen published her first book, *The Story of My Life*. Helen had worked hard to overcome her difficulties. She wanted to help others who were struggling with problems. She began traveling and lecturing about civil rights, capital punishment, and support for the deaf and blind. During World War I, she visited wounded American soldiers in Europe. After the war, she returned to Europe to help people resume their lives. She continued to write books, travel, and lecture until the age of eighty. She suffered several strokes and died on June 1, 1968.

Helen Keller's life story is proof that handicaps are part of life's obstacles. With support and understanding from society, these obstacles can be overcome. Freed from her solitary world, Helen believed that "Knowledge is happiness."

READ MORE ABOUT HELEN KELLER

- Hunter, *Helen Keller*. Bookwright Press, 1986.
- Tames, *Helen Keller*. Franklin Watts, 1989.
- Wepman, *Helen Keller: Humanitarian*. Chelsea House, 1987.

DISCOVERY ACTIVITIES

- Using reference sources, discover Anne Sullivan Macy. Who was she? How was she able to help Helen when all else had failed?
- Using reference sources, discover the services available today for the blind and deaf.
- Helen Keller said, "Knowledge is happiness." What do you think she meant by that?

Helen Keller: "Knowledge Is Happiness"

1. Did you know that there is a blind spot on the retina of each eye? This is the place where the tiny nerves of the retina unite to form the optic nerve.

DIRECTIONS Hold this page at arm's length. Close your left eye. Look with your right eye at the cross below. You can see the dot, too. Move the page toward you, slowly. The dot will disappear when the light reflected from it strikes your blind spot.

2. Did you know your brain will fuse two pictures?

DIRECTIONS Stand a 3″ by 5″ card on its longer edge on the line between the fish and the fishbowl below. Bend down until your nose touches the card. One eye sees the fishbowl, the other, the fish. Now, your brain will fuse the pictures. You will see the fish in the bowl.

3. Did you know that you can be left-eyed or right-eyed?

DIRECTIONS With both eyes open, point your finger at a point on the wall. Do not move your finger. Close your right eye. Is your finger still pointing to the spot? Close your left eye. Is your finger still pointing to the spot? If your finger seems to move when you close your right eye, you are right-eyed. If your finger seems to move when you close your left eye, you are left-eyed.

Meet Martin Luther King, Jr.: "I Have a Dream"

Three generations lived happily together in the Victorian house at 501 Auburn Street: Martin, called M.L.; brother A.D.; sister Willie Christine; their parents Daddy King and Mama Dear; as well as their grandparents, Mama and Grandfather Williams.

Martin Luther King, Jr., was born on January 15, 1929, in Atlanta, Georgia. His grandfather, then his father, was pastor of Ebenezer Baptist Church. During his school years, Martin excelled in academic work and sports as well as in debate and public speaking. While at Morehouse College, he felt he had received the call to become a minister. Martin graduated from Crozer Seminary and received his doctorate from Boston University. In Boston he met Coretta Scott, whom he married on June 18, 1953. Martin was pastor of Dexter Avenue Baptist Church in Montgomery, Alabama, from 1954 to 1959, when he resigned to work full time for civil rights. Martin believed in Mohandas Gandhi's philosophy of nonviolent protest: "Hate the sin, not the sinner," "Attack the wrong, not the wrong doer," and "Love is the answer, nonviolence the vehicle." From 1959 on, Martin played a major part in all civil rights projects and demonstrations. On April 4, 1968, Martin was assassinated while at the Lorraine Motel in Memphis, Tennessee.

Martin Luther King did not live to realize his now famous "I Have a Dream" speech, delivered on August 23, 1963, during the demonstration in Washington, D.C., attended by more than 200,000 people. But Martin never gave up. It was his hope to be remembered not for speeches given or prizes won, but for whatever good he had been able to achieve.

READ MORE ABOUT MARTIN LUTHER KING, JR.

- Adler, *Martin Luther King, Jr.: Free at Last.* Holiday House, 1989.
- Darby, *Martin Luther King, Jr.* Lerner Publications, 1989.
- DeKay, *Meet Martin Luther King, Jr.* Random House, 1989.

DISCOVERY ACTIVITIES

- Using reference sources, discover Rosa Parks and the Montgomery bus boycott in Montgomery, Alabama. Relate the happenings of that occurrence.
- Martin Luther King believed in "nonviolent protest." In your opinion, what is nonviolent protest, how is it accomplished, and what does it accomplish?
- Using reference sources, discover any civil rights accomplishments that have occurred since the death of Martin Luther King. If possible, make a time line and include rights that have been accomplished for all groups.

Martin Luther King, Jr.: "I Have a Dream"

On August 23, 1963, more than 200,000 people gathered at the Washington Monument to support civil rights legislation and to commemorate the freeing of the slaves. The last speaker of the day was Martin Luther King, Jr. His "I Have a Dream" speech came directly from his heart.

DIRECTIONS Read Martin Luther King, Jr.'s, "I Have a Dream" speech printed below. On a separate sheet of paper, explain what this speech means to you.

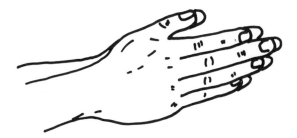

Five score years ago, a great American . . . signed the Emancipation Proclamation. . . . But one hundred years later, we must face the fact that the Negro is still not free.

I say to you today, my friends, that in spite of the difficulties and frustrations of the moment I still have a dream. It is a dream deeply rooted in the American dream. I have a dream that one day this nation will rise up and live out the true meaning of its creed: "We hold these truths to be self-evident; that all men are created equal." I have a dream.

I have a dream, that my four little children will one day live in a nation where they will not be judged by the color of their skin but by the content of their character.

Let freedom ring. Let freedom ring from the mighty mountains of New York. Let freedom ring from the heightening Alleghenies of Pennsylvania . . . but not only that, let freedom ring from Stone Mountain of Georgia. Let freedom ring from Lookout Mountain of Tennessee. Let freedom ring from every hill and molehill of Mississippi. From every mountaintop, let freedom ring.

When we let freedom ring, when we let it ring from every village and every hamlet, from every state and every city, we will be able to speed up that day when all of God's children, black men and white men, Jews and gentiles, Protestants and Catholics, will be able to join hands and sing in the words of the old Negro spiritual, "Free at last! Free at last! Thank God Almighty, we are free at last!"

© 1991 by The Center for Applied Research in Education

Meet Ray Kroc: "Mr. Big Mac"

Ray was a dreamer, but what he dreamed about, he tried to put into practice. He loved debating, discussions, and arguments. He loved being the center of interest and persuading people his view was right.

Ray Kroc was born on October 5, 1902, in Oak Park, Illinois. After graduating from high school, he became a salesman. He was selling Multimixers, a machine that mixed five milkshakes at once, when he received an order for eight Multimixers. Curious to know why a restaurant needed to mix forty milkshakes at one time, he visited the restaurant in San Bernardino, California. He found a small building with eight large windows. Long lines of people waited in front of each window. Ray joined a line and bought what he said was the best hamburger, fries, and shake he had ever eaten. The restaurant was called McDonald's. Ray dreamed of a chain of McDonald's across the country. He talked the owners, Maurice and Richard McDonald, into a partnership. On April 15, 1955, Ray opened his first McDonald's in Chicago, Illinois. By 1959, he had opened two hundred across the country. Ray bought out the partnership and began to build an empire. He wanted McDonald's to be a place where families would have fun eating together. Each McDonald's would be based on quality, service, and cleanliness. He planned special promotions for children and built play areas. Until his death on January 14, 1984, Ray visited a different McDonald's every day for lunch or dinner.

Today, McDonald's restaurants are located throughout the world. In each country, the menu reflects the customs of the people. For example, applesauce is served in Holland, and soup in Japan.

READ MORE ABOUT RAY KROC

- Kroc, *Grinding It Out: The Making of McDonald's.* Henry Regnery, 1977.
- Love, *McDonald's: Behind the Arches.* Bantam Books, 1986.
- Simpson, *Ray Kroc: Big Mac Man.* EMC Corporation, 1978.

DISCOVERY ACTIVITIES

- Ray won the Horatio Alger Award. Using reference sources, discover this award. On what basis is it awarded?
- McDonald's has become very successful. In your opinion, what have been the reasons for its success?
- McDonald's was the first to begin what is called the "fast-food" restaurant. What is McDonald's competition in the fast-food business in your area?

Ray Kroc: "Mr. Big Mac"

McDonald's plans special promotions throughout the year. If you had the chance to design a special "fast food" for the restaurant, what would you choose?

DIRECTIONS The logo of McDonald's is the "Golden Arches." Within the arches pictured below, design a "fast-food" menu to be featured at McDonald's for a special period of time.

Meet Juliette Low: "Be Prepared"

While pulling taffy one day, cousin Randy said, "Daisy's hair is the same color as the taffy. Let's braid it into her hair." Daisy thought that was great fun. But the taffy hardened. Daisy's hair had to be almost completely cut off.

Juliette Gordon Low, called Daisy, was born on October 31, 1860, in Savannah, Georgia. She had a happy childhood. Her family, cousins, and friends were full of spirit and mischief. Daisy married Willy Low on December 21, 1886. During the traditional rice shower, a grain of rice lodged in one ear, causing damage to the ear drum. As a childhood infection had damaged the other ear, Daisy became almost totally deaf. After Willy's death in 1905, Daisy began traveling to ease her restlessness. During a trip to England, she met Sir Robert Baden-Powell. She became very interested in his organization, called the Boy Scouts. While visiting friends in Scotland, Daisy organized a patrol for girls, called Girl Guides. She was asked to organize several patrols in London. When she returned to the United States in 1912, she began organizing Girl Guide patrols. Later the name was changed to Girl Scouts and the patrols were called troops. The main purpose of the Girl Scouts was for girls to make friends and to become useful citizens. In 1916, younger girls were invited to join Brownie troops, named for the helpful brownies in fairy tales. When Girl Scout troops began to be organized throughout the world, Daisy organized the International Council of Girl Scouts. By 1925, there were more than 100,000 Girl Scouts. Daisy organized the Girl Scout World Camp and remained active in the Girl Scout movement until her death on January 17, 1927.

Today, more than 50 million girls and women are, or have been, active in the Girl Scouts. Most Girl Scout leaders were Girl Scouts in their youth.

READ MORE ABOUT JULIETTE LOW

- Behrens, *Juliette Low: Founder of the Girl Scouts of America.* Childrens Press, 1988.
- Kudlinki, *Juliette Low: America's First Girl Scout.* Penguin, 1989.
- Radford, *Juliette Low: Girl Scout Founder.* Garrard, 1965.

DISCOVERY ACTIVITIES

- Using reference sources, discover where and when the first Girl Guide patrol was established in the United States.
- Using reference sources, discover when Sir Robert Baden-Powell organized the Boy Scouts in England.
- Using reference sources, discover and name the different groups within the Girl Scout organization. What are the age requirements for each group?

Juliette Low: "Be Prepared"

When a girl joins the Girl Scouts, she promises to live by the Girl Scout Law.

DIRECTIONS The Girl Scout Law is printed below. On the back of this sheet or on another sheet of paper, explain what you feel each part of the Girl Scout Law requires of all Girl Scouts.

I will do my best:

- to be honest
- to be fair
- to help where I am needed
- to be cheerful
- to be friendly and considerate
- to be a sister to every Girl Scout
- to respect authority
- to use resources wisely
- to protect and improve the world around me
- to show respect for myself and others through my words and actions

Meet Mary Lyon: Founder of Mount Holyoke College

"It is a shame you are not a boy," Schoolmaster Higgins told Mary. "I'd like to see what you could do if you could go to college."

Red-haired Mary Lyon was born February 28, 1797, in Buckland, Massachusetts. Mary had little primary education. She was needed to work on the farm. "The mountains were my first teachers," she said later in life. "They taught me patience." She could see Mount Holyoke from her window, standing like a sentinel guarding the Connecticut River. Mary had a quick, intelligent mind and managed to study for a short time at several schools.

At seventeen, Mary began teaching at Sherbourne Fall, Massachusetts. When a new school opened in Londonderry, New Hampshire, Mary taught there during the April to November session. She opened her own school in Buckland, which was in session from December through March. After a few years, she left both schools to teach at Ipswich Academy in Massachusetts.

In the 1800s, public education ended at the sixth grade. Higher education was available only at expensive private colleges. It was also common practice that if a teacher changed schools, his/her students would follow. Often a teacher was hired only if he/she could guarantee students. Mary wanted to open a college for girls from families of average means. She wanted her college to be a place where students came because of the curriculum.

On November 8, 1837, Mount Holyoke College for Women opened in South Hadley, Massachusetts. The curriculum was designed after the men's colleges, with more emphasis on math and science and less on instrumental music and needlework. Mary remained president of the college until her death on March 5, 1849. She was buried on the campus. Each year, the graduating class places a chain of ivy around her grave in tribute to her memory.

READ MORE ABOUT MARY LYON

- Banning, *Mary Lyon of Putnam's Hill.* Vanguard Press, 1965.
- Fleming, *Great Women Teachers.* Lippincott, 1965.

DISCOVERY ACTIVITIES

- Using reference sources, discover Mount Holyoke College today. Write a short report on how Mount Holyoke College has changed through the years.
- Emily Dickinson was a student for a short time when Mount Holyoke College opened. Read about Emily Dickinson, using the sheet on her in this book, and compare the lives of the two women.

Mary Lyon: Founder of Mount Holyoke College

When Mount Holyoke College opened, the philosophy of the college was

1. To open to women the highest educational opportunities.
2. That this education develop all the powers of the individual.
3. That this educational opportunity be used in service to others.

DIRECTIONS Using Mount Holyoke College's original philosophy, on the lines below compare that philosophy with the reasons you feel a college education would be of value to you as an individual.

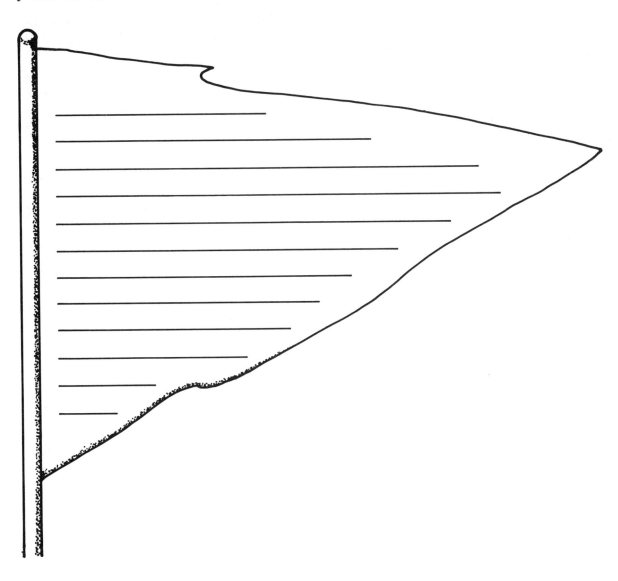

Meet Horace Mann: Father of Public Education

Horace was excited. His father had been chosen to be the keeper of the "treasure," the collection of books donated to the town by Benjamin Franklin. Horace believed the key to that treasure was reading.

Horace Mann was born May 4, 1796, in Franklin, Massachusetts. At his small school, the only book available for him to use was the *New England Primer*. Horace wanted to go to a private academy, but his father could not afford the tuition. At the age of twenty, he was accepted at Brown University. On graduation, his goal was to share his learning with everyone he could.

In 1837, Horace became secretary of the Massachusetts State Board of Education. He believed freedom was best guarded by education. He worked to have schools organized into grades and be attended by both boys and girls who would study the same subjects. He worked tirelessly for public education so that all children would be taught by well-trained teachers in good schools. He wanted a library in each school, believing that if children were to learn to read, there must be books for them to choose from to read. He felt there should be at least fifty books in each school library.

Horace opened the first school to train women as teachers in Lexington, Massachusetts, in July of 1839. He fastened large slates to the wall for teachers and students to write on with chalk. These "modern inventions" were known as blackboards.

In 1853, Horace became the first president of Antioch College in Yellow Springs, Ohio, where he remained until his death in 1859.

READ MORE ABOUT HORACE MANN

- Edwards, *Horace Mann: Sower of Learning.* Houghton Mifflin, 1958.
- Pierce, *Horace Mann: Our Nation's First Educator.* Lerner Publications, 1972.
- Treichler, *Horace Mann: Educating for Democracy.* Encyclopedia Britannica, 1962.

DISCOVERY ACTIVITIES

- Horace Mann believed that both boys and girls should study the same subjects. Using reference sources, discover how education and the curriculum differed for boys and girls during the 1800s.
- Horace Mann believed that freedom was best served through education. What do you believe that statement means?
- Using reference sources, discover what the responsibilities of the state board of education of your state are.

© 1991 by The Center for Applied Research in Education

Horace Mann: Father of Public Education

The people of Franklin, Massachusetts, named their town in honor of Benjamin Franklin. They wrote to him asking him to send them a bell for their meeting house. Instead, he sent them a collection of 116 books, with the explanation that "sense was better than sound." That collection became the "treasure."

DIRECTIONS Pretend you are Benjamin Franklin. Write a letter to the people of Franklin explaining why you are sending a collection of books in place of a bell they had requested.

Meet Sandra Day O'Connor: Supreme Court Justice

"I had thought to become a geologist because I loved being outdoors," Sandra said in later years. "But I really thought I might be running the ranch some day so I decided to study the law."

Sandra Day O'Connor was born in El Paso, Texas, on March 26, 1930. She grew up on the family ranch, a 260-square-mile spread on the Arizona–New Mexico border. The ranch had been owned by her family for over a hundred years. Her early playmates were the animals and the cowboys. As the ranch was so isolated, she spent each school year in El Paso, living with her grandparents and attending school with her cousin Flournay Davis. Both girls spent holidays and vacations at the ranch.

Sandra graduated from high school at age sixteen and was accepted at Stanford University. While working on the *Stanford Law Review,* she met John Jay O'Connor III. They were married on December 20, 1952. Sandra had difficulty finding a job, because women lawyers were not generally accepted. One firm offered her a job as a legal secretary. Rejecting that, she went to work as a deputy county attorney in California. In 1969, she was elected to the Arizona State Senate and became majority leader, the first woman majority leader in any state senate in the nation. In 1974, Sandra was elected to the Maricopa, Arizona, Superior Court.

When Potter Stewart resigned as a Supreme Court justice, President Reagan nominated Sandra to fill the vacancy. Her nomination was passed unanimously by the Senate. On September 25, 1981, Sandra Day O'Connor was sworn in as a Supreme Court justice, the first woman to serve on the highest court in the land.

READ MORE ABOUT SANDRA DAY O'CONNOR

- Fox, *Justice Sandra Day O'Connor.* Enslow Publishers, 1983.
- Woods, *Equal Justice: A Biography of Sandra Day O'Connor.* Dillon, 1985.

DISCOVERY ACTIVITIES

- Using reference sources, discover the duties and responsibilities of the Supreme Court justices.
- Using reference sources, discover the names of the other justices that serve on the Supreme Court.
- Supreme Court justices are appointed for life. Using reference sources, name the presidents who had the opportunity to nominate one or more Supreme Court justices.

Sandra Day O'Connor: Supreme Court Justice

DIRECTIONS The decisions handed down by the Supreme Court are very important and affect us all. What words would you use to describe the qualifications and characteristics that you believe the Supreme Court justices should possess in order to make these decisions? Write the words in the drawing below.

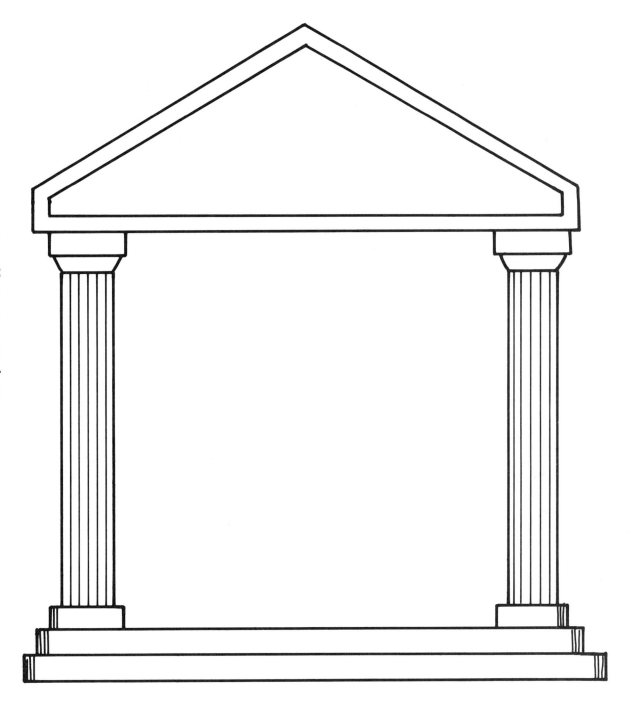

Meet Alice Freeman Palmer: College President

"Girls don't go to college," Alice's classmates scoffed. "And they only go to school to have something to do until they get married."

Alice Freeman Palmer was born in Colesville, New York, on February 21, 1855. The family moved to Windsor after her father became a doctor. Money was scarce, but Alice was determined to go to college. She was finally accepted on probation at the University of Michigan. She proved herself capable within six weeks. Due to financial problems, she left college during her junior year and accepted a position as a principal who would also teach Latin and Greek. She returned to college the following year and graduated with her class.

Alice held several teaching positions in the Midwest. She then came east to accept a position as head of the history department at Wellesley College for Women in Massachusetts. One year later, at the age of twenty-six, she became president of the college. She worked to improve the curriculum, had new dormitories built, and encouraged graduates to open schools to prepare girls for college.

Alice married George Palmer, a professor at Harvard College. She resigned as president of Wellesley College but remained active in the field of education. She served on the Massachusetts State Board of Education, founded the American Association of University Women, helped establish Radcliff College for Women, and served as Dean of Women at the University of Chicago.

Both Alice and George enjoyed traveling and were in great demand as speakers. While on a trip to France, Alice died in Paris in 1902.

READ MORE ABOUT ALICE FREEMAN PALMER

- Fleming, *Alice Freeman Palmer.* Prentice-Hall, 1970.
- Fleming, *Great Women Teachers.* Lippincott, 1965.

DISCOVERY ACTIVITIES

- It was unusual for a woman to be president of a college in Alice Freeman Palmer's day. Are there any women college presidents today? Using reference sources, make a list of the colleges in the United States that are headed by women.

- Alice Freeman Palmer founded the American Association of University Women. Using reference sources, discover the purpose of that organization.

- Using reference sources, discover how Wellesley College for Women has changed since Alice Freeman Palmer served as president.

Alice Freeman Palmer: College President

Education was different in the 1860s, when Alice Freeman Palmer attended school. Below is a list of words having to do with education during that time. Alice Freeman Palmer would be familiar with the terms.

DIRECTIONS Locate and circle the terms found below. The words will be found forward, backward, horizontally, vertically, and diagonally.

ACADEMY
ARITHMETIC
BELL
BENCHES
BLACKBOARD
CHALK
COPYBOOK
DISCIPLINE
DUNCE
GEOGRAPHY
HISTORY
HOMEWORK
LUNCH PAIL
MA'M
MCGUFFEY
PENMANSHIP
PRIMER
PUPILS
READING
RECESS
RECITATION
SIR
STOVE
TEACHER
WRITING

```
C Y R O T S I H W B G L S
I P Y E F F U G C M N U L
T D U N C E N S G V I N I
E N I L P I C S I D D C P
M E V O T S T M R R A H U
H B P I H S N A M N E P P
T L R R M O O M T P R A B
I W E H I B M R T I B I E
R C H N K M C E E H O L N
A H C C L L E B W C P N C
C A A Y H P A R G O E G H
G L E A C A D E M Y R S E
B K T H C O P Y B O O K S
```

Name _____ Date _____

© 1991 by The Center for Applied Research in Education

43

Meet Rosa Parks: The Spark That Ignited

When Rosa was young, she was afraid of the night. Groups of men called the Ku Klux Klan, wearing white hoods and sheets, terrorized the black community each night. Her grandfather kept watch with a shotgun. She spent each night listening, praying they would not come to her house.

Rosa Parks was born February 4, 1913, in Tuskegee, Alabama, but the family soon moved to a small farm outside Montgomery, Alabama. Rosa was a quiet, shy girl who loved to read and sew. She married Raymond Parks when she was nineteen and settled into a routine of home and job. She believed it was wrong to have special rules against black people, but she obeyed them.

On December 1, 1956, Rosa waited at the bus stop. She was tired from hunching over a sewing machine all day. She settled into a seat in the back of the bus where black people had to sit. The bus filled up. The driver told Rosa to give her seat to a white man. Rosa felt she had paid her fare, she had just as much right to a seat as the white man. She looked up at the driver and quietly said "No." She was arrested, put on trial, and found guilty. Her lawyer appealed to the Supreme Court. The black community vowed they would not ride a bus until they had the right to a seat anywhere on the bus. The bus company lost a lot of money. On December 20, 1956, the Supreme Court ruled that special rules for blacks were unconstitutional.

Although life has been difficult for Rosa, she has continued to work for civil rights for black people. She is given the credit for starting the Civil Rights Movement. All because a quiet, unassuming, tired woman had the courage to simply say, "No."

READ MORE ABOUT ROSA PARKS

- Altman, *Extraordinary Black Americans from Colonial to Contemporary Times.* Childrens Press, 1989.
- Greenfield, *Rosa Parks.* Thomas Y. Crowell, 1973.
- Stein, *The Montgomery Bus Boycott.* Childrens Press, 1986.

DISCOVERY ACTIVITIES

- Using reference sources, discover the special rules that were in effect against blacks prior to the Montgomery bus boycott.
- Using reference sources, discover the widespread effects the Montgomery bus boycott had on blacks throughout the United States.
- When Rosa Parks just said, "No," her life changed. Using reference sources, discover the changes in her life.

Rosa Parks: The Spark That Ignited

DIRECTIONS   The Montgomery bus boycott, sparked by Rosa Parks's refusal to give up her seat to a white man, was the beginning of the civil rights movement. On the lines below, list the effects the Montgomery bus boycott had on blacks in the United States.

BEFORE THE BUS BOYCOTT   **AFTER THE BUS BOYCOTT**

_____   _____
_____   _____
_____   _____
_____   _____
_____   _____
_____   _____
_____   _____
_____   _____
_____   _____
_____   _____
_____   _____

Meet Frances Perkins: The First Madame Secretary

Fanny loved being in school plays. Through acting she could try on different roles and escape the narrow confines her parents and society thrust upon her.

Frances Coralie Perkins was born in Boston, Massachusetts, on April 10, 1880. Growing up in Worcester, Massachusetts, she had difficulty accepting the role of the dutiful and loving daughter expected to live at home until she married and established her own home and family.

Frances was a people person. While at Mount Holyoke College, she organized a social club for young factory girls. This led her into a life of social service, working in the field of labor to improve working conditions for all people, but especially for women and children. Frances was able to reason with people. She did not cajole or demand. She was always prepared with facts and statistics that proved how her decisions would benefit both labor and management. Frances served in New York State as a member of the State Industrial Commission and as Chairman of the Labor Board. In 1933, President Franklin D. Roosevelt named Frances Secretary of Labor. She was the first woman member of the cabinet. During her tenure, Congress passed the Social Security Act. She retired from her cabinet post in 1945 but returned to Washington to serve as Civil Service Commissioner until 1952.

At age eighty-four, Frances retired to Maine. She began writing a biography of Alfred E. Smith, but soon suffered a stroke and died on May 14, 1965. A final tribute was awarded her with the words of George Meany, President of the AFL–CIO: "Madam Secretary was a great lady. We shall all miss her."

READ MORE ABOUT FRANCES PERKINS

- Mohr, *Frances Perkins: That Woman in FDR's Cabinet.* North River, 1979.
- Myers, *Madame Secretary: Frances Perkins.* Julian Messner, 1972.
- Severn, *Frances Perkins: Member of the Cabinet.* Hawthorne Books, 1976.

DISCOVERY ACTIVITIES

- Using reference sources, discover the working conditions of women and children in the early 1900s.
- Using reference sources, discover the effects of the Social Security Act of 1935 on the working public.
- Using reference sources, discover if any women since Frances Perkins have been members of the cabinet. Include name, date, and position.

Frances Perkins: The First Madame Secretary

Frances Perkins, the first woman in a president's cabinet, served as Secretary of Labor from 1933–1945.

The cabinet is a group of official advisors and assistants of the president. Cabinet members are appointed by the president.

DIRECTIONS Today there are fourteen cabinet members. Each member has a specific title. Using reference sources, find the titles of the fourteen members of the president's cabinet. Write the titles within the drawing below.

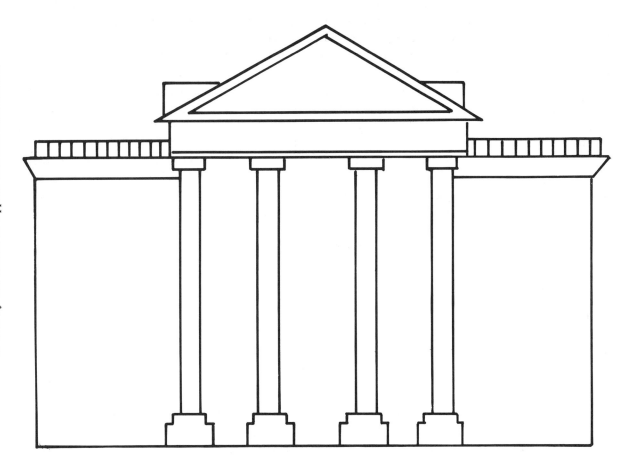

Meet The Ringling Brothers: The Greatest Show on Earth

After the Ringling brothers saw their first circus, they played circus every day "Don't worry," Papa told Mama. "This will pass. They will soon forget about the circus." But they never did.

There were seven boys, including baby Henry, in the Ringling family the day the circus docked at their river town of McGregor, Iowa, in 1870. Albert, August, Otto, Alfred, Charlie, and John loved every minute of that day. "Some day we shall have a circus of our own," vowed Albert. For years, they dreamed and practiced. They rode bareback, juggled kitchen plates, practiced tumbling, and walked a tightrope stretched across the hayloft. They talked Mama into dyeing their long underwear red, to resemble acrobats' tights. They staged neighborhood circuses. In 1884, they organized the Ringling Show and traveled through the Midwest in farm wagons, putting on shows. They added animals and circus artists and earned a reputation for honesty and fun. As each brother married, his wife joined the group and all the children grew up with the circus. By 1902, the Ringling Brothers Circus was the second-largest circus. In 1907, they bought out Barnum and Bailey's Circus and later joined the two circuses together to form the greatest show on earth. Fifteen hundred people and one thousand animals traveled by train across the country. The precircus parade stretched three miles traveling from station to fairgrounds. John outlived all his brothers and ran the circus until his death in 1936. The family operated the circus until 1967. They then sold it to new owners who kept the circus's original name.

Today, the Ringling Brothers and Barnum and Bailey Circus winters in Sarasota, Florida, preparing for the tour of America beginning each spring. The circus brings delight to people of all ages and a reminder of the brothers whose lives were changed the day the circus whistled into town.

READ MORE ABOUT THE RINGLING BROTHERS

- Booth, *At the Circus.* Raintree Publications, 1985.
- Cone, *The Ringling Brothers.* Thomas Y. Crowell, 1971.
- Weil, *Let's Go to the Circus.* Holiday, 1988.

DISCOVERY ACTIVITIES

- Using reference sources, discover more about the Ringling brothers, from the oldest to the youngest. How did so many brothers work together?
- Using reference sources, discover how the Ringling brothers changed the image and reputation of the circus.
- Using reference sources, trace the major changes in the circus from the early days to today.

The Ringling Brothers: The Greatest Show on Earth

DIRECTIONS The circus has universal appeal. If you have been to a circus, describe what you liked best on the lines below. If you have not been to a circus, describe what you would like to see.

Meet Anna Eleanor Roosevelt: Extraordinary First Lady

Eleanor was a tall, gawky child with big front teeth. Although she had beautiful blue-gray eyes, she thought herself ugly. Her beautiful mother laughingly called her "granny" because, "She is so shy and old-fashioned."

Anna Eleanor Roosevelt was born October 11, 1884, in a mansion in New York City. Her happy childhood ended at age seven when her mother died and her father went into a sanitarium. She was brought up by her grandmother, who cared only that Eleanor behaved properly. On March 2, 1905, Eleanor married her fifth cousin, Franklin Delano Roosevelt. Home, family, and Franklin's political career took up all her time until Franklin contracted polio in 1921. Eleanor became involved in politics to keep Franklin's name before the public until he could be active in politics again.

After being governor of New York State, Franklin was elected president in 1932. Eleanor became a very active First Lady. During Franklin's four terms, she lectured, wrote a daily newspaper column, and wrote a best-selling autobiography. During World War II, she traveled extensively, visiting wounded soldiers.

On April 12, 1945, Franklin died at Warm Springs, Georgia. Eleanor planned to retire to Hyde Park, New York, but President Harry Truman asked her to represent the United States at the United Nations. Eleanor worked for world peace until her death on November 7, 1962.

READ MORE ABOUT ANNA ELEANOR ROOSEVELT

- Faber, *Eleanor Roosevelt: First Lady of the World.* Viking Kestral, 1985.
- McKown, *Eleanor Roosevelt's World.* Grosset and Dunlap, 1964.
- Whitney, *Eleanor Roosevelt.* Franklin Watts, 1982.

DISCOVERY ACTIVITIES

- Using reference sources, discover how Eleanor kept Franklin's name before the public during the years he was recovering from polio.
- Franklin Delano Roosevelt served four terms as president. Using reference sources, discover the present rules governing the number of terms a president can serve. When and why were they put into effect?
- Eleanor worked for world peace. Using reference sources, discover what her accomplishments were in this mission.

Anna Eleanor Roosevelt: Extraordinary First Lady

Regardless of whether the president is from the Democratic party or the Republican party, the role of the First Lady is very important.

DIRECTIONS   On the lines below, answer this question: What do you think the role of the First Lady should be?

_____

_____

_____

_____

_____

_____

_____

_____

_____

_____

_____

_____

_____

Meet Sequoyah: The Cadmus of America

Tsis-kwa'ya knew by the age of ten that he had failed to prove himself a worthy Cherokee warrior. He accepted the nickname "Sequoyah," meaning "the lame one."

Sequoyah was born in Tennessee during the 1760s. He walked with a limp. The boys in his tribe proved themselves through games of strength and endurance. Sequoyah was always the first to be ready for the race, but he was the last to finish, if he was able to finish. He spent most of his time alone in the woods. One day, he idly drew some lines on a flat rock with a small stone and found that he could draw. At age fifteen, he became a painter. He then began to work with silver, designing bracelets, pendants, and earrings.

Sequoyah became a respected member of the tribe and was granted a seat on the tribal council. He worried that the Cherokee people were drifting away from the old ways. The Cherokees had no written language. He was afraid the tribal culture, passed verbally from generation to generation, would disappear.

Fascinated by the white man's written language, Sequoyah set for himself the goal of developing a written language for the Cherokees. He experimented for years. He neglected home and family, he was laughed at and scorned. Finally, in his middle fifties, he developed a simple syllabary. A syllabary differs from an alphabet in that each letter stands for a sound. His written language was accepted rapidly. Within a year, newspapers and books were printed.

Sequoyah believed that all Indians had a common language that had originated in Mexico. He set off to discover that origin. During August of 1843, he was discovered dead at San Fernando, Mexico. It is not known how he got there, how long he had been there, or what he might have discovered.

READ MORE ABOUT SEQUOYAH

- Campbell, *Sequoyah: The Story of an American Indian.* Dillon Press, 1973.
- Kohn, *Talking Leaves: The Story of Sequoyah.* Prentice-Hall, 1969.
- Oppenheim, *Sequoyah: Cherokee Hero.* Troll Associates, 1979.
- Patterson, *Sequoyah: The Cherokee Who Captured Words.* Garrard, 1975.

DISCOVERY ACTIVITIES

- Sequoyah is called the "Cadmus of America." Using reference sources, discover why and how Cadmus is compared to Sequoyah.
- The sequoia tree is named for Sequoyah. Using reference sources, discover this tree. Why do you think it was named for Sequoyah?
- Sequoyah feared the Cherokee tribal customs and culture would disappear. Using reference sources, discover what factors lead to this fear.

Sequoyah: The Cadmus of America

A Cherokee legend holds that whenever a new star appears in the sky with a tail streaming behind, do not be alarmed. It is only Sequoyah, the lame one, searching for the key to the mother tongue.

DIRECTIONS On the animal skin below, create an illustration for the legend of Sequoyah.

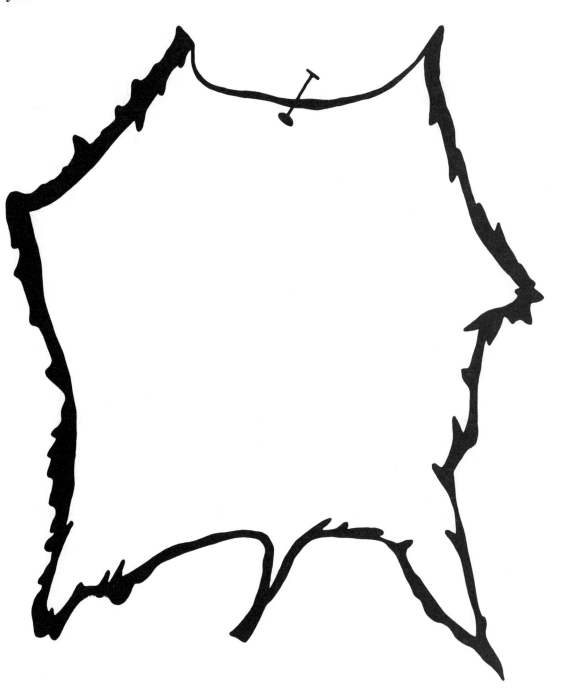

Meet Sojourner Truth: Traveler for Freedom

Isabella was sold three times before she was ten years old. Each time, she prayed to the Lord to help her please her mistress so that she would not be beaten.

Isabella Hardenburg was born in Ulster County, New York, during 1797 or 1798. Birth certificates were not issued for slaves. She was promised her freedom July 4, 1862, but her master reneged, claiming that she had not worked hard enough. Now married and mother of four children, Isabella took her own freedom and left. In 1827, New York passed a law freeing all slaves. Isabella dedicated her life to God. She took the name Sojourner, meaning one who goes from place to place, and Truth, as the Lord her master had the name of Truth. Sojourner spent many long years walking about the country talking about God's love and singing songs she wrote herself. She became a powerful speaker for freedom and women's rights. Sojourner spoke deep from within her heart and reached deep into the hearts of her audience. In 1863, she traveled to Washington to meet President Lincoln and stayed to help the freed slaves redirect their lives. In 1879, she returned to a little house in Battle Creek, Michigan, where she continued to work for civil rights for all people until her death on November 26, 1883.

Sojourner Truth spent her life speaking and singing in the fight for freedom. All she wanted was to be a faithful servant of God.

READ MORE ABOUT SOJOURNER TRUTH

- Ferris, *Walking the Road to Freedom: A Story About Sojourner Truth.* Carolrhoda Books, 1988.
- Krass, *Sojourner Truth.* Chelsea House, 1988.
- Lindstrom, *Sojourner Truth: Slave, Abolitionist, Fighter for Women's Rights.* Julian Messner, 1980.

DISCOVERY ACTIVITIES

- When we think of slavery, we think of the South. Using reference sources, trace the history of slavery in New York State from 1626 through 1827.
- Using reference sources, discover the Emancipation Proclamation. How did it free the slaves? Did it work? When were the slaves actually freed?
- Using reference sources, discover the arguments put forth by men against civil rights for women.

Sojourner Truth: Traveler for Freedom

Sojourner Truth traveled, mostly by walking, through more than twenty states in New England and the Midwest, speaking and singing for freedom and rights for all women.

DIRECTIONS If Sojourner Truth were to return today, what changes would she see? Do you feel she would be pleased? What might she feel still needs to be changed? Explain your feelings on the lines below.

Meet Harriet Tubman: A Woman Called "Moses"

Harriet was short and plump. She possessed physical grace and strength from working in the fields. Her deliberate, sullen expression hid a rebellious spirit.

Harriet was born Araminta Ross in Bucktown, Maryland, around 1821. As a slave, Harriet toiled in the fields. She had a sweet contralto voice and used it to pass on messages through the grapevine while her master or overseer thought she was just singing. Many slaves were trying to escape to freedom in the North. The escape route, helped by people opposed to slavery, was called the underground railroad. Harriet married John Tubman. He was a free man, but he had no ambition. When her master died, Harriet knew she would be sold. She fled, via the underground railroad, to Philadelphia. Harriet was free, but that was not enough for her. She had to rescue others. She went back to the South countless times to lead others to freedom. When Congress passed the Fugitive Slave Act, she led the people to Canada. Folklore grew up about Harriet. She was given the name Moses, after the leader in the Bible. During the Civil War, Harriet joined the Union Army and became a nurse, a scout, and a spy. There was a price on her head of $40,000 for her capture, dead or alive. After the Civil War, Harriet settled in Auburn, New York, where she built a home for her parents. She worked for education for all black people and rights for all women until her death on March 10, 1913.

Today, Harriet's home in Auburn has been rebuilt and is maintained as a memorial by the A.M.E. Zion Church. On a wall in the Cayuga County Courthouse, hangs a bronze memorial tablet, dedicated to a woman of rare courage.

READ MORE ABOUT HARRIET TUBMAN

- Ferris, *Go Free or Die: A Story About Harriet Tubman.* Carolrhoda Books, 1988.
- Kingel, *Women of America: Harriet Tubman.* Creative Education, 1987.
- Smith, *Harriet Tubman.* Messner, 1989.

DISCOVERY ACTIVITIES

- The underground railroad was patterned after the steam railroad. There were "stations" and "conductors." Using reference sources, discover how the underground railroad worked.
- Using reference sources, discover why to be free, escaped slaves had to go to Canada from the northern states after Congress passed the Fugitive Slave Act.
- Using reference sources, discover the Emancipation Proclamation. What was the effect of this proclamation on the people of the United States?

Harriet Tubman: A Woman Called "Moses"

The Civil War divided the United States into two opposing sides. One side was called the *United States of America,* and the other side was called the *Confederate States of America.*

DIRECTIONS Below is a map of the United States in 1861. Using reference sources:

1. Color the union states blue.
2. Color the confederate states gray.
3. Color the areas that had not yet achieved statehood green.

Meet Booker T. Washington: All Men Are Brothers

When Booker carried his owner's daughter's books to school, he peeked in the door. "Going to school must be heaven," he thought.

Booker T. Washington was born a slave in Hales Ford, Virginia, in 1856. After the Emancipation Proclamation, the family traveled two hundred miles in a donkey cart to join his stepfather in Malden, Virginia. Booker and his brothers went to work in the salt mines. Booker was determined to learn to read. His mother managed to buy him a copy of Webster's *Blue-Backed Speller.* When a school opened, Booker was allowed to attend, as long as he worked before and after school in the mines.

At school, Booker was asked for his last name, but he had no last name because slaves were given only first names. He chose the name Washington. At age sixteen, Booker set off on foot to find a school called Hampton Institute. He worked along the way and arrived at the school ragged and dirty. He was told to sweep a room. Booker thoroughly cleaned the entire room. He was accepted and trained to be a teacher.

Booker taught for a few years, then studied law. Later, he was asked to open a school in Tuskegee, Alabama. On July 4, 1881, the Tuskegee Normal and Industrial Institute opened in an old building with thirty students. Booker traveled the country raising funds for the school. In 1900, Booker published his autobiography, *Up from Slavery,* which became a bestseller. When George Washington Carver, a famous botanist, came to teach at Tuskegee, the two men became close friends.

Booker continued to travel throughout the country, seeking funds to build schools for black students. Early in 1915 he became ill. Booker returned to his beloved Tuskegee, where he died on November 14, 1915.

READ MORE ABOUT BOOKER T. WASHINGTON

- Patterson, *Booker T. Washington: Leader of His People.* Garrard, 1962.
- Washington, *Up from Slavery.* Foreword by William O. Douglass. Doubleday, 1963.
- Wise, *Booker T. Washington.* Putnam, 1968.

DISCOVERY ACTIVITIES

- Using reference sources, discover the meaning of the Emancipation Proclamation and how it freed all slaves.
- Using reference sources, discover why life was as difficult for the slaves after the Emancipation Proclamation as before.
- Using reference sources, discover the history of Tuskegee Institute from its beginning to the present day.

Booker T. Washington: All Men Are Brothers

A teacher at Hampton Institute taught Booker T. Washington how to give a speech. She taught him how to breathe and how to stand. Booker was very nervous. She suggested that he hold something. Booker tried holding a pencil. That worked. After that, Booker always held a pencil when giving a speech.

DIRECTIONS Booker traveled a great deal, giving speeches to raise funds for Tuskegee Institute. Write a speech that Booker might use to help raise funds for a special project for your school. If possible, use the speech to help the project. Use the back side of this sheet if you need more space.

TITLE OF THE PROJECT _____

Meet Noah Webster: Collector of Words

Red-haired Noah loved words—any words, all words, and especially long words. Every day, he copied words into homemade notebooks. When he found out the meaning of each word, he copied the meaning next to the word.

Noah Webster was born in West Hartford, Connecticut, on October 16, 1758. He was accepted at Yale University at the age of sixteen. After graduation, he discovered his father had mortgaged the farm to pay his tuition. He vowed to pay off the mortgage.

While he was working at various jobs, Noah wrote *The American Speller,* a spelling book he felt would interest as well as teach children. When the book was finally completed, Noah became worried. What if someone plagiarized his speller? Noah successfully campaigned for copyright laws. Noah could now protect his speller, but he could not find a publisher. He borrowed money to print the speller himself. The speller became a success, and Noah was able to pay off all his debts as well as the mortgage on his father's farm.

Noah spent the next twenty-eight years writing *The American Dictionary,* which was published in 1806. His second dictionary, *An American Dictionary of the English Language,* published in 1828, included 12,000 words and 40,000 definitions that had never been included in a dictionary.

In his later years, until his death on May 12, 1843, Noah's pockets were always bulging. Some were full of peppermints and raisins for his grandchildren. The others held notebooks and pencils for writing down words.

READ MORE ABOUT NOAH WEBSTER

- *The American Speller. An Adaption of Noah Webster's Blue-Backed Speller.* Illustrated by Barbara Cooney. Thomas Y. Crowell, 1960.
- Ferris, *What Do You Mean? A Story About Noah Webster.* Carolrhoda Books, 1988.
- Higgins, *Noah Webster: Boy of Words.* Bobbs-Merrill, 1961.

DISCOVERY ACTIVITIES

- Discover if there is a Webster's dictionary in your library. What edition is it? Make a time line from the first to the latest edition.
- Discover who publishes the Webster dictionaries today. Using reference sources, discover how that company received the copyright.
- Noah was influenced by the Charter Oak, in Hartford, Connecticut, and the Tree of Liberty, in Boston, Massachusetts. Using reference sources, discover what part these two trees played in the history of America.

Noah Webster: Collector of Words

DIRECTIONS Listed below are some words that Noah probably would have written into his notebook. Locate the meaning for each word. Write the meaning beside each word.

ANACHRONISM ——————————

FRONTISPIECE ——————————

PLAGIARISM ——————————

BOISTEROUS ——————————

WHIMSICAL ——————————

EXONERATE ——————————

OBLITERATE ——————————

JUXTAPOSITION ——————————

CANTANKEROUS ——————————

PANDEMONIUM ——————————

VACILLATE ——————————

TACITURN ——————————

GRATUITY ——————————

INALIENABLE ——————————

Literature & The Arts

As long as you keep a person down, some part of you has to be down there to hold him down, so it means you cannot soar as you otherwise might.

—*Marian Anderson*

There is no duty we so much underrate
As the duty of being happy.

—*Robert Louis Stevenson*

Name _____   Date _____

Meet Marian Anderson: World-Renowned Contralto

When Maestro Toscanini heard Marian sing in Salzburg, Austria, he told her, "Yours is a voice such as one hears once in a hundred years."

Marian Anderson was born in Philadelphia, Pennsylvania, on February 29, 1902. She loved singing and sang in church choirs from the age of six. After high school, Marian sang in concert in churches, theaters, and small colleges. Because so many doors were closed to her in the United States, Marian planned a concert tour through Europe. She was acclaimed everywhere she went.

On her return, Marian's debut was performed at Town Hall in New York City on December 30, 1935. She sang dressed in a long gown designed to conceal a cast covering a broken bone in her foot. A concert was planned at Constitution Hall in Washington D.C., but Marian was denied use of the building by the Daughters of the American Revolution, the building's owners. Instead, on Easter Sunday, April 9, 1939, Marian sang at the Lincoln Memorial, with Abraham Lincoln as her background for anyone who wished to come. The concert was attended by 75,000 people. On January 30, 1955, Marian sang in Verdi's *The Masked Ball* at the Metropolitan Opera House. She was the first black to appear on that stage.

Today, every door is opened to Marian, including Constitution Hall. She has appeared in concert throughout the world. Her rich, full, velvety voice, called a contralto, has a full range, reaching up to soprano and down to baritone.

READ MORE ABOUT MARIAN ANDERSON

- Anderson, *My Lord, What a Morning.* Franklin Watts, 1956.
- Tedard, *Marian Anderson.* Chelsea House, 1989.
- Tobias, *Marian Anderson.* Thomas Y. Crowell, 1972.

DISCOVERY ACTIVITIES

- Using reference sources, discover what is meant by a *contralto* voice, a *soprano* voice, and a *baritone* voice.
- Using reference sources, discover Maestro Arturo Toscanini. Who was he and why was his praise so important to Marian Anderson?
- During Marian Anderson's early career, she had difficulty being accepted because she was black. In her later career, she was accepted everywhere. Using reference sources, discover the reasons for the change.

© 1991 by The Center for Applied Research in Education

Name _____   Date _____

Marian Anderson: World-Renowned Contralto

There were many important milestones in Marian Anderson's life. Some of the most important are listed below in the musical notes.

DIRECTIONS Under the date in each musical note below write the event in Marian Anderson's life that took place on that date.

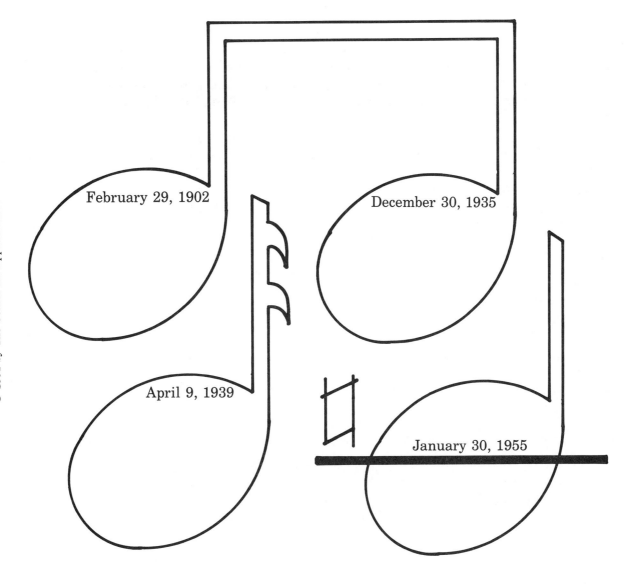

February 29, 1902

December 30, 1935

April 9, 1939

January 30, 1955

Meet John James Audubon: Painter of Birds

John did not want to go to school and study. He did not even want to take art lessons. He just wanted to be left alone, to paint birds in his own way.

A mystery clouds the birth and identity of John James Audubon. One belief is that he was born in Santo Domingo, Dominican Republic, on April 26, 1785, the son of Jean Audubon, a French sea captain, and a Haitian woman. The other belief is that he was the Lost Dauphin (eldest son) of the French king Louis XVI, dethroned during the French Revolution. Jean Audubon and his wife legally adopted John when he was eight and brought him up in France.

In 1803, John was sent to Pennsylvania to help manage a farm owned by his father. John had little interest in farming. He wandered the woods, painting birds. He married Lucy Blakewell on April 5, 1808. Lucy had great faith in John's artistic talents and supported him while he worked on what he called his "Great Work." This was to be life-sized paintings of all the birds of North America in their natural habitat. John spent the next thirty years traveling through North America painting birds. He returned home only occasionally. He suffered financial failure, personal hardship, and ridicule, but never faltered in his mission. On June 20, 1838, John's *Birds of America*, consisting of four huge leather-bound volumes was completed. This work brought him fame and fortune.

John and Lucy retired to a small estate in New York overlooking the Hudson River. His mission accomplished, John's strength slowly ebbed away. He died on January 27, 1851.

READ MORE ABOUT JOHN JAMES AUDUBON

- Kiernan, *John James Audubon.* E. M. Hale, 1954.
- Rourke, *Audubon.* Franklin Watts, 1936.
- Stevenson, *Painting America's Wildlife: John James Audubon.* Encyclopedia Britannica Press, 1961.

DISCOVERY ACTIVITIES

- Using reference sources, discover the Audubon Society. When was it formed? What are the purposes and objectives of this organization?
- Using reference sources, discover why the work of John James Audubon is considered so important today.
- Using reference sources, discover more about the mystery concerning the birth and identity of John James Audubon.

John James Audubon: Painter of Birds

When Audubon painted birds, he added branches, berries, and grasses to portray the birds in their natural habitat.

DIRECTIONS   Color the birds pictured below. Add branches, berries, or grasses to show the birds in a more natural setting.

Meet Mikhail Baryshnikov: Ballet Superstar

During his younger years, Misha worried about his height. "I was always the shortest boy in my class," he recalls wryly. "I finally realized it was ridiculous. Art is not a matter of height and size. I don't worry any longer."

Mikhail Baryshnikov was born on January 27, 1948, in Riga, Latvia, a province in the Soviet Union. As a child, Misha could not sit still. He loved to run, leap, jump, swim, and kick a ball. He was very involved in all sports. He began taking ballet lessons at the age of twelve at the Latvia Ballet School. He was selected to be a member of a dance troupe to tour Russia performing for students. While in Leningrad, he visited the famous Kirov Ballet School. He boldly asked to compete for admission. He was accepted and spent the next three years studying from nine in the morning until ten at night, six days a week. After graduation, Misha joined the Kirov Ballet Company as a soloist. During the next three years he won international acclaim and many awards. In 1974, Misha defected from the Soviet Union, requesting political asylum while in Canada. He said, "I left Russia for my artistic growth. Artistically, it was the only decision I could make." He joined the American Ballet Theater and became artistic director in 1980. Misha has enjoyed great success as a dancer, choreographer, and motion picture star.

Today, Misha attends dance class every morning, rehearses every afternoon, and performs most nights. He accepts guest roles when the theater is not in session. After the many years of having his life and activities planned for him, Misha values freedom to make his own decisions.

READ MORE ABOUT MIKHAIL BARYSHNIKOV

- Aria, *Misha: The Mikhail Baryshnikov Story.* St. Martin's, 1989.
- Butler, *Ballet for Boys and Girls.* Prentice-Hall, 1980.
- Goodman, *Baryshnikov: A Most Spectacular Dancer.* Harvey House, 1979.

DISCOVERY ACTIVITIES

- Mikhail Baryshnikov's style of dancing is called *bravura.* Using reference sources, discover what is meant by the *bravura* style.
- Mikhail Baryshnikov began ballet lessons at age twelve. That is considered a very advanced age at which to begin. Using reference sources, discover why twelve is old. What is the best age to begin ballet lessons and why?
- Using reference sources, discover the main differences between the work of male ballet dancers and that of female ballet dancers.
- Have you ever been to a performance of a ballet? Which one? Where? When? Describe your reaction to the performance.

Mikhail Baryshnikov: Ballet Superstar

Mikhail Baryshnikov said, "I left Russia for my artistic growth. Artistically, it was the only decision I could make."

DIRECTIONS What is your reaction to Mikhail's decision? Do you feel he made the right decision. What is the difference between his life today and his previous life in Russia? Write your opinion on the lines below. Continue on the back of this sheet if you need more room.

Meet Leonard Bernstein: American Maestro

Only a miracle could change a skinny, sickly, unhappy boy into a well-adjusted athlete and student. This miracle happened to Lenny, in the form of a piano.

Leonard Bernstein was born in Lawrence, Massachusetts, on August 25, 1918. His family moved many times to different neighborhoods within the Boston area. Lenny had trouble adjusting to the moves. He also suffered from many types of allergies and had difficulties making friends. One day, when Lenny was ten, he found a piano in the front hall. His aunt had asked to store the piano and other furniture in his parent's home. Lenny loved the piano. He taught himself to play and spent hours practicing. When he began piano lessons, his teachers discovered he was a gifted musician. The confidence gained from this ability changed his life. Lenny graduated from Boston Latin School and Harvard University with high honors. He was a brilliant composer, conductor, and pianist. Although he was urged to concentrate in one area, he could not make a choice and continued in all three areas.

Lenny served as music director of the New York Philharmonic Orchestra. He was famous for his musicals, especially *West Side Story,* and served as guest pianist and conductor in orchestras internationally. His television appearances helped young people gain a deeper appreciation of music. Music was Lenny's whole world, until his death on October 14, 1990.

Leonard Bernstein was an acknowledged genius. He possessed boundless energy and worked on several projects at the same time. Although he was highly acclaimed and world famous, he always worried about his work being good enough.

READ MORE ABOUT LEONARD BERNSTEIN

- Cone, *Leonard Bernstein.* Thomas Y. Crowell, 1970.
- Ewen, *Leonard Bernstein.* Chilton Book Company, 1967.
- Peyser, *Leonard Bernstein: A Biography.* Morrow, 1987.

DISCOVERY ACTIVITIES

- Using reference sources, discover and list the accomplishments of Leonard Bernstein.
- Using reference sources, discover the meaning of the term *Maestro.*
- Using reference sources, discover why most musicians concentrate on one area such as conducting, composing or playing. In your opinion, how was Leonard Bernstein able to accomplish all three?

Name _____ Date _____

Leonard Bernstein: American Maestro

Leonard Bernstein tells us in his book *The Joy of Music* that "people enjoy listening to organized sound."

There are sounds all around us. Usually we block them out because our minds are on other things. Listen to the sounds. They can grate on our nerves, they are out of order. But try putting them together in various ways; in other words, organize or arrange them. They can become music when put together in a pleasing way.

DIRECTIONS   Listen to the sounds in your classroom. Choose a high sound, a low sound, and two medium sounds that you can recreate. Arrange the sounds in various patterns, setting up a rhythm to each pattern.

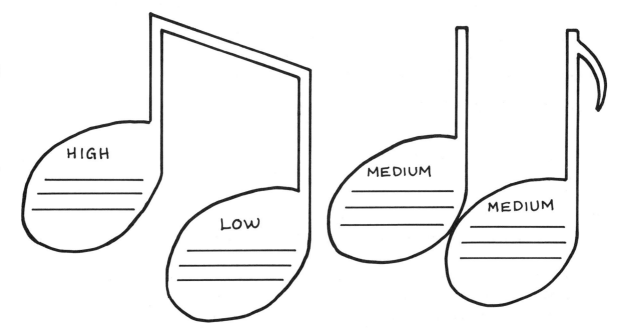

Which pattern do you like best?
Try this with several classmates. Which pattern does each like best?

Meet Judy Blume: "She Writes About Me!"

While Judy was growing up she read Nancy Drew books, biographies, and girl-loves-horse stories. She enjoyed them but wished there were books about the problems kids have that are difficult to share with parents and even with friends.

Judy Sussman was born on February 12, 1938, in Elizabeth, New Jersey. She spent rainy days in the attic or on the porch making up stories in which her dolls became the actors. Judy says she was really two people. On the outside she always did what was expected of her, was a straight-A student, and a "perfect" daughter. On the inside, she wanted to be a rebel, wanted to do things her parents would not approve of, but she did not dare. In 1959, Judy married John M. Blume and settled into a comfortable life as a housewife and mother. She took a course in children's writing and began writing and illustrating short, funny stories. Her first picture book, *The One in the Middle is the Green Kangaroo,* tells the story of a middle child who feels squashed like the peanut butter in a sandwich. Remembering her childhood wish, Judy began writing realistic fiction. *Are You There, God? It's Me, Margaret* was the first book for children about adolescent problems. Judy's books are based on real-life episodes and experiences.

Today Judy lives in Santa Fe, New Mexico. She continues to write in her first-person, natural style that helps the reader identify with the main character. She possesses a remarkable talent for writing in a matter-of-fact yet warm and humorous manner of the universal problems children face during the growing-up years.

READ MORE ABOUT JUDY BLUME

- Lee, *Judy Blume's Story.* Dillon Press, 1981.
- Blume, *Are You There, God? It's Me, Margaret; Blubber; Deenie; Freckle Juice; The Incredible Sheila the Great; It's Not the End of the World; The One in the Middle is the Green Kangaroo; Starring Sally J. Freedman as Herself; Superfudge; Tales of a Fourth Grade Nothing;* etc.

DISCOVERY ACTIVITIES

- Discover Judy Blume's books. Read at least two. What episodes or experiences in her life are the books based on?
- Read *The Summer of the Falcon* by Jean George and *Are You There, God? It's Me, Margaret* by Judy Blume. Compare the two books.
- Using reference sources, discover two more authors who write about young people and their problems. Read at least one book by each.

Name _____   Date _____

Judy Blume: "She Writes About Me!"

Judy Blume says, "I like nothing better than hearing a kid laugh while reading a book." Judy has the talent to turn embarrassing and true-life experiences into warm, humorous stories.

DIRECTIONS   Write a letter to Judy describing an experience that might make a good story. Also, try writing the story yourself.

Meet George Catlin: Mission with a Paintbrush

The Crow Indians said the buffalo would panic at the sight of even one human, but a wolf could wander peacefully through the herd. George covered himself in a wolf skin. He was so close to the buffalo as he painted them that he could feel their hot breath.

George Catlin was born in Wilkes-Barre, Pennsylvania, on July 27, 1796. His introduction to the Indian came through O-Gong-Way, an Oneida Indian, who taught George their culture and folklore. George was sure the way of the Indian would soon disappear. He believed his mission in life was to paint the Indian before this happened. He traveled through the west painting the Indian and the buffalo and began to collect Indian artifacts. George staged a successful Indian exhibit in Buffalo, New York. He tried unsuccessfully to interest Congress in buying the collection for a permanent exhibit. George then toured Europe with the collection. He became deeply in debt so he sold the collection to Joseph Harrison, who stored it in one of his factories. George painted his way through the Indian villages of Central and South America, then northwest Canada and Alaska. He was gone so long, he was presumed dead. He turned up in New York City shortly before his death on December 23, 1872.

Congress finally voted to purchase the collection, but most of it had been destroyed by moths and mice. The heirs of Joseph Harrison donated what was left to the Smithsonian. George had a great love for the Indians. That love shows the heart of a world lost forever, except through art. George Catlin's work ranks as one of the most important studies of North and South American Indians.

READ MORE ABOUT GEORGE CATLIN

- Millichap, *George Catlin.* Boise State University, 1977.
- Plate, *Palette and Tomahawk: The Story of George Catlin.* David McKay, 1962.
- Rockwell, *Paintbrush and Peacepipe: The Story of George Catlin.* Atheneum, 1971.

DISCOVERY ACTIVITIES

- Using reference sources, discover why George Catlin wanted to preserve the Indian way of life through art and artifacts.
- Using reference sources, discover how the bounty on the buffalo helped to extinguish the Indian way of life.
- George Catlin's daughters inherited all his paintings not in the collection sold to Joseph Harrison. Using reference sources, discover what they did with the paintings. How could you view these paintings today?

George Catlin: Mission with a Paintbrush

George Catlin feared that the everyday life of the American Indian was changing and would disappear as he knew it. That is why he believed his mission was to record the life of the American Indian through art and collecting artifacts.

DIRECTIONS If you believed the American way of life, as you know it, was in danger of being changed forever, what would you want to record? Either draw or list what you feel would be important to remember.

Meet William Henry Cosby, Jr.: Entertainer and Teacher

Bill Cosby's first audience was his mother. She listened to his jokes and encouraged his telling funny stories. However, she was not happy when he became the class clown.

Bill was born in North Philadelphia, Pennsylvania, on July 12, 1937. At the age of nine, he became the man of the family when his father enlisted in the Navy. Bill's mother worked twelve hours a day as a maid but still managed to find time to read books such as Mark Twain's novels to Bill and his brothers. Bill was an outstanding athlete, but was more concerned with living up to his nickname, "Cool Coz." He dropped out of school and enlisted in the Navy. While in the Navy, he earned his high school diploma and learned to balance work with play.

An athletic scholarship made it possible for Bill to enroll at Temple University. To supplement the scholarship, he worked part-time in a cafe as a comic. He became such a success that he dropped out of college to become an entertainer.

Today, Bill Cosby is a famous comedian. He has won an Emmy and six Grammy Awards. His TV program, "The Cosby Show," is one of the top-rated family shows. Bill has returned to college and earned a doctor's degree in education. He considers himself a teacher whose hope and dream is that if people can laugh together, perhaps they can learn to work together.

READ MORE ABOUT WILLIAM HENRY COSBY

- Adams, *The Picture Life of Bill Cosby.* Franklin Watts, 1986.
- Haskins, *Bill Cosby: America's Most Famous Father.* Walker, 1988.
- Kettlecamp, *Bill Cosby: Family Funny Man.* Messner, 1987.
- Martin, *Bill Cosby: Superstar.* Rourke Corporation, 1987.
- Woods, *Bill Cosby: Making America Laugh and Learn.* Walker, 1988.

DISCOVERY ACTIVITIES

- Bill Cosby did not become a star overnight. Using reference sources, make a time line of the various types of roles he played before "The Cosby Show."
- Bill Cosby is a famous and wealthy superstar. Why do you think he went back to college to complete his education?
- Bill Cosby laces his messages with humor. Watch one or more episodes of "The Cosby Show." What messages do you think he was trying to get across to the audience?

William Henry Cosby, Jr.: Entertainer and Teacher

Bill Cosby and his wife Camille have four daughters and one son. All their names begin with E: Erika, Erinn, Ensa, Evin, and Ennis. Bill says, "It's a way of reminding them each day throughout their lives that 'E' stands for excellence."

DIRECTIONS Using a dictionary, find as many words as you can beginning with "E" that have to do with excellence in education and life. Write the words in the "E" below. Share the list with another person, explaining how each word fits.

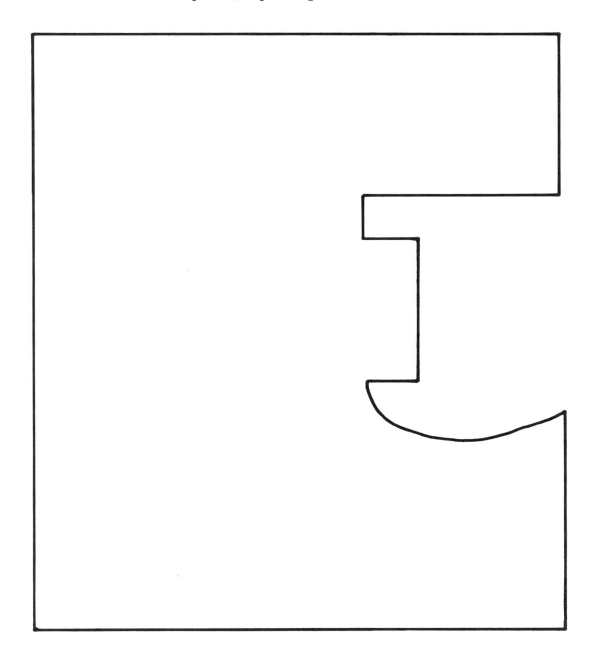

Meet Emily Dickinson: A Major American Poet

Although Emily would disappear upstairs when the front doorbell rang, she would come to the back door when children rang the bell. Often she would invite them in for fresh-baked cookies and listen to their secrets.

Emily Dickinson was born on December 10, 1830, in Amherst, Massachusetts. She enjoyed a close family life, although her father dominated the family. He considered only the Bible worth reading. Emily secretly read books by Charles Dickens and other authors. She enjoyed school and loved to write, but dreaded having to stand up and read before her classmates.

Emily loved all nature. She had difficulty with the Fundamentalist form of religion thrust upon her. She was expected to, but could not, publicly declare herself a true Christian, preparing for the afterlife. Emily believed this life was beautiful. She slowly retreated into her own world. Her poetry reveals her wonder and questions of what life is, could be, and should be. By age thirty, Emily was a complete recluse. She wrote long letters to friends, but would not see them. Emily did not want her poems published. She wrote for herself and for her friends, not for the public.

In 1884, Emily became ill with a kidney disease. She died May 15, 1886. After her death, it was discovered that she had written more than 1,700 poems. When her work was published, she was acknowledged a major American poet.

READ MORE ABOUT EMILY DICKINSON

- Barth, *I'm Nobody! Who Are You? The Story of Emily Dickinson.* Seabury, 1971.
- Longsworth, *Emily Dickinson: Her Letter to the World.* Thomas Y. Crowell, 1965.
- Thayer, *Emily Dickinson.* Franklin Watts, 1989.
- Wolff, *Emily Dickinson.* Addison Wesley, 1988.

DISCOVERY ACTIVITIES

- Emily Dickinson and Ralph Waldo Emerson are considered the most gifted American poets. Both were influenced by an American author. Using reference sources, discover this author and how he influenced them.

- Using reference sources, discover how an American war during her lifetime affected Emily Dickinson.

- Experts believe that what happens in one's adult life has its beginnings in one's childhood. Discover happenings in Emily Dickinson's childhood and young adulthood that might expain her becoming a recluse.

Name _____ Date _____

Emily Dickinson: A Major American Poet

During the year of 1862, Emily Dickinson wrote more than 365 poems she considered good enough to save in her bottom dresser drawer. One of these poems reveals her feelings about people and the world.

DIRECTIONS Read the poem by Emily Dickinson printed below. Write on the lines below what you feel this poem reveals about her.

I'm nobody! Who are you?
Are you Nobody too?
Then there's a pair of us?
Don't tell! They'd advertise you know!

How dreary to be Somebody!
How public like a frog
To tell one's name the livelong June
To an admiring Bog!

Meet Walt Disney: Creator of Mickey Mouse

Mickey was created during a train trip from New York to Los Angeles. Walt christened him Mortimer. Walt's wife, Lilly, did not like the name. By the time they reached Los Angeles, they had rechristened him Mickey Mouse.

Walter Disney was born December 5, 1901, in Chicago, Illinois. Walt's father was a tyrant, who did not believe in fun or toys for children. Walt had to work for his father, without wages, before and after school all through his school years. After high school, Walt worked for several companies, drawing animated cartoons. He created several successful series of cartoons for Charles Minz. On a trip to New York, Walt discovered Minz owned all rights to the cartoons. Walt would not receive any royalties. Walt created Mickey Mouse and using his own voice made his first Mickey Mouse sound film. Mickey was a huge success and won an Academy Award in 1931. When Walt made his first feature-length cartoon, *Snow White and the Seven Dwarfs,* everyone called it "Disney's folly," until it opened to great success. Walt opened a studio in Burbank, California, and worked to combine human actors and animation, as in *Mary Poppins,* the most acclaimed Disney film.

Walt's two small daughters loved amusement parks, but Walt was not pleased with the conditions at such places. He dreamed of creating a park with imaginative, safe rides; a place for the whole family. That dream came true with the opening of Disneyland in Anaheim, California, in 1955.

While planning the next of the Disney amusement parks, Disney World, Walt became ill. He died on December 16, 1966. During his lifetime he received more than 1,000 awards. To Walt, the most important was the first Oscar for Mickey Mouse, for that award made all the others possible.

READ MORE ABOUT WALT DISNEY

- Fisher, *The Walt Disney Story.* Franklin Watts, 1988.
- Larson, *Walt Disney: An American Original.* Creative Education, 1974.
- Montgomery, *Walt Disney: Master of Make-Believe.* Garrard, 1971.

DISCOVERY ACTIVITIES

- Using reference sources, make a list of as many Walt Disney films as you can. Make a checkmark beside the titles you have read or viewed.
- If you have been to Disneyland or Disney World, write a report of your visit.
- Many of Walt Disney's feature films have been adapted from books. Select a title to which you have access to both the book and the film. Read the book and view the film. In what ways does the film differ from the book? Which did you enjoy most and why?

Walt Disney: Creator of Mickey Mouse

Mickey Mouse was drawn from circles, rounding out into a pear-shaped body. Often cartoon characters come from smoothing out basic shapes.

DIRECTIONS Below are four basic shapes. Try creating an animated cartoon by starting with each basic shape and adding to it. Choose the one you like the best. Take several sheets of paper. Fold each sheet into four parts and cut along each fold. Draw your cartoon character on each page, changing the position of the arms and legs just a bit each time, always in the same direction. Staple the pages together to make a book. Flip through the pages and watch your character "move." That's animation.

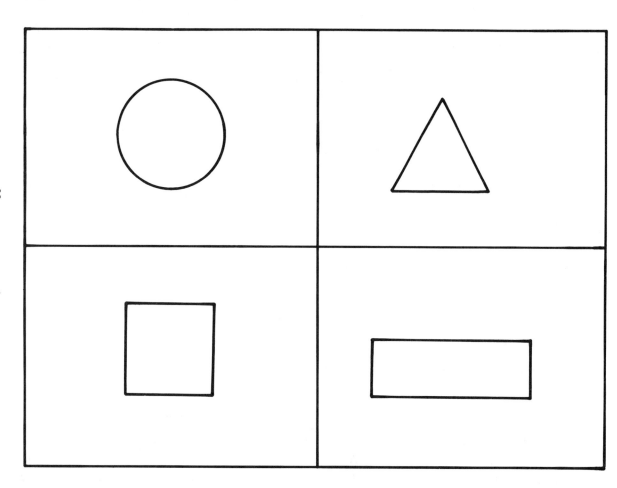

Meet Anne Frank: Het Achterhuis (The Diary)

Anne, who wanted to become a writer, received a diary on her thirteenth birthday. The diary became her closest friend and confidante. She practiced writing through recording her daily routine and deepest thoughts.

Anne Frank was born on June 12, 1929, in Frankfurt, Germany. When Hitler became Chancellor of Germany in 1933, he took away all rights and freedoms of the Jewish people, because he believed them inferior to Germans. Anne's father moved the family to Holland, where they lived happily in Amsterdam until Hitler invaded Holland. In July 1942, all Jewish people were rounded up and sent to concentration camps. The Frank family, along with four other people, moved into a hideout on the upper two floors of Mr. Frank's office building. They called it the "secret annex." They lived there, day and night, not even going near the windows, with the help of Dutch friends. On August 4, 1944, the Nazis, on a secret tip, raided the secret annex. All were arrested and sent to concentration camps. Mrs. Frank died of starvation. Anne and her sister, Margot, contracted typhus. Margot died in February and Anne died early in March of 1945. Mr. Frank was the only survivor.

When Mr. Frank visited the secret annex in June of 1945, friends gave him Anne's diary, which they had found after the raid. The diary was published in 1947 under the title *The Diary of a Young Girl.* The book has gone through more than fifty editions and sold more than eighteen million copies. The building housing the secret annex has become a museum, dedicated to freedom and the rights of all people.

READ MORE ABOUT ANNE FRANK

- Bull, *Anne Frank.* Hamish Hamilton, 1984.
- Frank, *The Diary of a Young Girl.* Doubleday, 1967.
- Leigh, *Anne Frank.* Bookwright Press, 1985.
- Tames, *Anne Frank.* Franklin Watts, 1989.

DISCOVERY ACTIVITIES

- Using reference sources, discover the reasons Hitler had a consuming hatred for all Jewish people.
- Using reference sources, discover the status of the Jewish people today in the countries occupied by Germany during World War II.
- In your opinion, what are the chances for the peoples of the world to live and work together in peace in the future? What do you believe will happen if people cannot live and work together in the future?

Anne Frank: Het Achterhuis (The Diary)

For two long years, Anne, her family, and four friends lived in several small rooms on the upper floors of a building. They were confined to this space day and night.

DIRECTIONS   If you were to experience Anne Frank's life during those two years, what would you find most difficult? On the diary pages below, write your feelings.

Meet Theodor Seuss Geisel: The Cat in the Hat Himself

Ted Geisel used his middle name when he began writing children's books and added the Dr. just for fun. He planned to save his real name for when he wrote adult or "important" books. At that time, writing for children was considered practice for writing "real" books. However, Ted soon discovered writing for children was important. Although he still uses Dr. Seuss, Ted considers writing children's books his serious work.

Theodor Seuss Geisel was born on March 2, 1904, in Springfield, Massachusetts. Ted had no formal art training but simply loved to draw all sorts of unusual characters and make up stories to go with them. After graduating from Dartmouth College, Ted wrote essays and drew cartoons for magazines. In 1928, he signed a contract with Standard Oil Company as an advertising cartoonist. This contract did not allow him to work for any other company, but Ted discovered that it did not forbid the writing of children's books. In 1936, he wrote *And to Think That I Saw It on Mulberry Street.* It was rejected by twenty-seven publishers because it was not like other children's books. Vanguard Press took a chance and published it. The book was an instant success. When Random House publishers asked Ted to write a story for beginning readers, *The Cat in the Hat* was born. Ted became president of Random House's Beginning Books Division. He also writes "I Can Read" books under the names Theo. LeSieg and Rosetta Stone.

Today, Ted lives on a hillside in La Jolla, California. He collects hats, many of which have a striking similarity to the hats in his stories. He has ideas and plans for many more books. Children love his books because they are fun. They also encourage children to read, help to develop self-confidence, and tickle the imagination.

READ MORE ABOUT THEODOR SEUSS GEISEL

- MacDonald, *Dr. Seuss.* Twayne Publishers, 1988.
- San Diego Museum of Art, *Dr. Seuss from Then to Now.* Random House, 1986.
- Dr. Seuss, *And to Think That I Saw It on Mulberry Street, The Cat in the Hat,* and more than forty other titles.

DISCOVERY ACTIVITIES

- Dr. Seuss won two Caldecott Honor Awards. Using reference sources, discover the titles and the year that these books won the silver medal.
- Using reference sources, discover why *And to Think That I Saw It on Mulberry Street* was so different from other children's books published at that time.
- Dr. Seuss has written more than forty-two books for children and adults. Using reference sources, find as many titles as possible.

Theodor Seuss Geisel: The Cat in the Hat Himself

Dr. Seuss's drawings are considered cartoons. A cartoon is a drawing that is amusing and exaggerated. Dr. Seuss' characters are imaginary but are completely believable. The stories that accompany the illustrations are bright, brash, and always optimistic. The problems that occur in the story are solved in a very satisfactory manner at the end.

DIRECTIONS To write or draw in the Dr. Seuss style, one must let the imagination flourish. Try thinking up an imaginary character. Draw this character in the space below and write a paragraph or two about the character. Let your imagination take over!

Meet Johannes Gutenberg: The Father of Printing

"If only books could be printed in some way, such as pictures are printed from woodcuts," thought Johannes. *"Then books could be as cheap as pictures."*
Johannes Gutenberg was born in Mainz, Germany, in the early 1390s. In those days, all books were hand-copied. This process was very expensive, so there were very few books and little reason for people to learn to read.

After years of experimenting, Johannes developed movable metal letters, based on the raised lines of a woodcut. The letters could be put together to form words and lines for a page. After each printing, the letters could be reset for another page. The printing press Johannes developed was adapted from a machine used to press grapes or cheese. Johannes mastered every technical detail of this first printing press. The first book he printed was the Bible. The few copies of the Gutenberg Bible in existence today are considered by experts to be magnificent examples of the forty-two-line page. One copy is owned by the Library of Congress. It is housed under glass and is on exhibition.

Johannes lived to see the printing press used throughout Germany and the rest of Europe. He saw the number of books double, triple, and quadruple. As the number of books available grew, so did the number of people learning to read them.

READ MORE ABOUT JOHANNES GUTENBERG

- Harris, *Johannes Gutenberg and the Invention of Printing.* Franklin Watts, 1972.
- McMurtrie. *Wings for Words: The Story of Johannes Gutenberg and His Invention of Printing.* Tower Books, 1971.
- Smith, *Johannes Gutenberg.* Row, Peterson, 1951.

DISCOVERY ACTIVITIES

- Using reference sources, discover some of the differences between Johannes's press and modern printing presses.
- If you have access to a printing set, experiment with printing a letter to Johannes, telling him about today's printing process.
- Many people in Johannes's day feared the printing press. They called it a "black art from Satan." Using reference sources, discover why they felt this way.
- In your own opinion, why do you think it is important for all people to be able to read for themselves, rather than just a few people?

Johannes Gutenberg: The Father of Printing

Johannes Gutenberg's printing press, made from a machine used to process grapes or cheese, was very crude compared to modern presses. Johannes might be confused hearing terms used today in the modern process.

DIRECTIONS Locate and circle the terms listed below. The words may be found forward, backward, horizontally, vertically, and diagonally.

```
B  F  O  H  L  D  U  M  M  Y  N  S  W
S  T  A  B  G  N  I  D  P  B  T  X  H
S  F  C  M  L  O  G  O  T  Y  P  E  O
H  R  O  K  G  I  C  T  R  E  I  L  F
E  T  E  L  E  D  Q  H  R  N  R  P  F
N  G  R  T  I  J  C  U  M  H  C  K  S
S  V  L  P  C  O  T  M  E  B  S  B  E
C  R  A  S  H  A  T  B  U  L  L  E  T
R  B  U  F  N  D  R  N  L  N  P  K  B
E  F  S  G  N  I  C  A  P  S  C  G  E
E  W  I  D  O  W  T  I  H  O  R  M  R
N  S  V  Q  B  D  H  L  T  C  G  L  N
B  S  R  R  O  T  I  S  O  P  M  O  C
```

BULLET	Large dot used as an ornamental device
CHARACTERS	Individual letters
COMPOSITOR	Person who sets the type
COPY	Manuscript material; written words to be set into type
CRASH	Thick cloth gauze used to form the "hinges" of a hard book cover
DELETE	To take out
DINGBATS	Typographic decorations
DUMMY	Layout showing arrangement
FOLIO	Page number
LOGOTYPE	Signature or trademark
OBLIQUE	Letters that slant to the right; also called *italic*
OFFSET	Printing from a flexible metal plate using a photographic process (how this book was printed)
SCREEN	Fine dot pattern
SIGNATURE	Group of pages printed on one sheet
SPACING	Space between letters and words
STOCK	Paper used for printing
THUMBNAILS	Small rough sketches
VISUAL	A layout
WIDOW	A short line of type

Meet Winslow Homer: Yankee Painter

At age twenty-six, Winslow's future as an artist depended on one painting. "If my dealer sells it, I will continue my art," he told his brother Charles. "If he does not, I shall find another business." The painting sold and Winslow continued his art. Years later, he discovered that Charles had bought the painting.

Winslow Homer was born February 24, 1836, in Boston, Massachusetts. His earliest drawings, sketched on his textbooks, showed strength and character. He always signed and dated his work. After working for a printmaker, Winslow moved to New York City. In two years he became a well-known illustrator. Winslow wanted to change to painting. After what he thought was the successful sale of the painting, he began to experiment with watercolors and oils. He did not copy anyone's technique or style; he painted what he saw as he saw it.

By age twenty-nine, Winslow was a recognized artist. He moved to Prouts Neck, Maine. He built a portable studio, with glass windows, stove, and wheels. He could paint what he wished, when he wished, where he wished. People began to call him a recluse. He just didn't have time for adults, but children were invited in to watch him paint.

In 1910, Winslow was stricken by a cerebral hemorrhage. He died on September 30, 1910. An artist whose main theme was the relationship between man and his environment, Winslow Homer's work has continued to grow in importance through the years.

READ MORE ABOUT WINSLOW HOMER

- "The Yankee Individualist: Winslow Homer." Freedgood, *Great Artists of America.* Thomas Y. Crowell, 1963.
- Judge, *Winslow Homer.* Crown, 1986.
- Ripley, *Winslow Homer.* Lippincott, 1963.

DISCOVERY ACTIVITIES

- Using reference sources, view a selection of Winslow Homer's watercolors and oils. Which do you prefer and why?
- Winslow Homer became practically a recluse. Using reference sources, discover whether you feel his lack of contact with people affected his paintings.
- Winslow Homer would not talk to adults, but he welcomed children and talked to them. Why do you think he would associate with children, but not with adults?

Winslow Homer: Yankee Painter

Winslow Homer enjoyed working with watercolors, but felt that they often had a washed-out look. He tried streaking dark lines on trees to emphasize the trunk and branches. He tried opaque white paint to bring out highlights. Then he tried leaving spots of the white paper in place of the opaque paint. He believed these techniques gave his watercolor paintings more sparkle and vigor.

DIRECTIONS Two copies of this activity are needed.

1. Paint the picture below with water colors.
2. Using the second copy, paint the picture the same way, except:
   a. Leave spots of white paper where you would like highlights.
   b. Streak dark lines on the trunk and branches.
3. Compare the two pictures.

Meet Langston Hughes: "Minstrel Man"

Langston's grandmother told him stories of how his people fought for freedom from slavery. Langston was filled with a fierce pride for his people.

James Langston Hughes was born on February 1, 1902, in Joplin, Missouri. His father left the family to seek opportunities in Mexico. Although Langston had contact with his father at various times, he and his father never became close. Langston and his mother moved from city to city as she sought work, so he received his education from many different schools and colleges. He became very conscious of the problems his people faced in their daily lives and how they tried to face these problems with love and humor. The feelings this awareness evoked filled up inside him, and he began to write poetry to express them. Langston wrote stories, books, plays, and poetry. His best work was written when he was filled with sadness. During the brief happy times of his life, he did not write. His work reflects the changing attitudes of people toward other people during his life time. Langston traveled all over the world, reading his poetry and instilling love and inspiration into the hearts of people. When he died on May 22, 1967, his friends mourned him with music and poetry and rejoiced that they had known him.

Langston Hughes spoke for black people. He showed that they could laugh, even when they were sad and always thought this ability made them very special. He has been called "the poet of his people."

READ MORE ABOUT LANGSTON HUGHES

- Haskins, *Always Movin' On: The Life of Langston Hughes.* Franklin Watts, 1976.
- Hughes, *The Best of Simple, The Big Sea, The Dream Keeper, I Wonder as I Wander, The Panther and the Lash.*
- Myers, *Langston Hughes: Poet of His People.* Garrard, 1970.
- Walker, *Langston Hughes: American Poet.* Thomas Y. Crowell, 1974.

DISCOVERY ACTIVITIES

- Using reference sources, discover the people who had the greatest influence on Langston Hughes's life.
- Langston Hughes's favorite place was Harlem, New York. Read about Langston and discover what attracted him to Harlem.
- Read the poetry of Langston Hughes. Select several of his poems and write what they mean to you.

Langston Hughes: "Minstrel Man"

Langston Hughes wrote "Minstrel Man" to "show the presence of tragedy behind the Negro's smiling mask."

DIRECTIONS The theme of "Minstrel Man" is universal. Many people hide behind a personal mask. On the lines below "Minstrel Man," write what the poem means to you.

Because my mouth
Is wide with laughter
You do not hear
My inner cry?
Because my feet
Are gay with dancing
You do not know
I die?

_____

_____

_____

_____

_____

_____

_____

_____

_____

_____

_____

_____

_____

Meet Joseph Rudyard Kipling: Storyteller

Five-year-old Ruddy was excited when his parents planned his first trip back to England. He did not know that he and his younger sister, Trix, would not be returning to India with them.

Joseph Rudyard Kipling was born in Bombay, India, in 1865. His father taught at the JJ Art School in Bombay. English parents living in India sent their children back to England to be educated. When the family went to England on leave, they left the children to board with a family and attend day school. Ruddy had seven years of cruel treatment. When he started bumping into things, a doctor discovered he was half blind. His mother came back from India and took the children on a long country holiday. Ruddy was enrolled in boarding school, where he made his first friends.

After graduation, Rudyard returned to India to work on a newspaper. He began to write and publish stories. Forty of these stories were successfully published in a book, *Plain Tales from the Hills.* He returned to England to write and married Caroline Balestier. They moved to Brattleboro, Vermont, to live near her family. After an argument with Caroline's brother over land use, the Kiplings returned to England. Rudyard loved to tell stories to his children. His daughter, Elsie, insisted he tell the stories the same each time, never changing a word. "The stories must be told just so," she stated. When the stories were published, Rudyard titled them *Just So Stories.* Rudyard published many books, but *The Jungle Book, The Second Jungle Book,* and *Just So Stories* were his most popular and successful ones.

In 1907, Rudyard became the first English writer to win the Nobel Prize for Literature. He continued to write until his death in 1936. His ashes were placed in Westminster Abbey, along with those of England's most-honored writers.

READ MORE ABOUT JOSEPH RUDYARD KIPLING

- Kamin, *Kipling: Storyteller of East and West.* Atheneum, 1985.
- Sutcliff, *Rudyard Kipling.* Walck, 1961.

DISCOVERY ACTIVITIES

- Read the *Just So Stories.* Which is your favorite and why?
- Read *The Jungle Book* or *The Second Jungle Book.* Write a book report.
- Using reference sources, discover the time period when a great many English people lived and worked in India. Compare their lifestyle with that of most of the Indian people.

Joseph Rudyard Kipling: Storyteller

Many of Rudyard Kipling's stories told how certain animals got their unusual characteristics, a "before-and-after" type of story.

DIRECTIONS Write a "just so" story of your own. Some examples could be

- How the porcupine got its quills
- How the skunk got its odor
- How the giraffe got its long neck
- How the pig got its curly tail

Or think of a title of your own. Draw a "before-and-after" picture in the outline below and write your story on a separate piece of paper.

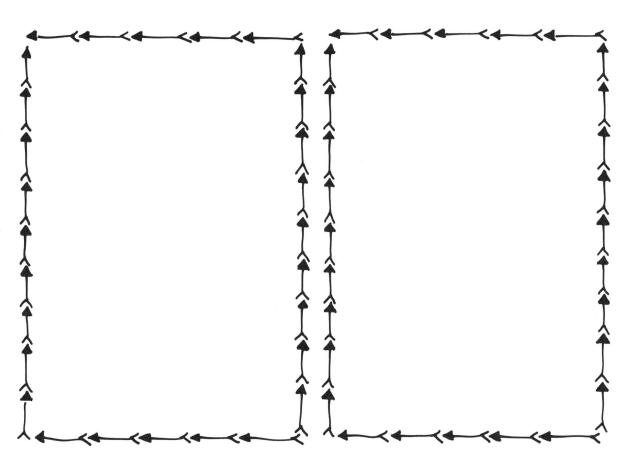

Meet Emma Lazarus: Poet for the Statue of Liberty

On December 3, 1883, a collection of writings was auctioned in New York City. The money was to be used to complete the pedestal for the Statue of Liberty. Included in this portfolio was a poem entitled, "The New Colossus," by Emma Lazarus. The portfolio was not heard of again for twenty years.

Emma Lazarus was born in New York City on July 22, 1849. Her father was a wealthy businessman whose ancestors were among the original group of Spanish Sephardic Jews to come to New Amsterdam in 1654. Emma lived a sheltered life, reading Greek and Roman classics and writing poetry. All the inspiration for her writing came from within her, until 1881. After the death of the czar, thousands of Jews emigrated to America to escape persecution in Russia. Emma directed her total energies to helping them with time, money, and her pen. The desperate plight of her people gave her the inspiration to write "The New Colossus." At the time of her death, on October 28, 1886, Emma was still involved helping her people settle in their new land.

In 1903, Georgina Schuyler, a patroness of the arts, was browsing in a New York City used-book store. She picked up a portfolio of writings and began reading. She rediscovered, "The New Colossus." Believing this poem expressed the true symbol of the Statue of Liberty as the Mother of Exiles, she arranged along with the War Department to have the poem engraved on a plaque. The plaque was placed inside the second story of the pedestal of the Statue of Liberty. Today, the last five lines of the poem have become one of the most famous poems in history.

READ MORE ABOUT EMMA LAZARUS

- Lefer, *Emma Lazarus.* Chelsea House, 1988.
- Levinson, *I Lift My Lamp: Emma Lazarus and the Statue of Liberty.* Lodestar Books, 1986.
- Maestro, *The Story of the Statue of Liberty.* Lothrop, Lee and Shephard, 1986.
- Schappes, *Emma Lazarus: Selections from Her Poetry and Prose.* Emma Lazarus Federation of Jewish Women's Clubs, 1982.

DISCOVERY ACTIVITIES

- Using reference sources, discover Frederic Auguste Bartholdi. Document in a time line his connection to the Statue of Liberty.
- Using reference sources, read the entire poem "The New Colossus." Which lines are the most famous?
- Using reference sources, discover what happened to the Jews who emigrated to America during Emma's lifetime. Specifically, how did Emma help them?

Emma Lazarus: Poet for the Statue of Liberty

DIRECTIONS Below is a copy of the poem, "The New Colossus," by Emma Lazarus. Underline the part of the poem that has become famous. Learn that part and recite it to your teacher, someone at home, and one friend.

The New Colossus

Not like the brazen giant of Greek fame,
With conquering limbs astride from land to land;
Here at our sea-washed, sunset gates shall stand
A mighty woman with a torch, whose flame
Is the imprisoned lightning, and her name
Mother of Exiles. From her beacon hand
Glows world-wide welcome; her mild eyes command
The air-bridged harbor that twin cities frame.
"Keep ancient lands, your storied pomp!" cries she
With silent lips. "Give me your tired, your poor,
Your huddled masses yearning to breathe free,
The wretched refuse of your teeming shore.
Send these, the homeless, tempest-tost to me,
I lift my lamp beside the golden door!"

Meet Anna Mary Robertson Moses: Grandma Moses

Anna Mary's brothers scoffed when she drew her colorful "lamb scapes" as she called them. They preferred to draw steam engines.

Anna Mary Robertson was born September 7, 1860, on a farm near Eagle Bridge, New York. She had only a basic schooling of reading and writing. Children were expected to learn needed life skills from their parents. Between chores, Anna Mary enjoyed sleigh rides, coasting, and skating in the winter and country fairs, berry picking, and roaming the fields in the summer. Her father, a hard-working farmer, had a love of beauty and art. He brought home large sheets of newsprint and encouraged his ten children to draw.

After marrying Thomas Moses in 1886, farm and family took all Anna Mary's time. She could only dream "lamb scapes" in her mind. When Thomas died in 1927, Anna Mary went to live with a son. She began embroidering pictures with worsted wool. When rheumatism stiffened her fingers, she began painting again. At first, she copied other pictures and photographs. Soon, though, she began painting the countryside and the scenes stored in her mind. At the age of eighty, Anna Mary, known as Grandma Moses, was becoming famous. Her paintings were exhibited everywhere. She continued to paint until her death on December, 13, 1961.

Grandma Moses' folk art reflects the simple, timeless pleasures of a world that was peaceful and happy, full of the joy of being alive. A time that one cannot go back to—indeed, may not want to—but it rests one's mind to think about it and visualize it through her paintings.

READ MORE ABOUT ANNA MARY ROBERTSON MOSES

- Liang, *Grandma Moses: The Grand Old Lady of American Art.* SamHar Press, 1972.
- Oneal, *Grandma Moses: Painter of Rural America.* Viking Kestral, 1986.
- Thompkins, *Grandma Moses.* Chelsea House, 1988.

DISCOVERY ACTIVITIES

- Using reference sources, discover why Grandma Moses' paintings are so popular today.
- Grandma Moses lived to be one hundred and one years old. She lived during an era of many exciting discoveries but chose to paint from her childhood. Using reference sources, discover why.
- Grandma Moses had very little education and no training at all in art. Using reference sources, discover how a person with no training and at such an advanced age was able to become so famous.

Anna Mary Robertson Moses: Grandma Moses

Grandma Moses is called a primitive or folk artist, which means she had no formal art training. She usually worked on several paintings at one time because it was a more practical way to use paints. She mixed her paints in preserve jar lids. She always framed her pictures. She felt a painting was not "dressed" without a frame. She often cut the Masonite board to fit a frame. Her work is divided into four seasons with one color dominating.

DIRECTIONS In the boxes below, draw the same scene showing the four seasons, using the dominant color and adding others. Draw a frame to complete each picture.

White for WINTER

Light green for SPRING

Deep green for SUMMER

Brown for AUTUMN

Meet Georgia O'Keeffe: Poet of Art

The first time Georgia saw her work displayed, she was upset. The teacher had printed G. O'Keeffe in dark, thick letters at the bottom of each painting. "The name was more noticeable than the painting," she complained. From that point on, Georgia never signed her work. Her paintings would identify themselves.

Georgia O'Keeffe was born in Sun Prairie, Wisconsin, on November 15, 1887. By the age of twelve, she knew she would become an artist. Georgia attended several art schools for short periods of time, but she felt her work was becoming a composite of the work of her teachers. She must find her own technique. Using reams of paper and soft charcoal, she worked until she found the style that was deep inside her. At her first showing, critics could not agree about her work. The strong, simple, flowing shapes growing out of vibrant colors had an energy of their own.

After marrying Alfred Steiglitz in 1924, Georgia painted in New York City and Lake George. In 1929, she began spending summers in New Mexico. She moved there permanently after Steiglitz's death in 1938. She loved the great expanse of land against an endless sky, the clear air, and the ever-changing, brilliant desert colors.

Georgia was a very private person who devoted her total energy to art. She believed in herself and dared to paint bold and original subjects. She continued to paint until her death on March 6, 1986, at the age of 98. She is considered one of the most important women in the history of American art.

READ MORE ABOUT GEORGIA O'KEEFFE

- Barry, *Georgia O'Keeffe.* Chelsea House, 1989.
- Gherman, *Georgia O'Keeffe: The "Wideness and Wonder of Her World."* Atheneum, 1986.
- Lisle, *Portrait of an Artist: A Biography of Georgia O'Keeffe.* Washington Square Press, 1987.

DISCOVERY ACTIVITIES

- Using reference sources, view Georgia O'Keeffe's paintings. Which ones do you like or dislike and why?
- Georgia O'Keeffe lived for almost a century. Using reference sources, discover the important changes that took place during her lifetime. Did any of these changes affect her work?
- Georgia O'Keeffe was called a great woman artist, but she objected to the word "woman." Using reference sources, discover why?

Georgia O'Keeffe: Poet of Art

Georgia O'Keeffe went through a stage of painting flowers. She painted pansies, the black iris, sunflowers, petunias, jack-in-the-pulpits, poppies, and morning glories. She magnified the flowers instead of painting them delicately as was the custom. At times, she would magnify just one part of the blossom. These paintings were very startling to people.

DIRECTIONS   Below are drawings of some of the types of flowers Georgia experimented with. Select a section of one or more of the flowers. On a separate sheet of paper, draw an enlarged version of the section. Show the drawings to others in your classroom. Note their reaction.

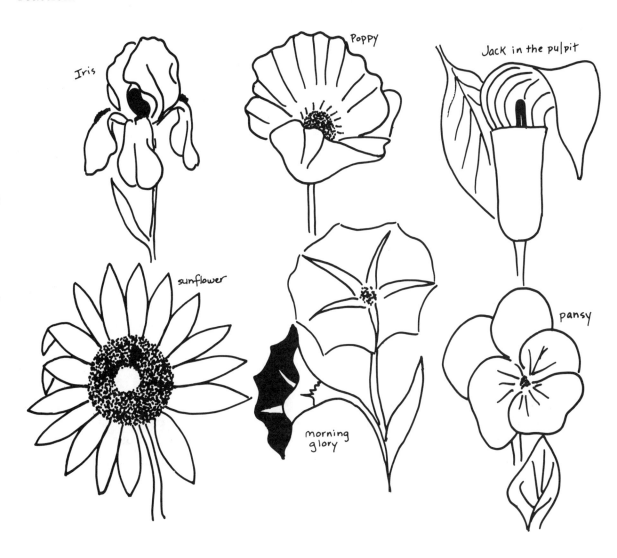

Meet Steven Spielberg: Mr. Movies

When Steven was a boy, he delighted in making up scary stories and objects to entertain his younger sisters. Was he practicing for the day when he would create the movie, E.T., The Extra-Terrestrial?

Steven Spielberg was born on December 18, 1947, in Cincinnati, Ohio. He had a difficult time in school. He did not make friends easily, he was not good in sports, and he was considered "different" by his classmates. Steven loved to make movies. When his family moved to Phoenix, Arizona, Steven joined the theater arts group at Arcadia High School. For the first time, he felt that he belonged. Here were kids who were interested in the same things as he. He was no longer "different."

At age sixteen, Steven made his first full-length movie, *Firefly.* He was script writer, photographer, editor, director, and producer. Steven's family moved again, this time to San Jose, California. Steven had his first inside look at a major movie studio. He liked what he saw so much that he spent a whole summer studying every part of filming movies and TV shows. Dressed in a suit and tie and carrying a briefcase, he walked right past the guard every morning. No one questioned him. After that summer, Steven knew that writing and directing movies would be his whole purpose in life.

Steven's successes include *Jaws, Close Encounters of the Third Kind, Raiders of The Lost Ark,* and *E.T.,* considered to be the most popular movie of all time. Steven is a dreamer. He brings his dreams to life through the movie camera. His future plans are to direct a film a year and possibly create a sequel to *E.T.*

READ MORE ABOUT STEVEN SPIELBERG

- Collins, *Steven Spielberg: Creator of E.T.* Dillon Press, 1983.
- Mabery, *Steven Spielberg.* Lerner Publications, 1986.

DISCOVERY ACTIVITIES

- Using reference sources, discover the education and on-the-job training one should have to become a movie director.
- Although Steven Spielberg created the movie *E.T.,* he did not create the story. Using reference sources, discover the author, title, publisher, and copyright date of the book *E.T., The Extra-Terrestrial.*
- Using reference sources, discover all the Steven Spielberg movies. Create a time line of the films, including the role Steven Spielberg played in each.

Steven Spielberg: Mr. Movies

DIRECTIONS Steven Spielberg is looking forward to making many more movies, and perhaps even a sequel to *E.T., The Extra-Terrestrial*. On the lines within the letters, write a synopsis of what you would like to see happen with Elliot and E.T.

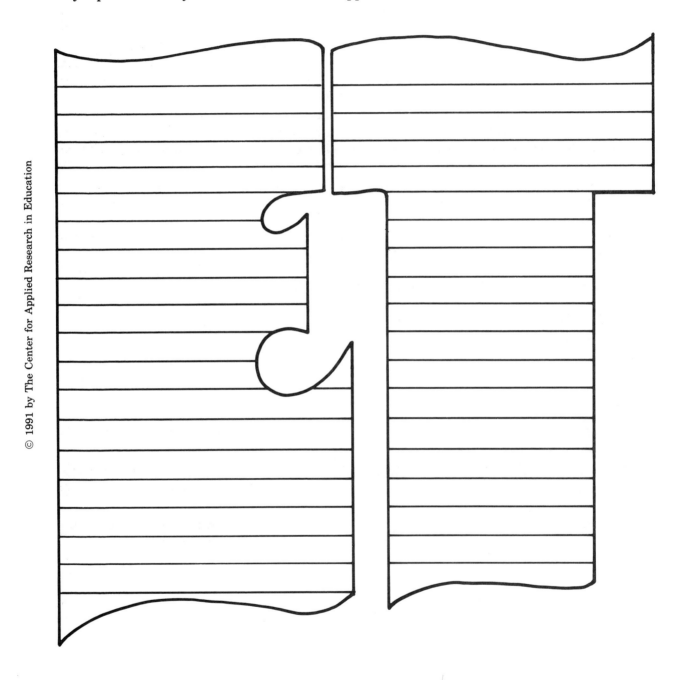

Meet Robert Louis Stevenson: Novelist and Poet

When Louis wrote law essays, he needed an audience so he could read them aloud. His thirteen-year-old stepson, Lloyd, complained, "Why don't you try writing something interesting?" With that remark, Treasure Island *was born.*

Robert Louis Balfour Stevenson was born on November 13, 1850, in Edinburgh, Scotland. As an only child he had his parents undivided attention. Louis's health was very poor, forcing him to spend as much time in bed with colds, coughs, and pneumonia as he spent at school. He loved to read and write though, and he always carried two books, one to read and one to write in. As Louis grew older, his health problems increased. He spent most of his time in warm, sunny places, returning to Scotland only for visits. He married Fanny Osborne, an American widow with two children.

Louis began successfully to write essays and articles. After Lloyd's complaint, he wrote a tale of pirates and buried treasure, which grew into *Treasure Island,* still read and loved today. His other best-known works include *Kidnapped, The Strange Case of Dr. Jekyll and Mr. Hyde,* and *A Child's Garden of Verses,* poems based on his childhood.

The south seas climate seemed beneficial to Louis. He built a house in Samoa and lived there until he died of a stroke on December 3, 1894. He had been loved and was mourned by the islanders. The chiefs buried Louis on top of Mount Vaea, as he had requested.

READ MORE ABOUT ROBERT LOUIS STEVENSON

- Furnas, *Voyage to Windward: The Life of Robert Louis Stevenson.* West, 1980.
- Peare, *Robert Louis Stevenson: His Life.* Henry Holt and Company, 1955.
- Stevenson, *Treasure Isaland, Kidnapped, The Strange Case of Dr. Jekyll and Mr. Hyde,* and *A Child's Garden of Verses.*

DISCOVERY ACTIVITIES

- Read one of the novels by Stevenson. How did Stevenson's life experiences help him write the book.
- *A Child's Garden of Verses* is based on Stevenson's childhood. Read the book. Find examples of poems he wrote about the times of sickness and the times when his health was good.
- Why was Stevenson not able to become an engineer as his father wanted, and what happened to his law career?

Robert Louis Stevenson: Novelist and Poet

Many of Robert Louis Stevenson's poems are based on a simple fact. He does not have to explain the fact; the understanding comes to us as we read the poem.

DIRECTIONS Below is an example of a poem based on a fact. Read the poem carefully. On the lines, explain the fact behind the poem.

Bed in Summer

In winter I get up at night
And dress by yellow candle light.
In summer, quite the other way,
I have to go to bed by day.

I have to go to bed and see
The birds still hopping on the tree.
Or hear the grownup people's feet
Still going past me in the street.

And does it not seem hard to you,
When all the sky is clear and blue,
And I should like so much to play,
To have to go to bed by day?

_____

_____

_____

_____

_____

_____

_____

_____

_____

_____

_____

_____

_____

Meet Maria Tallchief:
First Internationally Recognized American Indian Ballerina

On her twelfth birthday, Maria gave a performance of piano and dance. She felt torn in two. She loved both but knew she must choose one over the other.

Elizabeth Marie Tallchief was born on January 25, 1925, in Fairfax, Oklahoma, on the Osage Indian reservation. She began piano lessons at age three and ballet lessons at age four. The family moved to Los Angeles, California, when Betty Marie was eight. The new ballet teacher claimed Betty Marie had been taught wrong and insisted she begin again. Her mother wanted her to be a concert pianist, but Betty Marie loved ballet. She tried to be perfect at both. At age sixteen she performed in a ballet. A tall, slim, serious girl, Betty Marie felt strong and gloriously alive. She chose ballet over the piano.

After joining the Ballet de Monte Carlo in New York City, Betty Marie toured with the company. She was asked to take a stage name. She took the name Maria, but refused to change her last name. She married George Balanchine, choreographer and founder of the New York City Ballet. She performed internationally to great acclaim. Although famous, Maria felt a lack in her life. She ended her marriage and at age thirty-one married again and had a daughter. Later, she toured with the American Ballet Theater as prima ballerina. In 1966, she "hung up her shoes" to be at home with her husband and daughter.

Maria's love for the ballet continued, and she worked to establish the Chicago City Ballet. She served as artistic director from 1980 until 1987.

READ MORE ABOUT MARIA TALLCHIEF

- Butler, *Ballet for Boys and Girls.* Prentice-Hall, 1980.
- Krementz, *A Very Young Dancer.* Knopf, 1976.
- Tobias, *Maria Tallchief.* Thomas Y. Crowell, 1970.

DISCOVERY ACTIVITIES

- Using reference sources, discover what the first ballet was. Who created it? When and where was it performed?

- Using reference sources, discover the best age to begin ballet lessons. What are the ideal physical and mental characteristics of a ballet dancer?

- Using reference sources, discover the notable ballet companies in the United States. What state has the largest number of companies. What ballet company is closest to your home?

- Have you ever been to a performance of a ballet? Which one? Where? When? Describe your reaction to the performance.

Maria Tallchief:
First Internationally Recognized American Indian Ballerina

ACROSS

4. Composition of steps, movements, and dance patterns.
6. Costume worn by female dancer.
8. Full bend of the knees in any position
10. The height to which a dancer can jump
11. Female "star" dancer.
12. One-piece practice knit suit.

DOWN

1. Fixed wooden rail used for practice.
2. Famous ballet usually performed in December.
3. A story expressed in dancing.
5. Dancing on the toes.
7. The number of basic positions in ballet.
9. A turn or turns on one foot.

Meet Laura Ingalls Wilder: A True Pioneer

Small Laura was afraid there would be no Christmas that year. The creek was flooded; no one could get across. But Laura hung up her stocking anyway. On Christmas morning, the bulging stocking held a shiny tin cup, a candy stick, a gleaming new penny, and a sweet cake. Mr. Edwards had swum the creek, bringing the gifts. He said Santa had left them on the other side. Bursting with happiness, Laura knew no Christmas could ever be better.

Laura Ingalls Wilder was born on February 7, 1867, in Pepin, Wisconsin. Her father had the restless spirit of the pioneer. Her mother was a true pioneer wife, working side by side with her husband, building a home and family life wherever they might be. The Ingalls family was always one of the first to move into a new area. At age fifteen, Laura became a teacher of five students in a one-room schoolhouse. When Laura married Almanzo Wilder on August 25, 1885, they became homesteaders on a farm where their daughter, Rose, was born. The years that followed were not always easy, but Laura and Almanzo faced their problems with love and courage. Laura began comparing modern life with the days of her childhood. She wanted to bring them back through stories. In 1930, she began writing *The Little House in the Big Woods,* a fiction story based on her true life. Published in 1932, the book was so successful she continued until the series of eight books was completed with *These Happy Golden Years,* published in 1943. Laura's last years were spent in the company of thousands of letters from children who loved her books. Laura Ingalls Wilder died on February, 10, 1957.

Laura Ingalls Wilder said, "Running through all my stories is a golden thread of courage, independence, cheerfulness, and humor, the values of the pioneer."

READ MORE ABOUT LAURA INGALLS WILDER

- Blair, *Laura Ingalls Wilder.* Putnam, 1981.
- Wilder, *On the Way Home.* Harper and Row, 1962.
- Zochert, *Laura: The Life of Laura Ingalls Wilder.* Henry Regnery, 1976.

DISCOVERY ACTIVITIES

- Read the "Little House" books in order from *The Little House in the Big Woods* through *These Happy Golden Years.*
- Draw a map showing the setting of each "Little House" book. Compare those places with the places Laura Ingalls Wilder actually lived.
- Using reference sources, discover how fiction and nonfiction are woven together in the "Little House" books.

Laura Ingalls Wilder: A True Pioneer

The advice given to all beginning writers is to write about what you know. Laura Ingalls Wilder did just that. Drawing on her own childhood, she wrote fiction books based on fact, but not limited just to the facts. Fiction and nonfiction are closely woven throughout her stories.

DIRECTIONS Practice weaving fiction and nonfiction together. Write a short paragraph about something that actually happened to you. Then on the back of this sheet or on a second copy, rewrite the paragraph, keeping the basic facts but coloring them with imagination or fiction.

Meet Frank Lloyd Wright: Master of Light and Shadow

When Frank was born, his mother decided he would become an architect. She hung prints of famous European cathedrals in his nursery to influence him. But it was Frank himself who was determined to be the world's greatest architect.

Frank Lloyd Wright was born on June 8, 1869, in Richland Center, Wisconsin. During his early teens, he worked summers on his uncle's farm. This experience gave him a love for natural things. After a year at the University of Wisconsin studying engineering, Frank left college and went to Chicago.

He was hired as a tracer to trace blueprints in a architect's office. Frank was extremely confident in his own ability. He believed that "American architecture should not be a copy of ancient forms, but should grow out of the conditions and needs where it was to be built." His outstanding contributions included the prairie-style house that blended into its surroundings; the Imperial Hotel in Tokyo, built to withstand Japan's earthquakes; the Guggenheim Museum in New York, a controversial seven-layer inverted spiral; and California's Marin County Civic center.

Frank created the Taliesin Fellowship, where students flocked to study with him in Wisconsin and Arizona. He worked on hundreds of projects, many of which were completed and some that never left the drawing board, because society frowned on his lifestyle, which affected his being hired. Frank was a complete egotist and never changed his opinions. In later years, all sorts of honors were bestowed on him. During April of 1959, Frank became ill. Despite an emergency operation, he died two months before his ninetieth birthday. Frank Lloyd Wright has been acknowledged to be America's greatest architect.

READ MORE ABOUT FRANK LLOYD WRIGHT

- Gill, *Many Masks: A Life of Frank Lloyd Wright.* Putnam, 1987.
- Jacobs, *Frank Lloyd Wright: America's Greatest Architect.* Harcourt, 1965.
- Storrer, *The Architecture of Frank Lloyd Wright: A Complete Catalog,* 2nd. ed. MIT Press, 1978.

DISCOVERY ACTIVITIES

- Using reference sources, discover the differences between Wright's "prairie" houses and the Victorian houses of the late 1800s.
- Using reference sources, discover the controversy surrounding the Guggenheim Museum.
- Using reference sources, discover how Wright was able to design and build the earthquake-proof Imperial Hotel in Tokyo.

Frank Lloyd Wright: Master of Light and Shadow

Frank Lloyd Wright believed that form, the design, should follow function, how the design is to be used. Think of how you use your bedroom. Do you study there? Read? Watch TV? Work on hobbies? Have your friends over?

DIRECTIONS Design a room reflecting your personality and how you use or would like to use your bedroom, having form follow function.

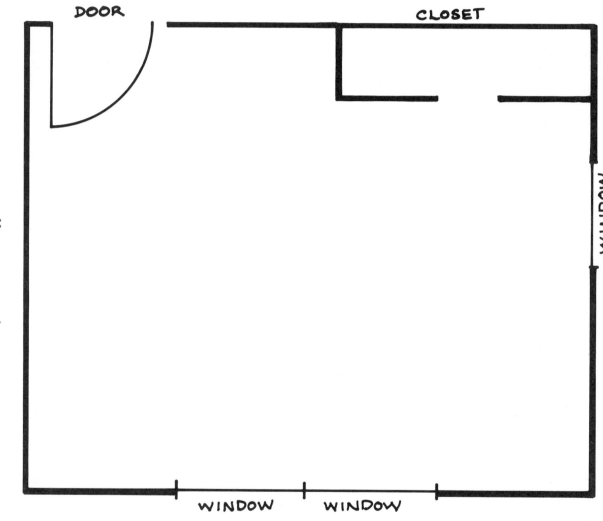

Science & Discovery

Chance favors the prepared mind.

—*Louis Pasteur*

Every kind of peaceful cooperation among men is primarily based on mutual trust and only secondarily on institutions such as courts of justice and police.

—*Albert Einstein*

Meet Frederick Banting: The Mysterious Hormone X

Fred and Jane were close childhood friends. When Jane died from diabetes, Fred vowed to become a doctor. He had to learn more about this mysterious disease that caused the death of children.

Frederick Banting was born in Alliston, Ontario, Canada, on November 14, 1891. His father inspired in his five children a respect for religion, a love of music, and a desire for knowledge. After becoming a doctor, Fred set up a practice of orthopedic surgery. A shy, reserved man with adults, Fred was at ease with children. His small patients loved him and called him Uncle Doctor Fred. In addition to his practice, Fred taught at the University of Western Ontario. One day he prepared for a lecture on the pancreas, a small gland whose function is necessary for the body to use sugar. The inability of the body to use sugar causes "sugar sickness" or diabetes. The time-dimmed memories of Jane washed over him.

Fred seriously researched this age-old disease. Together with Dr. James Collip and Dr. John Mcleod, Fred isolated a hormone from the pancreas of animals, which when injected into the body controlled diabetes. This hormone was named insulin. Insulin cannot cure diabetes, but when used properly enables diabetics to lead near-normal lives. Fred continued his research and guided and encouraged young scientists in cancer studies until his death in a plane crash on February 21, 1941. Today, the research of Sir Frederick Banting continues at the Banting Research Institute in Toronto.

READ MORE ABOUT FREDERICK BANTING

- Covelli, *Borrowing Time: Growing Up With Diabetes.* Thomas Y. Crowell, 1979.
- Levive, *The Discoverer of Insulin: Dr. Frederick Banting.* Messner, 1959.
- Silverstein, *Runaway Sugar: All About Diabetes.* Lippincott, 1981.

DISCOVERY ACTIVITIES

- Using reference sources, discover the difference between childhood diabetes and adult diabetes.
- Using reference sources, discover how the islets of Langerhans played such an important part in the discovery of insulin.
- The discovery of insulin was not a cure for diabetes. Using reference sources, discover the rules and routines a diabetic person must follow in order to maintain health.
- Using reference sources, discover any newer techniques used in controlling diabetes that have been developed since Dr. Banting's discovery of insulin.

Frederick Banting: The Mysterious Hormone X

DIRECTIONS Below are some terms and definitions people use when discussing diabetes. After reading the terms and becoming familiar with the definitions, locate the terms in the puzzle. The terms may be found forward, backward, horizontally, vertically, and diagonally.

```
S  L  L  E  C  A  T  E  B  H  B  S  C
A  A  W  G  F  L  R  D  S  N  E  H  V
E  J  M  P  K  P  H  C  L  I  R  N  T
R  S  C  O  V  H  X  O  D  C  O  H  B
C  U  O  F  C  A  C  O  R  G  D  C  P
N  G  L  C  N  C  B  R  A  M  J  R  S
A  A  P  G  U  E  I  C  A  N  O  I  E
P  R  C  B  N  L  U  T  F  T  N  N  T
L  C  M  O  T  L  G  D  E  S  S  R  E
F  A  T  C  G  S  F  I  U  B  G  T  B
N  E  H  R  B  G  N  L  R  M  A  K  A
K  C  O  H  S  N  I  L  U  S  N  I  I
B  T  R  B  A  N  T  I  N  G  C  L  D
```

ALPHA CELLS	Pancreatic cells that produce glucagon
BANTING	Doctor who discovered insulin
BETA CELLS	Pancreatic cells that produce insulin
DIABETES	Disease caused by the inability of the body to use sugar properly
FAT	High-energy food substance found in butter, oils, and meat
GLUCAGON	Hormone that increases the amount of sugar in the blood
GLUCOSE	The most common kind of sugar in the blood
HORMONE	Body chemical that controls the organs and systems
INSULIN	Hormone that decreases sugar in the blood and increases sugar in the liver
INSULIN SHOCK	Reaction to too much insulin in the blood
KETONE BODIES	Chemicals formed when the body burns fat for energy
PANCREAS	Gland that produces insulin and glucagon
PROTEIN	Food substance used to build body structures
STARCH	Food substance that the body breaks down into sugar
SUGAR	Quick-energy food substance

Name ———————————————— Date ————————————

Meet Alexander Graham Bell: Scientist and Educator

Alexander Graham Bell was twenty-seven years old when he invented the telephone. Alexander's father invented "visible speech," a code of symbols that helped the deaf to speak. Alexander and his two brothers helped demonstrate this device.

Born in Edinburgh, Scotland, in 1847, Alexander moved with his parents to Ontario, Canada, after both his brothers died from tuberculosis, and Alexander's health was threatened. Alexander opened a school for the deaf in Boston. He developed the idea for the telephone while trying to send several telegraph messages over a single line at one time. Alexander believed that if sound could travel along a wire, voices could also. He hired Thomas A. Watson, who became his lifelong friend, to help with the electrical work.

Alexander was issued a patent for the telephone on May 7, 1876. When he exhibited the first telephones at the Centennial Exposition in Philadelphia in June of 1876, many men tried to claim they had already invented the telephone. This led to many lengthy law suits, and although Alexander proved his patent was the first, he had to spend a great deal of time defending his invention.

Alexander became a citizen of the United States in 1882 but spent most of his later years at his estate on Cape Breton Island, Nova Scotia, until his death on August 2, 1922.

READ MORE ABOUT ALEXANDER GRAHAM BELL

- Farr, *Thomas Edison—Alexander Graham Bell.* Pendulum Press, 1979.
- Johnson, *The Value of Discipline: The Story of Alexander Graham Bell.* Oak Tree Publications, 1985.
- Montgomery, *Alexander Graham Bell.* Garrard, 1963.

DISCOVERY ACTIVITIES

- Alexander's patent proved that he was the first to invent the telephone. Using reference sources, discover the definition of a patent. How does a person obtain a patent? How does a patent protect a person and an invention?
- Alexander exhibited his telephones at the Centennial Exposition. Using reference sources, discover what an exposition is. What is its purpose? Where and how often are expositions held?
- Make your own telephone with two tin cans and some string. With the help of an adult, cut off the tops of two medium cans. Punch a hole in the bottom of each. Thread the ends of the strings through the holes and knot the string inside each can. Each of you takes a can and moves apart until the string is tight. Speak through the open end. Your voice should travel along the string and be heard by the other person, who holds the open end of the can to the ear.

Alexander Graham Bell: Scientist and Educator

The telephone has changed a great deal since Alexander Graham Bell was issued a patent in 1876.

DIRECTIONS   Call Mr. Bell and tell him about the different types of telephones and how the telephone can be used today.

Hello, Mr. Bell, this is _____ calling.

_____

_____

_____

_____

_____

_____

_____

_____

_____

_____

_____

I have enjoyed talking to you, but I must go now. Goodbye, Mr. Bell.

Meet Louis Braille: Real Books for the Blind

Louis, blinded by an accident at the age of three, longed to be able to read real books. His classmates were happy to read his lessons to him, but Louis needed the independence of being able to read for himself.

Louis Braille was born in 1809 in Coupvray, France. He entered the Royal Institution for the Blind in Paris at the age of ten. He finally had books to read, but they were great big books with raised letters. The students traced the letters with their fingers, spelling out the words. Because the books were so expensive to make, each class had only two or three at best to read each year. Louis heard of a code of raised dots that was used by soldiers on the combat field. The messages could be decoded without light. Louis was positive that the concept of raised dots could be developed into a reading system for the blind.

After graduation, Louis remained at the school as a teacher. He continuously worked on his idea. Each letter of the alphabet would be represented by a group of dots, grouped to fit under a finger tip. The blind reader's fingers could glide across the page, a line at a time, as does a seeing reader's eye. After years of trial and error, he developed a system not only for reading, but for math and music as well. Louis taught the system to his students with great success. Gradually, Louis's dot system, known today as the braille system, spread throughout the world.

Louis remained at the school, which he called his home and family, until his death in 1852. He felt the greatest happiness in his life came from the fact that there could now be libraries filled with books for those who read with "seeing fingers."

READ MORE ABOUT LOUIS BRAILLE

- Davidson, *Louis Braille: The Boy Who Invented Books for the Blind.* Scholastic, 1974.
- DeGering, *Seeing Fingers: The Story of Louis Braille.* David McKay, 1962.
- Keeler, *Louis Braille.* Franklin Watts, 1986.

DISCOVERY ACTIVITIES

- Using reference sources, discover the device known as a braille writer. What is its purpose and how does it work?
- Using reference sources, discover the hardware and software available to the blind today.
- Using reference sources, discover the purpose and functions of the American Association of the Blind.

Louis Braille: Real Books for the Blind

The braille code is based on a cell of six dots. There are sixty-three possible arrangements of the dots. Louis Braille worked out an alphabet, punctuation marks, numerals, and a system for writing music using this code.

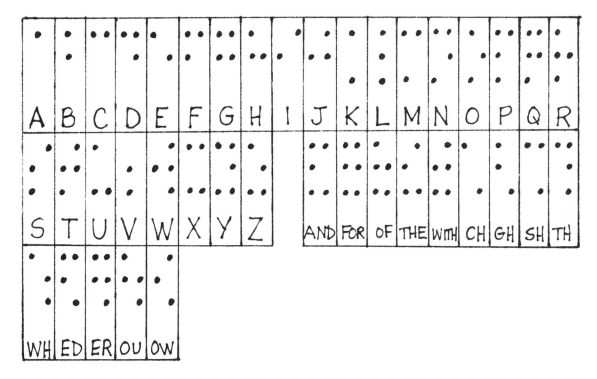

DIRECTIONS Write a message in braille in the lines below.

_____

_____

_____

_____

_____

_____

_____

_____

_____

_____

Meet Rachel Carson: Protector of Our Resources

"All living things are dependent upon one another in a natural cycle," Rachel Carson stated. "If one is destroyed all will be damaged."

Rachel Carson was born in Springdale, Pennsylvania, in 1907. She loved to read about the sea. She planned to be a writer, but as a student at Pennsylvania College for Women, she took a course in biology that changed her life. She knew that she had to become a marine biologist. After graduation, Rachel had difficulty finding a job, as marine biology was a man's field. When she passed the national exam for junior aquatic biologist, she was the only woman to take that test. She was hired by the Bureau of Fisheries, now the Fish and Wildlife Service, to write fish stories for their radio program, as none of the male biologists were writers.

Rachel believed that humans and their industry were polluting the air and the sea. She wrote several books, which became bestsellers, to alert the public to these problems. Her book *Silent Spring* spelled out these problems and shocked the nation into belief. Angry pesticide companies fought back. They claimed the planet was too large and the seas too vast to become polluted.

Rachel's books helped to bring about restrictions on the use of pesticides and increased people's awareness of the problems of pollution. Rachel Carson worked to protect our environment until her death in 1964. Since then, many of her predictions have proved, unfortunately, to be true.

READ MORE ABOUT RACHEL CARSON

- Carson, *Under the Sea Wind.* Simon and Schuster, 1941.
- Carson, *The Sea Around Us.* Oxford Press, 1951.
- Carson, *The Edge of the Sea.* Houghton Mifflin, 1955.
- Gartner, *Rachel Carson.* Ungar, 1983.
- Jexer, *Rachel Carson.* Chelsea House, 1988.
- Latham, *Rachel Carson.* Garrard, 1973.
- Graham, *Since Silent Spring.* Houghton Mifflin, 1970.

DISCOVERY ACTIVITIES

- Using research sources, what types of pollution are threatening the air and seas today? In your opinion, what can be done about it?
- Rachel Carson worked for the National Fish and Wildlife Service. Using reference sources, discover the duties and responsibilities of this agency.
- Using reference sources, discover what and where the Rachel Carson National Wildlife Refuge is?

Rachel Carson: Protector of Our Resources

Rachel Carson's early love for the sea came from reading. She did not actually see the ocean until she was an adult.

Throughout history, the sea has held a great fascination for many people.

DIRECTIONS On the lines within the shell below, write why you think people read about, write about, or are drawn to the sea.

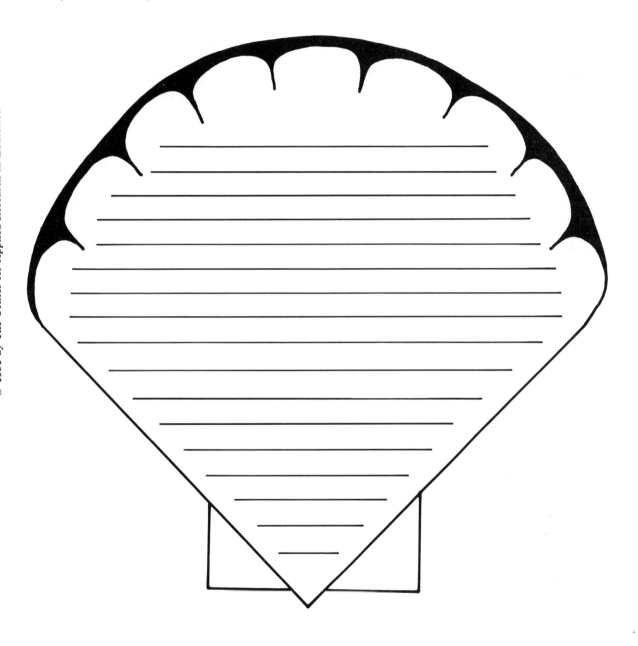

Meet George Washington Carver: Agricultural Scientist

"Plant goobers!" The farmers were scornful. "Goobers are only good for munching on at a fair." But George proved them wrong.

George Washington Carver was born in 1864 near Diamond, Missouri. As a baby, he and his mother were kidnapped. George was returned, but his mother was never found. George was reared by Moses and Susan Carver, his former owners. George loved plants. He talked to them; they were his friends.

At age twelve, George began his education. After attending several schools, he went to Simpson College in Indianola, Iowa. He received his master's degree from Ames Agricultural College in Ames, Iowa.

In April of 1896, George received a letter from Booker T. Washington of the new Tuskegee Institute asking simply, "Will you come and teach for us?" George had just been invited to join the faculty at Ames and could look forward to a distinguished career. However, his reply to the letter was, "Yes."

George believed that both the land and the people in Alabama were undernourished. He planted peanuts—known locally as "goobers." The crop flourished. George began experimenting and developed more than thirty products from the peanut. News of his success spread. He was asked to speak at functions, but he declined. A quiet and reserved man, he wished only to work with his students in the laboratory and help his people. He set up a traveling laboratory and toured the countryside, bringing new scientific methods to the farmer.

At the time of his death on January 5, 1943, George had developed more than three hundred uses for the peanut. The "goober" had become a strong economic product for the South.

READ MORE ABOUT GEORGE WASHINGTON CARVER

- Collins, *George Washington Carver.* Mott Media, 1981.
- Mitchell, *A Pocketful of Goobers: A Story About George Washington Carver.* Carolrhoda Books, 1986.
- Stocker, *George Washington Carver.* Moody, 1987.

DISCOVERY ACTIVITIES

- Using reference source, discover why the South needed a crop besides cotton.
- Using reference sources, discover the origin and past importance of goobers.
- Using reference sources, list the awards and honors given to George Washington Carver.

George Washington Carver: Agricultural Scientist

DIRECTIONS Locate and circle the products using peanuts in the puzzle below. The words may be found forward, backward, vertically, horizontally, and diagonally.

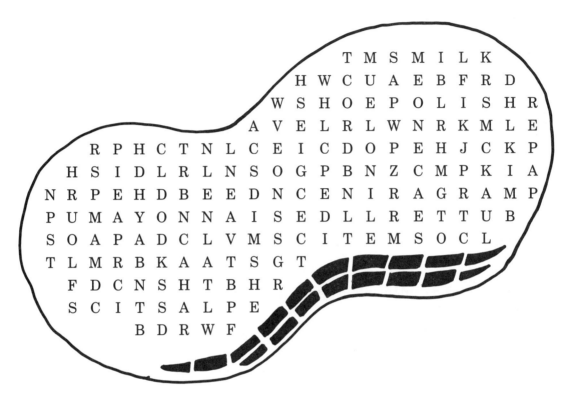

BUTTER   FERTILIZER   MAYONNAISE   SALAD OIL
CHEESE   FLOUR   MILK   SHAVING CREAM
COSMETICS   INK   PAPER   SHOE POLISH
CREAM   LINOLEUM   PICKLES   SOAP
DYES   MARGARINE   PLASTICS   WALLBOARD

Meet Captain James Cook: Explorer of the Pacific Ocean

James tried to apply himself to the business of an apprentice in a general store. However, the ships passing the shop, located on the shore of the North Sea, claimed more of his attention than the goods to be weighed and measured. James longed to go to sea.

James Cook was born in 1728 in Marten, England. He quit his apprenticeship at the age of fourteen and signed on a ship as a deckhand. He learned quickly through the practical method of experience and at age twenty-two commanded his own ship. A tall, well-built man, quiet, but with a sense of humor and fairness, James earned the respect of his crew. He was the first to include special foods in the crew's daily diet to prevent scurvy. He charted, or mapped, the St. Lawrence River during the French and English War and was the first to chart New Zealand and the east coast of Australia. He sailed around the Cape of Good Hope, Africa, and into the Antarctic Circle. He proved there was no sea passage between the Pacific Ocean and Hudson's Bay. He visited Tahiti and Hawaii several times. He treated all natives with friendliness and respect, but the natives had a great desire for anything made of iron and would lie, cheat, or steal to obtain it. On February 17, 1779, a fight broke out between the crew and the Hawaiians. James tried to stop the fight but was stabbed to death by a native with an iron dagger. The natives regretted the action and built a funeral pyre for James, lamenting the death of the white chieftain.

James Cook won fame throughout England as the first to chart the South Pacific and the first to prove crews could maintain good health on long voyages by including foods rich in vitamin A in their daily diet.

READ MORE ABOUT CAPTAIN JAMES COOK

- deLeeuw, *A World Explorer: James Cook.* Garrard, 1963.
- Selsam, *The Quest of Captain Cook.* Doubleday, 1962.
- Syme, *Captain Cook: Pacific Explorer.* William Morrow, 1960.

DISCOVERY ACTIVITIES

- Using reference sources, discover scurvy. What were the causes of the disease, the symptoms, and the prevention.
- Using reference sources, discover why the men who prepared maps in the 1700s believed there were vast lands in the Southern Hemisphere?
- King George III, known as the Farmer King, gave Captain Cook seeds and animals to introduce into New Zealand. Using reference sources, discover what happened to the seeds and animals.

Name _____

Date _____

Captain James Cook: Explorer of the Pacific Ocean

Captain James Cook made three main voyages, the first from 1768 through 1769, the second from 1772 through 1775, and the third from 1776 through 1779.

DIRECTIONS Using reference sources, discover the routes of Captain James Cook's three main voyages. Draw the routes on the world map below. Use a different color for each route.

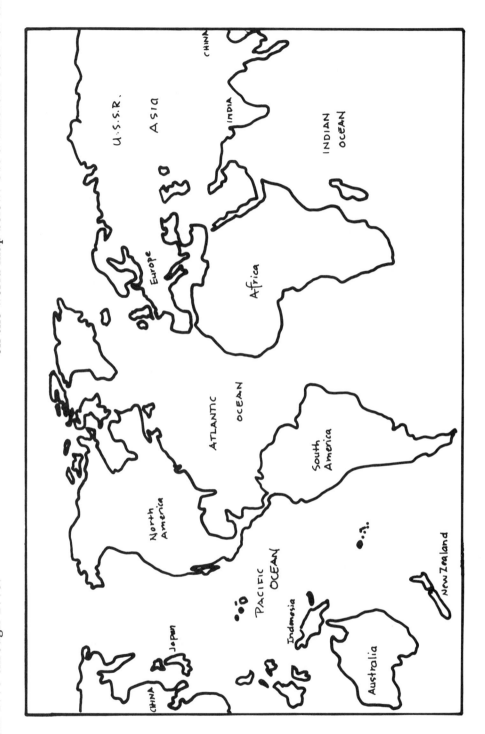

Meet Jacques Yves Cousteau: Skipper of the Calypso

"Life is too short," Jacques said recently. "I must hurry to do all that I want to do."

Jacques Yves Cousteau was born June 11, 1910, in Saint Andre de Cubzac, France. Due to his father's work, the family traveled a great deal. Jacques attended so many schools that he lost interest in his studies. He learned to apply himself, however, and in 1933 graduated from the French Naval Academy, second in his class of one thousand. Later, Jacques was in an automobile accident and fractured both arms. His doctors wanted to amputate one arm due to infection. Jacques refused to give permission. The infection cleared, but he had no movement in that arm. After working on it for eight months, he could move one finger. He kept trying until finally he had normal movement in the whole arm.

One day, Jacques borrowed a pair of underwater goggles and discovered the world beneath the sea. He knew then that he would spend his life exploring the sea. He invented the aqualung, which gave him underwater freedom. In 1950, Jacques bought the *Calypso* and remodeled it into a modern research vessel. Jacques has made underwater films and TV specials; located the sunken wreck of the *Britannica*, sister ship of the *Titanic;* and searched in vain for the legendary lost island of Atlantis. He is the author of several books on the sea.

Today, Jacques is concerned with pollution of the seas. The earth is washed clean by the rains, and all pollution ends up in the sea. He has passed the age of eighty but is still diving and exploring. He travels more than a thousand sea miles a year. He is always in a hurry, trying to do all that he wants to do.

READ MORE ABOUT JACQUES YVES COUSTEAU

- Cousteau, *The Silent World.* N. Lyons Books, 1987.
- Cousteau, *The Living Sea.* N. Lyons Books, 1988.
- Iverson, *Jacques Cousteau.* Putnam, 1976.
- Westman, *Jacques Cousteau: Free Flight Undersea.* Dillon, 1983.

DISCOVERY ACTIVITIES

- Using reference sources, discover:
  1. how an aqualung works.
  2. how a bathyscape works.
  3. the meaning of "rapture," a problem in deep-sea diving.
- Using reference sources, discover how divers deal with sharks and other problem fish.
- Read about Rachel Carson and compare the lives of these two people who have concerned themselves with pollution of the seas.

Jacques Yves Cousteau: Skipper of the *Calypso*

Let's pretend Jacques Cousteau is planning a year-long trip on the *Calypso,* sailing the oceans of the world, studying the effects of pollution on marine life. Four students are to be invited to accompany him.

DIRECTIONS You would love to be one of the four students. Write a letter to Captain Cousteau explaining why you should be one of the four students chosen. If you need more space, you may use the back of this sheet.

Meet Marie Curie: Discoverer of Radium

Marie's family's small apartment was noisy and crowded. Her parents boarded and tutored boys to add to their teaching salaries. Marie escaped through reading stories and her father's math and physics textbooks.

Marie Salomee Sklodowska was born in Warsaw, Poland, on November 7, 1867. She loved to study. A shy child with serious gray eyes, Marie was always the top student in her class. After high school, she worked as a governess to earn money for college. Because the University of Warsaw did not admit women, Marie studied at the Sorbonne in Paris, where she earned master's degrees in both physics and mathematics. In 1895, Marie married Pierre Curie, a noted scientist, and returned to the Sorbonne to study for a doctor's degree in physics.

While searching for a subject for her thesis, Marie became interested in uranium. Scientists knew uranium sent out radioactive rays far in excess of what could be in the uranium itself but did not know why. Using pitchblende, a very radioactive ore, Marie and Pierre removed the nonradioactive elements, leaving two radioactive elements. They named the first element polonium and the second radium. They studied the radium and found that it could cure tumors and some cancers. In 1903, they shared a Nobel Prize in physics for the discovery of radium. In 1906, Pierre was killed in an accident. Marie was offered his position, becoming the first woman professor at the Sorbonne. Marie continued to work with radium. In 1911, she was awarded a Nobel Prize in chemistry, the fist person ever to be awarded two Nobel Prizes. Marie Curie died on July 4, 1934, of leukemia, caused by overexposure to radium.

READ MORE ABOUT MARIE CURIE

- Birch, *Marie Curie: The Polish Scientist Who Discovered Radium and Its Life-Giving Properties.* Garett Stevens, 1988.
- Brandt, *Marie Curie: Brave Scientist.* Troll Associates, 1983.
- Greene, *Marie Curie: Pioneer Physicist.* Childrens Press, 1984.

DISCOVERY ACTIVITIES

- Marie and Pierre did not patent their discoveries, even though most of their life they lived in poverty. If you had discovered radium, would you have patented it and the process used to extract it? Why or why not?
- Marie used a ton of pitchblende to extract thirty-five ten thousandths of an ounce of pure radium. Using reference sources, discover how radium is extracted today.
- Using reference sources, discover how radium is both a lifegiving and deadly element.

Marie Curie: Discoverer of Radium

Radium is an element, a substance of which all matter is made. An element is made up of atoms that are all alike and cannot be changed by chemical means. Some of the more familiar elements are

Carbon   Copper   Gold   Iron   Lead   Oxygen   Silver   Sodium

DIRECTIONS The 1990 World Almanac lists 105 elements including the ones above.

1. How many more elements can you name?
2. Check the World Almanac or another reference source. List the elements that you have heard of before.

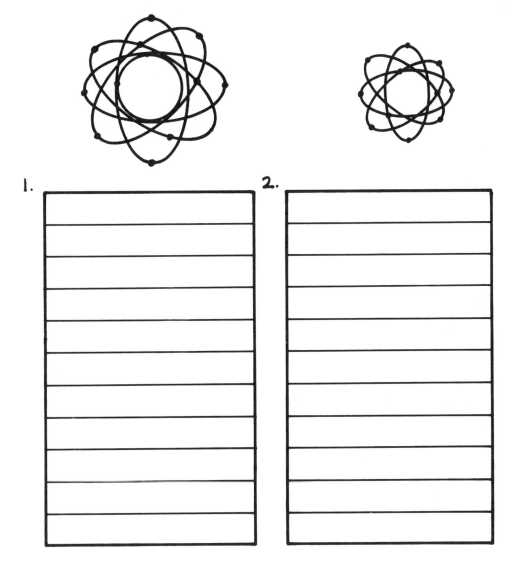

1.

2.

Meet Thomas Alva Edison: The Wizard of Menlo Park

Thomas Alva Edison is considered to be one of the all-time great inventors. Born in 1847, Thomas had a great curiosity about the world and a most unusual memory for facts. Thomas's formal schooling lasted three months. Because he did not learn in the manner in which children were taught at school, his teacher made fun of him. His mother took him out of school and taught him herself. Thomas loved to read, and his mother encouraged him to find in books the answers to his constant questions.

Thomas's great love was experimenting. He always managed to set up a small laboratory wherever he worked. He spent every free minute working out the ideas that were always forming in his mind. Finally, Thomas was able to set up a real laboratory at Menlo Park in New Jersey. Although Edison was granted hundreds of patents for his inventions, he is remembered mainly for inventing the microphone, the camera, the stock ticker, and most famous of all, the electric light bulb.

Thomas suffered a serious degree of deafness from the age of twelve but refused to have an operation. He felt his deafness helped him by closing out the noise and distraction of the outside world.

Although Thomas's main love was work, he did enjoy automobile touring and camping with friends. He entertained them by telling tall tales in a booming laughing voice. Shortly after his eighty-fourth birthday, Thomas became ill. He died in 1931, the fifty-second anniversary of the electric light bulb.

READ MORE ABOUT THOMAS ALVA EDISON

- Cousins, *The Story of Thomas Alva Edison: Young Inventor.* Children's Press, 1981.
- Green, *Thomas Alva Edison: Bringer of Light.* Bobbs-Merrill, 1983.
- Guthridge, *Thomas Alva Edison: Young Inventor.* Random House, 1981.

DISCOVERY ACTIVITIES

- Using reference sources, choose two of Thomas Edison's inventions and discover how they have changed since the original invention.
- Thomas Edison said, "Genius is one percent inspiration and ninety-nine percent perspiration." How would you explain that statement?
- Using reference sources, list the ways that Thomas Edison's inventions changed everyday life.

Thomas Alva Edison: The Wizard of Menlo Park

Thomas Alva Edison's inventions changed the everyday lives of people. He invented the electric light bulb, the phonograph, and the microphone. He made important changes and improvements in the telephone, the typewriter, and the camera.

DIRECTIONS Create an invention of your own that could change your life and the lives of others. Describe your invention on the lines below, then draw a picture of it in the space below.

My invention is _____

_____

_____

_____

_____

_____

_____

_____

Meet Albert Einstein: An Artist of Science

Albert had a poor record at school. He was curious about mechanical things but he had difficulty with verbal skills. His teachers stated, "He'll never be a success at anything."

Albert Einstein was born in Ulm, Germany, on March 14, 1879. He grew up in Munich. He loved mathematics but failed every other subject. When his family moved to Milan, Italy, Albert stayed behind to earn his school diploma. Six months later, he joined the family without the diploma. In 1896, Albert was accepted at the Swiss Polytechnic Institute in Zurich, Switzerland. He was brilliant in math and physics but refused to study any other subject. In 1905, Albert began publishing his own ideas about math and physics. By 1916, he had published his greatest works, *Special Theory of Relativity* and *General Theory of Relativity.* These theories concern the physical universe. Scientists had believed that properties such as mass, energy, time and space were separate and could not be changed. Albert proved they were related. Albert became world famous and received many awards, including the Nobel Prize for physics in 1921. An absent-minded man, Albert was interested only in his work, classical music, and playing the violin. He was visiting in the United States when Hitler came to power. As he was a Jewish pacifist, he never returned to Europe. He accepted a position at Princeton University, where he worked on his theories until his death on April 18, 1955.

Most of Albert's ideas could not be proven during his lifetime. Today, as sophisticated technology is developed, more and more of his theories are being demonstrated. We are still in the process of realizing what Albert gave to science. He has been called one of the greatest thinkers of the ages.

READ MORE ABOUT ALBERT EINSTEIN

- Ireland, *Albert Einstein.* Silver Burdett, 1989.
- Santrey, *Young Albert Einstein.* Troll Associates, 1989.
- Smith, *Albert Einstein.* Simon and Schuster, 1989.

DISCOVERY ACTIVITIES

- Using reference sources, discover the various schools and colleges at which Albert Einstein taught. How long did he spend at each place?
- It is obvious to us today that Albert Einstein was a genius. Why do you think he had such a poor academic record during his early school years?
- Using reference sources, discover how Albert Einstein's theories are being proven today?

Albert Einstein: An Artist of Science

Albert Einstein had a very difficult time during his early school years. He did not respond to lessons as did the other students. School rules were very strict and all students were taught the same lessons in the same manner.

DIRECTIONS Schools have changed considerably since Albert Einstein's day. In your opinion, how might Albert Einstein's early school years have been more successful if he were a student at your school?

$E = MC^2$ $E = MC^2$

$E = MC^2$

$E = MC^2$

$E = MC^2$

$E = MC^2$

$E = MC^2$

$E = MC^2$

Meet Sigmund Freud: Explorer of the Subconscious Mind

When Sigmund was born, an old woman prophesied that he would become a great man. His parents believed this prophesy and gave to him more love and attention than to his brothers and sisters.

Sigmund Freud was born May 6, 1856, in Freiberg, Moravia. His every wish was granted by his parents, who taught him to read and write and instilled in him a love of books and learning. After graduation from the University of Vienna, Sigmund studied in Paris and became a doctor of neurology. He practiced hypnotism. He believed that many mental illnesses, called hysteria, in adults were caused by experiences that had occurred in childhood. Use of hypnotism allowed the patient to talk about these problems that were deeply buried in the subconscious mind. Sigmund developed the "talking cure" which helped patients clear their minds of these painful memories, and "free association" in which a patient said whatever came into the mind, enabling him or her to describe what was frightening to even think about. Sigmund created a new science called psychoanalysis. He believed that dreams are a normal part of life, that the mind is not on guard during sleep, and that buried problems that a person does not want to remember or cannot deal with slip out in dreams. He published many books on the causes of mental illness. When Adolf Hitler came to power in 1933, Sigmund's books were publicly burned. Sigmund moved to London, where he put his theories into practice until his death on September 23, 1939.

The old woman's prophesy did come true. Sigmund Freud was an explorer of the mind. He left a legacy of ideas that scientists continue to study, to understand, and in some cases, to challenge.

READ MORE ABOUT SIGMUND FREUD

- Klagsbrun, *Sigmund Freud.* Franklin Watts, 1967.
- Lager, *Sigmund Freud: Doctor of the Mind.* Enslow Publishers, 1986.
- Neimark, *Sigmund Freud: The World Within.* Harcourt Brace Jovanovich, 1976.

DISCOVERY ACTIVITIES

- Read a book about dreams. Do you agree with what the book says? Tell about a dream you have experienced lately. What do you think it means?
- Using reference sources, discover some of the problems with using hypnotism to bring buried experiences to the conscious mind.
- Using reference sources, discover why Adolf Hitler burned the books written by Sigmund Freud.

Sigmund Freud: Explorer of the Subconscious Mind

Emotions play a very important role in mental health. Talking about, thinking about, and writing about them can help people understand and deal with their reactions to them. Everybody reacts to different emotions in a different way.

DIRECTIONS   Below is a list of seven common emotions. Beside each, write how you react when you are experiencing that emotion.

ANGER _____

_____

FEAR _____

_____

FRUSTRATION _____

_____

HATE _____

_____

JOY _____

_____

LOVE _____

_____

SORROW _____

_____

Meet Robert Goddard: Rocket Pioneer

Bob had an inexhaustible sense of curiosity. He wanted to know about everything, especially about the sky. How high was it? What lay beyond it? He wanted so much to fly up and find out.

Robert Hutchings Goddard was born in Worcester, Massachusetts, on October 5, 1882. An only child, his parents encouraged his every interest and supplied the materials needed to satisfy his curiosity. On October 19, 1899, Bob climbed a cherry tree to trim branches. He experienced a strange daydream. He knew his life would be spent studying space exploration. Bob called that day Anniversary Day and celebrated it quietly, by himself, for the rest of his life. Bob graduated from Worcester Polytechnic Institute and received his graduate degrees from Clark University. He experimented with rockets and proved that it was possible for a rocket to operate in the vacuum of outerspace. In 1914, Bob patented a multistage rocket, based on the same principles that propel modern rockets. He published articles, but the scientific world, with the exception of Germany, paid little attention. The German V-2 rockets, used to launch attacks on London during World War II, were based on Bob's patents and principles. Bob built and set off rockets using liquid fuel. In 1926, his first rocket rose to a height of 164 feet, while traveling at a speed of 60 mph. His final rocket flight, in 1935, streaked to 7,550 feet, traveling at a speed of 700 mph. During World War II, Bob worked for the United States Navy, developing weapons until his death on August 10, 1945.

The extent of Bob's achievements were not realized until long after his death. Honors were heaped upon him, including the Congressional Medal of Honor and the Langley Gold Medal.

READ MORE ABOUT ROBERT GODDARD

- Dewey, *Robert Goddard: Space Pioneer.* Little, Brown, 1962.
- Lehman, *Robert Goddard: Pioneer of Space Research.* Da Capo, 1988.
- Verral, *Robert Goddard: Father of the Space Age.* Prentice-Hall, 1963.

DISCOVERY ACTIVITIES

- Using reference sources, discover the first spacecraft to go into orbit around the earth. Who launched that spacecraft and when was it launched?

- In your opinion, what does the future hold for space travel? Do you have a desire to travel into space? Why or why not?

- Using reference sources, discover the United States space program. Where are the rockets launched? Where is the control center? Where do the different types of space vehicles land?

Robert Goddard: Rocket Pioneer

Modern rockets are based on the principles of Robert Goddard's 1914 patent for a multi-stage rocket.

DIRECTIONS   The diagram below shows the main sections of a rocket. To the left of the diagram are the names of the sections. Draw a line matching up the name with the section.

First stage

Second stage

Third stage

Command module

Liquid
hydrogen
fuel tank

Liquid
oxygen
fuel tank

Kerosene
fuel

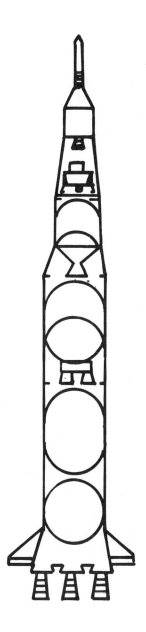

Meet Samuel F. B. Morse: Instant Communication

"I am so lonely," Samuel wrote to his family from Europe. "I wish it did not take so long for letters to reach me."

Samuel F. B. Morse was born in Charlestown, Massachusetts, on April 27, 1791. He wanted to be an artist and studied art at Yale University and in Europe. Samuel had only average success as an artist. He had to travel great distances, as he worked on a commission basis painting portraits of people in their homes.

Samuel had always been fascinated by the power of electricity. He experimented with the horseshoe electromagnet. He knew electricity passed instantly over a wire. Samuel believed that intelligence could be transmitted over a wire. He reasoned that if the flow of electricity were interrupted, a spark would appear. A spark and the absence of a spark could be signs that could be made into a code. This code could travel any distance along a wire. On September 2, 1837, Samuel successfully demonstrated his device, called the American electromagnet telegraph.

Samuel offered the rights to the telegraph to Congress, but they refused the offer. Most members of Congress felt the telegraph was a toy with no practical value. Ten years later, Congress grudgingly granted money for a test line between Baltimore and Washington. Samuel organized The Magnetic Telegraph Company, which slowly grew and prospered.

Samuel had a telegraph wire hooked up from his study to a public telegraph near his home. Until his death in 1872, he could communicate instantly across the country and throughout most of Europe. Samuel no longer had to wait for letters.

READ MORE ABOUT SAMUEL F. B. MORSE

- Hays, *Samuel Morse and the Telegraph.* Franklin Watts, 1960.
- Latham, *Samuel F. B. Morse.* Garrard, 1961.

DISCOVERY ACTIVITIES

- Samuel Morse wished that letters could reach him more quickly. Using reference sources, discover what types of mail services were available in the 1800s.
- Samuel Morse believed that "God created the forces of nature for the benefit of man." What do you think he meant by that statement.
- Using reference sources, discover the first message Samuel Morse tapped out on the completed telegraph line between Baltimore and Washington, D.C., on May 24, 1844.

Samuel F. B. Morse: Instant Communication

The American Morse code is based on the use of dots, dashes, and spaces. The dot is made by a quick press and release of the key. A short dash is twice the length of a dot. A long dash is four dots. The space between dots and dashes used to make up a letter is as long as a dot. The space between letters equals three dots. Any space that is part of a letter combination equals two dots. Morse designed the American Morse code alphabet as follows.

DIRECTIONS Using the American Morse code pictured above, decode the first message Samuel Morse tapped over the completed telegraph line from Baltimore to Washington, D.C., on May 24, 1844.

MESSAGE _____

_____

Meet John Muir: Protector of the Wilderness

Young John and his brother Davie played a game they called "Scootcher." This game consisted of daring each other into feats of great physical strength and courage, like climbing out of a third floor dormer window to straddle the roof at midnight and climbing the Tower of Dunbar, knowing the loose stone could give way and dash them into the sea.

John Muir was born in Dunbar, Scotland, on April 21, 1838. In 1848, John and Davie came with their father to a farm in Wisconsin to prepare a home for the rest of the family. John worked from dawn to dusk but trained himself to wake up in the middle of the night in order to have time to read. Freed from his father's rule at age twenty-one, John worked his way through college. He packed a knapsack and explored the majesty and beauty of the northwest. He loved the Yosemite and High Sierra country. He discovered living glaciers but also forests stripped bare by man and sheep. Although first scoffed at as an ignorant fanatic, famous learned men, including President Theodore Roosevelt, came to realize John was a keen, practical man dedicated to preserving our natural resources. He is largely responsible for large tracts of lands becoming national parks, forests, and monuments. Until his death on December 24, 1914, John lived to protect nature against the economic interests of man.

John Muir loved the mountains and forests. Only there did he find complete freedom. He loved pitting his strength against and becoming one, with nature, learning her best-kept secrets.

READ MORE ABOUT JOHN MUIR

- Douglas, *Muir of the Mountains.* Houghton Mifflin, 1961.
- Swift, *From the Eagle's Wing: A Biography of John Muir.* William Morrow, 1962.

DISCOVERY ACTIVITIES

- Using reference sources, discover why John felt the balance of nature would be threatened if humans kept stripping the forest and keeping sheep.

- Many places have been named in honor of John Muir, discover these monuments.

- John wrote his articles with a quill pen formed from the feathers of a golden eagle. When he had trouble finding the right words to express his feelings, he relaxed and let the eagle guide his way. Why and how do you think that worked for John?

- John founded the Sierra Club. Using reference sources, discover when and why he founded this club. What is the status of this club today?

John Muir: Protector of the Wilderness

John Muir felt the destruction of the giant sequoias for lumbering was an evil waste. He said, "When felled, the sequoia breaks like glass. From 25 to 50 percent is unfit for the mill." It was his opinion that the sequoia is the most majestic of all trees and should be protected from destruction by law.

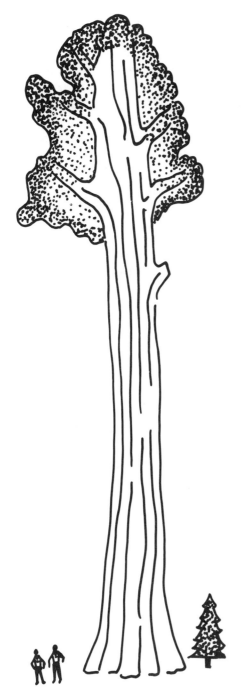

DIRECTIONS Using reference sources, discover the sequoias. On the lines below, write a report on them.

_____

_____

_____

_____

_____

_____

_____

_____

_____

_____

_____

_____

_____

_____

_____

_____

_____

_____

_____

_____

_____

Meet Alfred Nobel: Construction and Destruction

"I can get As in school in everything but attendance," Alfred told his mother. "If only I could get an A in attendance."

Alfred Nobel was born in Stockholm, Sweden, on October 21, 1833. He suffered from a variety of health problems, namely headaches, colds, poor digestion, and a weak heart. When he could not go to school, Alfred spent hours drawing and working out mechanical devices in his mind. When Alfred was eleven, the family moved to St. Petersburg, Russia, where his father was working on various types of explosives.

When the family returned to Stockholm, Alfred experimented with nitroglycerin, a shock-sensitive explosive. He thought that its great explosive power could be an important aid in construction. His first patented nitroglycerin explosive was too shock-sensitive and many accidents and deaths resulted from its use. When he absorbed the nitroglycerin in a porous clay, he produced an explosive that could be handled safely but that produced the same explosive power. He patented this product under the name dynamite.

When dynamite was used in making weapons, Alfred felt responsible for his inventions causing destruction rather than aiding construction. Several years before his death on December 10, 1896, he set up a trust fund of about nine million dollars. The interest from this trust was to be used to award prizes to outstanding individuals for the contributions in the field of science, literature, and peace.

READ MORE ABOUT ALFRED NOBEL

- Gray, *Champions of Peace: The Story of Alfred Nobel, the Peace Prize, and the Laureates.* Two Continents, 1976.
- Halasz, *Nobel: A Biography of Alfred Nobel.* Orion Press, 1959.
- Meyer, *Dynamite and Peace: The Story of Alfred Nobel.* Little, Brown, 1959.

DISCOVERY ACTIVITIES

- Using reference sources, discover the subcategories within the prize fields of science, literature, and peace.
- Using reference sources, discover how a person is nominated for and awarded a Nobel Prize. What is the monetary award connected with each prize?
- Alfred Nobel invented dynamite for peaceful purposes. Using reference sources, discover how dynamite is used during war and peace.

Name _____   Date _____

Alfred Nobel: Construction and Destruction

Alfred Nobel was very concerned that dynamite was used for war when he wanted it to be used for peace. Today, the world is still striving for peace.

DIRECTIONS   Write a letter to Alfred Nobel stating how a person of your age feels peace could be attained in your lifetime.

Dear Alfred Nobel,

I feel peace could be attained in my lifetime if _____

_____

_____

_____

_____

_____

_____

_____

_____

_____

_____

_____

_____

_____

_____

_____

Meet Louis Pasteur: "Slow Learner" or Genius?

Young Louis was always the last to complete his schoolwork. He formed each letter perfectly. He thought out and explained each answer. His teachers claimed he was a slow learner. They did not encourage further academic study.

Louis Pasteur was born in Dôle, France, on December 27, 1822. He was fifteen before his teachers realized that the great care with which he did everything produced the highest results in the class. Louis was studying to be a teacher, but switched to research in chemistry. His ambition was to find out what made people sick and to cure them. He was scoffed at by doctors and surgeons, for he was only a chemist. His method was to follow a disease to its source and begin from there. He worked on his theories until he obtained proof. While studying crystals, he founded the science of stereochemistry, and while trying to discover what made good wine turn to vinegar, he founded the study of bacteriology and biochemistry. He proved that the change was caused by bacteria and developed pasteurization, a method of heating a liquid to kill the bacteria, a method still used today. He developed vaccines for anthrax and rabies. He proved that anything grown in contaminated soil became contaminated and caused disease in man and animals. On October 23, 1887, Louis suffered a stroke, which affected his speech. He continued working at the Pasteur Institute until he developed kidney disease, which caused his death on September 28, 1895.

Louis's discoveries continue to influence modern scientists as they work to unravel the mysteries of microbes and viruses. This "slow learner" was in fact a genius.

READ MORE ABOUT LOUIS PASTEUR

- Bains, *Louis Pasteur.* Troll Associates, 1985.
- Mann, *Louis Pasteur: Founder of Bacteriology.* Scribner's, 1964.
- Sabin, *Louis Pasteur: Young Scientist.* Troll Associates, 1983.

DISCOVERY ACTIVITIES

- Using reference sources, define the following terms:
  Bacteriology
  Biochemistry
  Stereochemistry
  Anthrax
  Rabies
- Using reference sources, discover why the method known as pasteurization is so important.
- Using references sources, discover the Pasteur Institute. Where is it located? When was it built? Why was it built? Who was its first director?

Louis Pasteur: "Slow Learner" or Genius?

Modern medicine has changed a great deal since Louis Pasteur's day. He would be amazed at the weapons that exist today to fight disease.

DIRECTIONS   Using the library's resources, choose four books you think would interest Louis that tell how disease is being cured and controlled today.

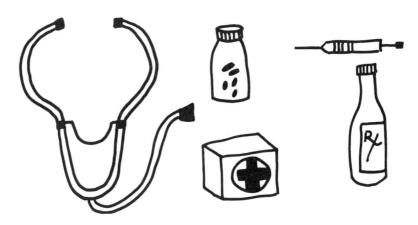

1. Author _____

   Title _____

   Publisher _____ Copyright Date _____

2. Author _____

   Title _____

   Publisher _____ Copyright Date _____

3. Author _____

   Title _____

   Publisher _____ Copyright Date _____

4. Author _____

   Title _____

   Publisher _____ Copyright Date _____

Meet Sacagawea: Interpreter for Lewis and Clark

On April 7, 1805, Sacagawea set off with the Lewis and Clark expedition to the Big Water (Pacific Ocean). No longer was she just a captured slave. She was a part of a great adventure.

Sacagawea was a Shoshone Indian born around 1787. As a young girl, she was captured by a Hidatsas tribe while on a buffalo hunt and taken to their village. She was given as wife to Charbonneau, a Frenchman. They had a son called Pomp. In 1804, the Lewis and Clark expedition wintered at their village on the Missouri River. Charbonneau offered their services as interpreters. Sacagawea was a great ally to the expedition. She knew which roots and berries were edible and cooked nourishing meals. She could "read" signs of earlier occupation of areas by tribes, such as who had been there and how many. When they reached Shoshone territory, she arranged for horses and guides. Her presence proved the expedition came in peace, for war parties never traveled with a woman and child. Her physical strength, sunny nature, and adventurous spirit helped during the long, hard sixteen-month journey over the mountains, along the Columbia River to the Pacific Ocean and back. She was appreciative of the consideration and respect shown her by the men. As an Indian squaw, she did not expect this treatment.

Little is known of Sacagawea's life following the expedition. It is thought that she died in 1812. She never knew that through the journals kept by Clark that she became an important part of American history and lore.

READ MORE ABOUT SACAGAWEA

- Brown, *Sacagawea: Indian Interpreter to Lewis and Clark.* Childrens Press, 1988.
- Gleiter, *Sacagawea.* Raintree Press, 1987.
- Jassem, *Sacagawea: Wilderness Guide.* Troll Associates, 1979.

DISCOVERY ACTIVITIES

- Using reference sources, discover what events happened in the United States in 1804 and 1805, while Sacagawea was a part of the Lewis and Clark expedition.
- Sacagawea was of the Shoshone Indian tribe. Using reference sources, discover her tribe. Write a short report on the Shoshone Indians.
- Using reference sources, discover the honors awarded to Sacagawea, in the form of memorials and places named for her.

Sacagawea: Interpreter for Lewis and Clark

Pomp was less than one year old when Sacagawea accompanied Lewis and Clark on the expedition. He probably made the trip in the Indian baby carrier pictured below.

DIRECTIONS Color the picture of the Indian woman and baby below. Caring for a child takes time. On the back of this sheet write how you think Sacagawea was able to make such a long trip with a small child.

Meet Albert Schweitzer: Missionary Doctor

Throughout his childhood, Albert was only an average student. However, once he set his mind on a goal, he did not stop until he reached it.

Albert Schweitzer was born on January 4, 1875, in Kaysersberg, Alsace, a section of Germany that is today a part of France. A quiet, shy boy with a great shock of unruly hair, Albert led a happy life studying in France and Germany. At age twenty-one, he felt he must devote his life to helping people. He decided he would study and work within the areas of his own interest until the age of thirty, then determine how he would reach this goal. During these years, Albert became a scholar, a preacher, a university professor, a musician, and an author. He became accomplished in each of these fields and became famous throughout the world. At age thirty, Albert set his goal. He would become a missionary doctor and work in Africa. After receiving his medical degree, Albert began his practice in Lambarene, French Equatorial Africa, today Gabon. His first clinic was held in a converted chicken coop. Over the years, Albert built a large medical hospital complex. He received the Nobel Peace Prize in 1952 and used the prize money to build a leper colony near the hospital. Albert continued working at the complex until his death on September 4, 1965.

Albert gave up a career of fame and fortune to help cure human suffering and misery. His love and reverence for life have made him a legend in the history of mankind.

READ MORE ABOUT ALBERT SCHWEITZER

- Bently, *Albert Schweitzer: The Doctor Who Gave Up a Brilliant Career to Serve the People of Africa.* Gareth Stevens, 1989.
- Cremaschi, *Albert Schweitzer.* Silver Burdett, 1985.
- Johnson, *The Value of Dedication: The Story of Albert Schweitzer.* Oak Tree Publications, 1979.

DISCOVERY ACTIVITIES

- Using reference sources, discover the status of Doctor Schweitzer's medical clinic in Lambarene today.
- In 1957, Albert Schweitzer received Great Britain's Order of Merit award. Using reference sources, discover that award. What is the award, who has received it, and what are the qualifications for the award?
- Using reference sources, discover why Albert Schweitzer has been called one of the greatest Christians of his time.

© 1991 by The Center for Applied Research in Education

Albert Schweitzer: Missionary Doctor

At age twenty-one, Albert Schweitzer believed that because he had been privileged to lead such a happy life while there was so much sorrow, suffering, and anxiety in the world, he must devote himself to helping others.

DIRECTIONS   If you or any other person set a goal of helping people today, what form do you believe that goal should take? On the lines below, explain what and where, in your opinion, is the greatest need of people today.

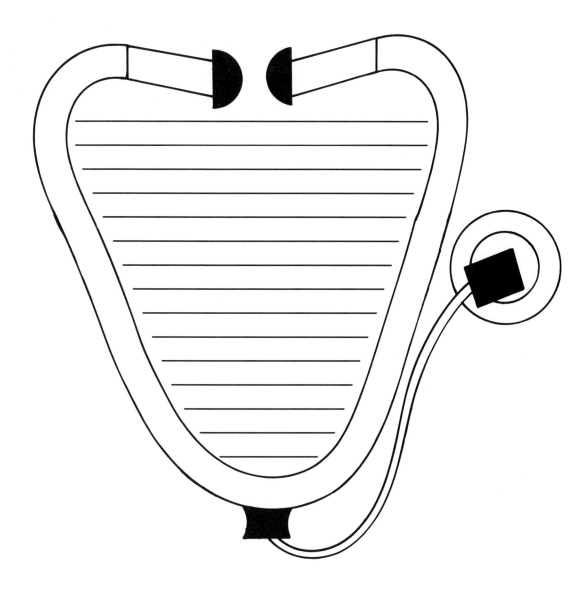

Meet Eli Whitney: Mechanical Genius

Eli Whitney played a dual role in history. Although he is known chiefly for the invention of the cotton gin, he is also the father of mass production. Born in Westboro, Massachusetts, on December 8, 1765, young Eli just had to take things apart to see what made them work. However, he could also put them back together again as well or better than they had been before.

After graduating from Yale College in 1792, Eli went to Georgia to teach but could not find a job. He heard farmers complaining that they would like to increase cotton planting but the slow process of hand picking out the seeds made it impractical. He invented a machine, called the cotton gin, that would separate the cotton from the seeds. He applied for a patent but before it could be granted the idea was stolen and imitated. Eli sued and after years of court battles was granted the rights a year before the patent expired. He applied for a renewal but Congress refused to extend the patent.

In 1798, the United States government asked Eli to manufacture 10,000 muskets. Eli perfected a way to make the parts interchangeable so that the muskets could be mass produced.

In his later years, Eli was awarded recognition for his contribution to the cotton industry and to military weapons. Now that he had some leisure time, Eli delighted in constructing all sorts of mechanical toys for his grandchildren. Eli's contributions gave him great wealth, which he enjoyed until his death in 1825.

READ MORE ABOUT ELI WHITNEY

- Green, *Eli Whitney and the Birth of American Technology.* Little, Brown, 1965.
- Latham, *Eli Whitney: Great Inventor.* Garrard, 1963.
- Latham, *The Story of Eli Whitney.* Harper and Row, 1962.

DISCOVERY ACTIVITIES

- Many products we use today are made of cotton. Using the list of types of cotton found on the puzzle page, make a list of the types found in your home; for example, canvas—backpack.
- After the seed is removed from the fiber, the seed is used for a variety of products. Using reference sources, discover what products are made from cottonseed.
- Even the cotton linters, the short fuzz on the seed, are used. Using reference sources, discover what products are made from the linters.

Eli Whitney: Mechanical Genius

Eli Whitney's cotton gin made cotton the South's most valuable crop. The United States uses about two-and-one-half-billion pounds of cotton fiber a year. Some type of cotton clothing is worn by at least three of every four persons in the world.

DIRECTIONS Below is a listing of some of the different types of cotton fabrics. Locate and circle the terms in the puzzle. The terms may be found forward, backward, vertically, horizontally, and diagonally.

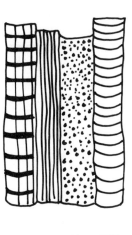

```
P V E M C R F L A N N E L
B H W C U X O M I N E D T
A M T C A S U S B D G A C
T E N O E L L I N E H C A
I L F E L T A I N B V O M
S A V N A C R I N T E R B
T C Y O R U D R O C L B R
E R D Y G R A A R V V C I
Z E K H A V M B O H E A C
U P H B L T A L B R T L F
A N A R Y E S R E J B I J
G G K T I C K I N G T C R
N G I N G H A M E L I O V
```

BATISTE	FOULARD
BROADCLOTH	GABARDINE
BROCADE	GAUZE
CALICO	GINGHAM
CAMBRIC	JERSEY
CANVAS	KHAKI
CHENILLE	LACE
CORDUROY	MUSLIN
DAMASK	PERCALE
DENIM	TICKING
FELT	VELVET
FLANNEL	VOILE

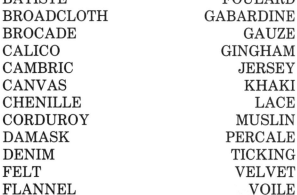

Meet Daniel Hale Williams: Pioneer of Heart Surgery

Dan admired his father's hands as they surely and skillfully cut beards and trimmed mustaches. "Someday, I will be a great barber," he promised himself. "My hands will be as good as father's."

Daniel Hale Williams was born in Hollidaysburg, Pennsylvania, on January 18, 1856. At age nine, his happy childhood ended when his father died. Dan was apprenticed to a shoemaker, but he ran away to join his mother in Illinois. Dan attended school and worked in a barber shop. After deciding to be a doctor rather than a barber, he graduated from the Chicago Medical School in 1883 and started a family practice. Dan was a quiet, thoughtful man with a deep love, patience, and understanding for his patients. His years of sewing shoe leather and barbering afforded his hands great strength and dexterity. He directed the organization of the Provident Hospital in Chicago. On July 9, 1893, he performed the first heart operation, on a man who had been stabbed in the chest. It was the first time a doctor had successfully cut into the chest wall, repaired the damage, and sewed up the incision. In 1894, Dan became surgeon general at Freedman's Hospital in Washington, D. C. He helped organize the Negro Medical Organization and assisted in setting up training hospitals throughout the South. Dan practiced medicine and worked for equality for black doctors and nurses until his death on August 4, 1931.

Dr. Daniel Hale Williams battled prejudice and professional jealousy. He was a pioneer in surgery and a crusader in bringing hospital care into the modern age.

READ MORE ABOUT DANIEL HALE WILLIAMS

- Fenderson, *Daniel Hale Williams, Open-Heart Doctor.* McGraw-Hill, 1971.
- Meriwether, *The Heart Man: Dr. Daniel Williams.* Prentice-Hall, 1972.
- Patterson, *Sure Hands, Strong Heart: The Life of Daniel Hale Williams.* Abingdon, 1981.

DISCOVERY ACTIVITIES

- Using reference sources, discover the close connection between barbering and doctoring in history.
- Using reference sources, discover why people would not go to the hospitals in the early days.
- Compare the medical training of a doctor in Daniel Hale Williams's day with the medical training of a doctor today.

© 1991 by The Center for Applied Research in Education

Daniel Hale Williams: Pioneer of Heart Surgery

Daniel Hale Williams was the first doctor to perform surgery on the heart. Today, heart surgery is performed daily with great success.

DIRECTIONS Below is a drawing of the heart. A list of the major parts of the heart is included below the drawing. Using reference sources, label the parts of the heart included on the list, on the lines provided.

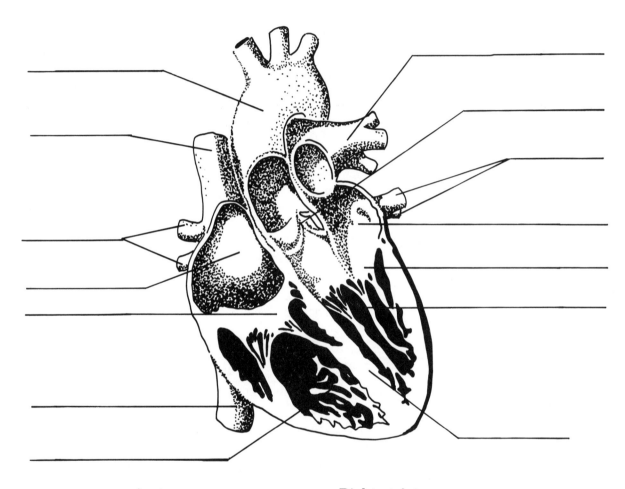

Aorta

Bicuspid valve

Inferior vena cava

Left atrium

Left pulmonary veins

Left ventricle

Pulmonary artery

Right atrium

Right pulmonary veins

Right ventricle

Semilunar valve

Septum

Superior vena cava

Tricuspid valve

Meet Wilbur and Orville Wright:
American Aviation Pioneers

Wilbur and Orville's mother was not like other mothers of that day. She took them on picnics, fishing, and for long walks in the woods. She answered their questions and taught them to make a pattern or design before starting to build. She told them, "If you get it right on paper, it will be right when you build it."

Wilbur Wright, born April 16, 1867, and his brother Orville, born August 19, 1871, were close friends and companions growing up in Dayton, Ohio. They designed a sled on paper, and when they built it the result was so good that the sled was the envy of all the boys in town.

Both boys were fascinated with flying. They experimented with and built kites. They started a printing business with a homemade press, moved on to print a weekly newspaper, then opened a bicycle shop. All their spare time and money was spent learning about flight. They dreamed about and designed gliders.

When Orville developed typhoid fever in 1896, Wilbur spent a year reading to him all the books and information he could find about aviation. Finally they built a gasoline-powered glider, took it apart, and transported it from Dayton, Ohio, to Kill Devil Hill in Kitty Hawk, North Carolina. On December 17, 1903, they made their first flight. They flew 120 feet in 20 seconds. They made two more trips to Kitty Hawk, where they made longer and higher flights. They proved the gasoline-powered airplane was practical.

After Wilbur's death of typhoid fever in 1912, Orville worked on alone until his death in 1948.

READ MORE ABOUT WILBUR AND ORVILLE WRIGHT

- Johnson, *The Value of Patience: The Story of the Wright Brothers*. Oak Tree Press, 1976.
- Reynolds, *The Wright Brothers*. Random House, 1981.
- Sabin, *Wilbur and Orville Wright: Young Fliers*. Alladin Books, 1986.

DISCOVERY ACTIVITIES

- Dayton, Ohio, was a long distance from Kitty Hawk, North Carolina, in 1903. Using reference sources, discover why Wilbur and Orville chose Kitty Hawk.
- Using reference sources, discover what happened to the original plane.
- Draw a picture of the original plane and a picture of a modern plane. Compare similarities and differences.

Wilbur and Orville Wright: American Aviation Pioneers

Wilbur and Orville Wright's original airplane is on display at the National Air and Space Museum in Washington, D.C. That airplane has little resemblance to today's modern aircraft.

DIRECTIONS Choose two books on aircraft that you would recommend Wilbur and Orville read to bring them up to date on the status of air travel today.

1. Author _____

   Title _____

   Publisher_____ Copyright Date _____

   This book would help Wilbur and Orville because _____

   _____

   _____

   _____

   _____

2. Author _____

   Title _____

   Publisher_____ Copyright Date _____

   This book would help Wilbur and Orville because _____

   _____

   _____

   _____

   _____

At the beginning of the World Series of 1947, I experienced a completely new emotion when the National Anthem was played. This time I thought, it is being played for me, as much as for anyone else. This is organized major league baseball, and I am standing here with all the others, and everything that takes place includes me.

—*Jackie Robinson*

Meet Henry Aaron: Baseball's Quiet Hero

The Jacksonville Tars were trailing 4–2 in the bottom of the ninth inning that day in 1953. Henry came up to bat. One of his teammates yelled, "Get a hold of one, Hank!" Henry pulled a double, starting a rally that led to victory. Since that day, Henry has been called Hank.

Henry Louis Aaron was born February 5, 1934, in Mobile, Alabama. He lived near Hartwell Field, where major league exhibition games were played. Hank went to all the games and dreamed of playing baseball like his hero, Jackie Robinson. At age fifteen, Hank signed with the Mobile Black Bears. He soon attracted the attention of the major leagues. In 1952, both the New York Giants and the Boston Braves offered him a contract. He signed with the Braves because they offered him more money. Hank played for the Braves from 1952 to 1974. He holds the major league record of 2,297 runs batted in. On April 8, 1974, Hank beat Babe Ruth's record of 714 home runs and went on to hold the all-time record of 755 home runs.

Hank played for the Milwaukee Brewers from 1974 until his retirement in 1976. He won the Springarn Medal in 1975 and in 1982 was elected to the Baseball Hall of Fame. In a quiet, determined manner, Hank turned prejudice, jealousy, and envy into acceptance and respect by doing what he does best, playing baseball. He was always willing to listen, to accept change, and to cooperate with the team.

READ MORE ABOUT HANK AARON

- Gutman, *Hank Aaron*. Grosset and Dunlap, 1973.
- Milverstedt, *The Quiet Legend: Henry Aaron*. Raintree Editions, 1975.
- Young, *The Picture Story of Hank Aaron*. Julian Messner, 1974.

DISCOVERY ACTIVITIES

- Hank signed with the Boston Braves in 1952. The Braves have moved several times. Using reference sources, discover and write a brief history of the Braves from the time they were the Boston Braves through today.

- Although Hank was a member of the team, in the early days he could not travel, eat, or room with the team. Using reference sources, discover whether there has been a change in these conditions for black players today.

- Hank was elected to the Baseball Hall of Fame. When, where, and why was it organized? How are players elected to the Baseball Hall of Fame?

Hank Aaron: Baseball's Quiet Hero

Many young people play Little League baseball. Some are Little League "stars." But few of these go on to become major league baseball players.

DIRECTIONS   What are the talents and qualifications necessary to become a major league baseball player? On the lines below, describe how a person might become a major league baseball player. Continue on to the back of this sheet if more room is needed.

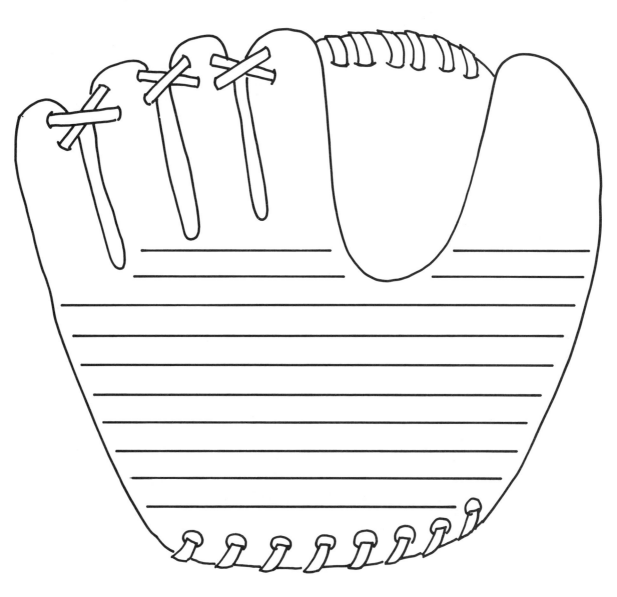

Meet Kareem Abdul-Jabbar:
"My Biggest Resource Is My Mind"

Lew was six feet tall in sixth grade. The first day of school, the teacher asked him to please sit down. "I am sitting," Lew reluctantly replied.

Ferdinand Lewis Alcindor, Jr., was born April 16, 1947, in New York City. His ancestors came from Trinidad, in the West Indies. His grandfather was six feet, eight inches tall. Lew was active in athletics from an early age, winning trophies and honors in many sports. His classmates at Holy Providence School in Pennsylvania talked him into playing basketball because of his height. From that point on, basketball was his game. He loved the speed, the skill, and the shouts of the spectators at each basket scored. Although a talented celebrity all through high school and college, Lew was often at odds with his classmates and teammates due to his height, race, values, and philosophy. He converted to the Islamic religion and in 1971 legally changed his name to Kareem Abdul-Jabbar. Kareem played center for the Milwaukee Bucks and the Los Angeles Lakers from 1969 until his retirement in 1989. He became one of the greatest centers in basketball history. Statistics show that he scored 38,387 regular-season points, played in 1,560 regular-season games, and was named the league's most valuable player six times.

Kareem is a sensitive, brave, deeply religious man who has proven himself a rare role model for young people. Although he will miss professional basketball, he looks forward to new experiences and projects that will utilize his many other talents. "I am not just a basketball player," he said recently. "My biggest resource is my mind."

READ MORE ABOUT KAREEM ABDUL-JABBAR

- Abdul-Jabbar and McCarthy, *Kareem.* Random House, 1989.
- Burchard, *Kareem Adbul Jabbar: The Story of Lew Alcindor.* Putnam, 1972.
- Haskins, *From Lew Alcindor to Kareem Abdul-Jabbar.* Lothrop, Lee and Shephard, 1972.

DISCOVERY ACTIVITIES

- Kareem was brought up in the Catholic faith. Using reference sources, discover the reasons for his conversion to the Islamic religion.
- Kareem won the Most Valuable Player award six times. Using reference sources, discover who the other players are that have won the award multiple times.
- As of 1990, Kareem has not been included in the Basketball Hall of Fame in Springfield, Massachusetts. Give the pros and cons, in your opinion, of why Kareem should or should not be included.

Kareem Abdul-Jabbar: "My Biggest Resource Is My Mind"

When Kareem reached his full height, he was seven feet, two inches tall. A person of that height often must face many everyday, practical problems.

DIRECTIONS On the lines below, list the everyday practical problems a person of that height might face that would not be problems for people of average height.

_____
_____
_____
_____
_____
_____
_____
_____
_____
_____
_____
_____
_____
_____
_____
_____
_____
_____
_____
_____
_____

Meet Muhammad Ali: "Worthy of All Praise"

When Cassius was twelve, his bicycle was stolen. He told a policeman, "If I find out who stole it, I'm going to beat him up." The policeman answered, "If you're going to do that, you better take boxing lessons. Come to my gym."

Cassius Clay was born on January 17, 1942, in Louisville, Kentucky. He did not like fighting and always left a gathering if it seemed a fight might break out. However, he took the policeman's offer and found he had a natural ability for boxing. At seventeen, he won the light-heavyweight title in the Golden Gloves Tournament in Louisville. He set his goal on a world boxing title. After winning the gold medal for the light-heavyweight division in the 1960 Olympics at Rome, Italy, Cassius turned professional and defeated all challengers. Cassius craved attention and began writing short jingles, which he read on TV. This helped him build up a huge following of fans, which had a psychologically negative effect on his opponents. In 1964, he defeated Sonny Liston to become the world heavyweight champion. Cassius joined the Black Muslim religion and was given the name Muhammad Ali, meaning "worthy of all praise." He refused to join the army as Black Muslims do not believe in war. The World Boxing Association took away his title. He appealed to the Supreme Court, which ruled in his favor. In 1971, he lost the title to Joe Frazier but won it back again in 1975. In 1977, he lost the title to Leon Spinks and hung up his boxing gloves.

Muhammad has the courage of his beliefs. He lives each day by his Muslim promise: "I will always walk tall, walk straight, lead a clean life, and stay with my people."

READ MORE ABOUT MUHAMMAD ALI

- Lipsyte, *Free to Be Muhammad Ali.* Harper and Row, 1977.
- Olsen, *Muhammad Ali: "I Am the Greatest."* Educative Systems, 1974.
- Wilson, *Muhammad Ali.* Putnam, 1974.

DISCOVERY ACTIVITIES

- Using reference sources, discover the reasons behind Muhammad's change to the Black Muslim religion.
- The jingles Muhammad wrote were short and catchy. Using reference sources, discover the poetry of Muhammad Ali.
- During the time Muhammad's case was before the Supreme Court, he could not engage in boxing in the United States. Using reference sources, discover how he occupied this time.

Muhammad Ali: "Worthy of All Praise"

Boxing is considered to be one of the oldest known sports. Records show that men have engaged in boxing for over 5,000 years.

DIRECTIONS Research the sport of boxing using encyclopedias or other sources. Write a short history of the sport of boxing on the lines provided below.

Meet Paul "Bear" Bryant: Winningest Coach in History

Paul would do anything to win attention and recognition. At age thirteen, he accepted a challenge to wrestle a bear on stage for one dollar a minute. During the match, the bear's muzzle worked loose and the bear bit Paul's ear, causing a great deal of blood. Paul broke loose and bolted. He received no money, but from that day forward he was always called "Bear."

Paul Bryant was born on September 11, 1913, in Moro Bottom, Arkansas. Because his father was ill, Bear and his eight brothers and sisters helped their mother run the farm. Before he was six, Bear drove the mule-driven, produce-laden wagon to town. The town kids made fun of his worn, patched, hand-me-down clothes. That caused Bear to be very sensitive to "put downs" all his life. Bear began playing football in high school and won an athletic scholarship to the University of Alabama. Football was evolving from a game of merely brute strength into a game involving skill, strategy, and deception. Bear set his sights on becoming a coach. After several assistant coach positions, Bear became head coach at the University of Alabama in 1958. He was a controversial figure. Some sportscasters and parents called him gruff, cruel, and a tyrant. His teams called him a dedicated coach, completely involved with bringing out the best in each player. During his twenty-five years at Alabama, his teams won 323 games, making Bear the "winningest coach in history." Six weeks after announcing his retirement, Bear died of a heart attack, on December 15, 1982.

Bear's work was his life. He completely dedicated himself to coaching football. Ten thousand people, including famous players, sportscasters, coaches, as well as alumni and fans, attended his funeral.

READ MORE ABOUT PAUL "BEAR" BRYANT

- Jones, *In Good Hands.* Albright, 1985.
- Peterson, *Bear Bryant: Countdown to Glory.* Scribner's, 1983.
- Smith, *Bear Bryant: Football's Winning Coach.* Walker, 1984.

DISCOVERY ACTIVITIES

- Using reference sources, discover the famous football players who were coached by Bear Bryant at the University of Alabama.
- Bear Bryant had had no experience when he played his first football game. Describe that first game Bear played with the Red Bugs of Fordyce High.
- Using reference sources, discover the awards won by Bear Bryant. Include the year each award was won.

Name _____ Date _____

Paul "Bear" Bryant: Winningest Coach in History

Today, college and professional football is considered big business. There are many ways to be involved in football other than being a player.

DIRECTIONS On the lines below, list the career possibilities that a person could aspire to, other than being a player.

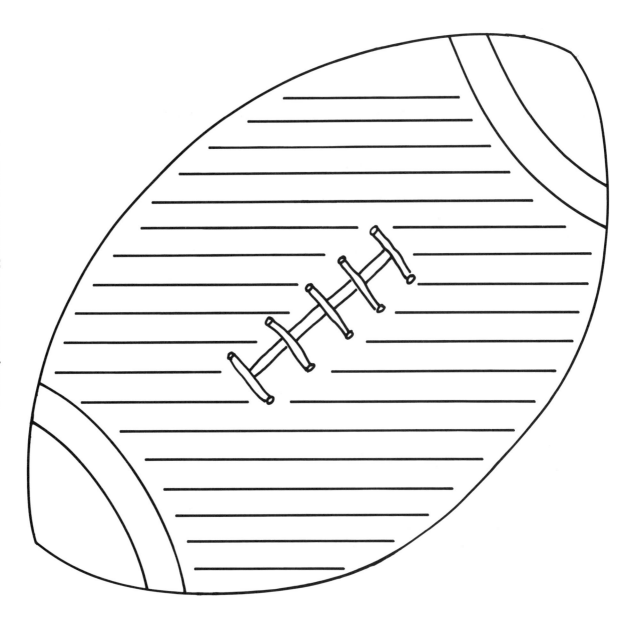

Meet Rod Carew: A Dream and a Goal

Rod and the kids in his neighborhood loved to play baseball. They used broomsticks for bats, tennis balls for baseballs, and paper bags for gloves. But after the kids went home, Rod threw the ball against a pair of steps and caught it, again and again.

Rod Carew was born on October 1, 1945, on a train. His mother was traveling to the hospital, but Rod arrived en route, in the Canal Zone of Panama. His childhood years were spent in Gatum and Gamboa, small towns along the canal. He played baseball and acted out radio broadcasts of major league games, dreaming of becoming a major league player. In 1961, Rod joined his mother in New York City, where he enrolled at George Washington High School and set himself to learn to read, write, and think in English. He was a shy, quiet boy with little confidence and few friends. In the spring of 1964, Rod began playing weekends with the Cavaliers, in the Bronx Federation League. A few months later, Herb Stein, a scout for the Minnesota Twins, watched Rod and was impressed with his ability. He arranged for Rod to try out for the Twins. In June of 1964, Rod signed a contract with the Minnesota Twins and began playing in their farm leagues. In 1967, Rod became a second baseman for the major league team. Rod was a loner and although he was well-liked and respected, he was never close friends with any of his teammates. During his career with the Twins, Rod won seven batting titles and the Most Valuable Player Award. In 1979, Rod was traded to the California Angels with whom he played until his retirement in 1986.

The love and support of Rod's wife, Marilynn, and their three daughters has helped Rod slowly crack the protective shell he had long built around himself. He has found happiness and contentment along with accomplishing his dream and goal of becoming a major league baseball player.

READ MORE ABOUT ROD CAREW

- Buchard, *Sports Hero: Rod Carew.* Putnam, 1978.
- Hahn, *Rod Carew: A Promise and a Dream.* EMC Corporation, 1978.
- Mueser, *The Picture Story of Rod Carew.* Julian Messner, 1980.

DISCOVERY ACTIVITIES

- Rod Carew was discovered by Herb Stein, a scout for the Minnesota Twins. Using reference sources, discover the job of a scout.
- If a Little League baseball player has hopes and dreams of becoming a major league player, what is the best path for him to follow?
- Using reference sources, discover the history of baseball. Write a short report of baseball in the United States.

Rod Carew: A Dream and a Goal

DIRECTIONS The diagram below shows a baseball field. The positions of the players are marked by a small circle. Selecting from the word bank below the diagram, write the position next to the circle.

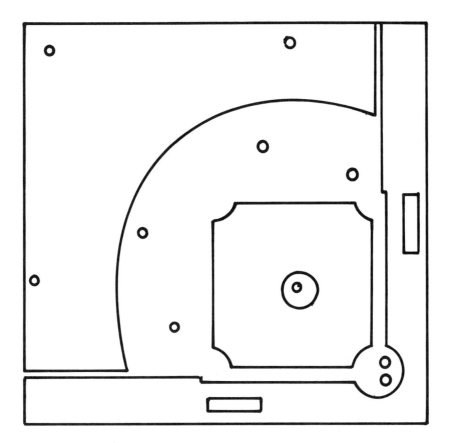

Batter	Pitcher
Catcher	Right fielder
Center fielder	Second baseman
First baseman	Shortstop
Left fielder	Third baseman

Meet Roberto Clemente: Prince of the Pittsburgh Pirates

One day, a small, skinny kid stood outside the fence, watching the San Juan Senators play. Monte Irvin popped a high foul behind home plate. The ball cleared the fence and Roberto caught it. He slept that night with the ball clutched in his hand beneath his pillow.

Roberto Clemente was born August 18, 1934, in San Juan, Puerto Rico. As a boy, he was taught that a person must be honest, must work for what he or she needs, and he or she must share what he or she has with others. Roberto was considered the best athlete ever to graduate from Vizarrondo High School. His great love was baseball. No matter what else he had to do, Roberto always found time to play baseball. In 1954, Roberto signed with the Pittsburgh Pirates, with whom he played throughout his career. Roberto was a shy, sensitive man. Although he was plagued with many muscle problems, he always gave 100 percent to the team. His honors included batting champion of 1961, Most Valuable Player of the National League in 1966, Roberto Clemente Night on July 27, 1970, and being the eleventh player in the history of baseball to achieve three thousand hits. Roberto was loved by the people of his country and was considered a living symbol of the island of Puerto Rico.

In December of 1972, Roberto organized a relief committee to aid earthquake-stricken Managua, Nicaragua. On New Year's Eve, he left San Juan Airport with a load of supplies. Moments after takeoff, there were explosions and the plane crashed into the sea. A memorial service had to be held, as his body was never recovered. The Atlantic Ocean became Roberto's final resting place.

READ MORE ABOUT ROBERTO CLEMENTE

- Brondfield, *Roberto Clemente: Pride of the Pirates.* Garrard, 1976.
- Hano, *Roberto Clemente: Batting King.* Putnam, 1968.
- Walker, *Pride of Puerto Rico: The Life of Roberto Clemente.* Harcourt Brace Jovanovich, 1988.

DISCOVERY ACTIVITIES

- Using reference sources, discover if the Pittsburgh Pirates won any World Series while Roberto Clemente was playing on the team.
- Roberto Clemente's dream was to build a facility called *Cuidad Deportiva.* Using reference sources, discover the status of this facility today.
- Roberto Clemente was the eleventh player to achieve three thousand hits. Using reference sources, discover whether any players since 1972 have achieved or surpassed that number of hits. If any players have achieved that honor, name them.

Roberto Clemente: Prince of the Pittsburgh Pirates

DIRECTIONS Choose four books about baseball, fiction or nonfiction, that you feel would be "hits" with your classmates. Fill in the information below. Recommend the books to your classmates.

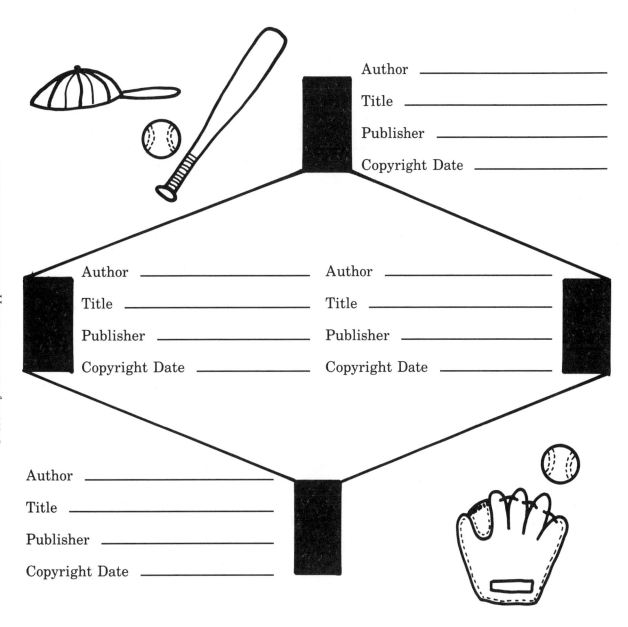

Author _____

Title _____

Publisher _____

Copyright Date _____

Author _____

Title _____

Publisher _____

Copyright Date _____

Author _____

Title _____

Publisher _____

Copyright Date _____

Author _____

Title _____

Publisher _____

Copyright Date _____

Meet Mary Decker: Fast and Feminine

It all started on a whim, just for something to do. Mary and a friend entered a local track meet. Mary discovered a fierce, competitive desire deep within herself to win. She won the event easily, far ahead of the others. The friend dropped out, but at age ten, Mary began her career in running.

Mary Teresa Decker was born in Bunnvale, New Jersey, on August 4, 1958. When the family moved to Garden Grove, California, Mary entered competition. She trained with Don DeNoon, who believed Mary had great potential because of her natural speed and form along with a positive, competitive spirit. At age fifteen, Mary was touring with the United States track team. By 1983, she held records for the 800, 1,500, 3,000, 5,000 and 10,000 meter races. Her only rival was the clock. Mary does not set the pace during a race. She stays in the middle of the group, gauging the ability of the pace setters, saving that extra burst of energy to pull ahead to win, just before the finish line. Mary is a very feminine athlete and always attractively groomed. She wears fingernail polish, earrings, and gold chains while racing. Although Mary has won acclaim as one of the greatest women racers, she has not yet achieved her dream of winning an Olympic medal. In 1972, she qualified but was too young. In 1976, an injury prevented competition. In 1980, President Carter boycotted the Olympics. In 1984, a collision with a South African runner eliminated her chances.

Today, Mary is in training for the 1992 Olympics to be held in Barcelona, Spain. Mary's philosophy is to never dwell on past or future races. She believes, "The present race is my only concern. Now is when I have to win. Now is when I have to do my best."

READ MORE ABOUT MARY DECKER

- Henkel, *Mary Decker: America's Nike.* Childrens Press, 1984.
- Jacobs, *Mary Decker: Speed Records and Spaghetti.* EMC Corporation, 1975.

DISCOVERY ACTIVITIES

- Young Mary Decker spent her fifteenth birthday far from home. Using reference sources, discover where Mary spent her fifteenth birthday and what the special gift was that made it all worthwhile.

- It is believed that Mary Decker would have won an Olympic Medal in 1984 at Los Angeles had not an unfortunate incident occurred. Using reference sources, discover the incident, who caused it, and the repercussions that followed.

- Using reference sources, discover who holds the records for the 800–10,000 meter races today.

Mary Decker: Fast and Feminine

DIRECTIONS The United States won a gold medal in the following track-and-field events listed below. Using reference sources, discover the name of the Americans who won the medals.

100-meter run

1928 _____
1936 _____
1960 _____
1968 _____
1984 _____
1988 _____

200-meter run

1960 _____
1964 _____
1984 _____
1988 _____

400-meter run

1984 _____

800-meter run

1968 _____

Meet Janet Guthrie: "Racing Is My Passion"

With few children living nearby, books became Janet's playmates. Her inner core of daring and adventure helped her identify with the characters' bold escapades.

Janet Guthrie was born on March 7, 1938, in Iowa City, Iowa. Her father, a pilot for Eastern Airlines, moved his family to Miami, Florida. Janet loved airplanes and flying. By the age of eighteen, she had earned a commercial and instructor's license. A tall, quiet, self-composed girl, Janet majored in physics at the University of Michigan and became an engineer.

In 1962, Janet bought a Jaguar XK–120. She loved the sense of driving a powerful car. She wanted to test the Jaguar's ability in a race. She joined a local sports car club and began competing. After attending the Sports Car Club of America School, she bought a Jaguar XK–140. She worked at night in an unheated barn with only a flashlight to learn how to take the engine apart and replace it perfectly. From 1963 through 1974, Janet raced, earning a reputation as a talented driver who was daring but careful, calm but quick thinking, and possessed superior timing. In 1975, Janet was invited to try to qualify for the Indianapolis 500. She qualified but could not race, as her car broke down. In 1977, she qualified again, started the race, but could not finish, as her car broke down. In 1978, she qualified, completed the course, and placed ninth.

Janet Guthrie has placed her mark on auto racing, the first woman to accomplish this feat, and has opened the way for other women. For as Janet says, "Racing is a matter of spirit, not strength. It is a matter of doing your best at all times, plus a very intense desire to keep going."

READ MORE ABOUT JANET GUTHRIE

- Dolan, *Janet Guthrie: First Woman Driver at Indianapolis.* Doubleday, 1978.
- Fox, *Janet Guthrie: Foot to the Floor.* Dillon Press, 1981.
- Olney, *Janet Guthrie: First Woman at Indy.* Harvey House, 1978.

DISCOVERY ACTIVITIES

- Using reference sources, discover why a driver must attend the Sports Car Club of America or some other school in order to qualify to compete.
- Using reference sources, discover what is meant by the "big three" types of auto racing.
- Using reference sources, discover the history of the Indianapolis 500. When did it start, what are some of the highlights of its history, and who are some of the competitors who have become famous?

Janet Guthrie: "Racing Is My Passion"

DIRECTIONS Below is a map of the Indianapolis Motor Speedway. Complete the following activities.

1. Color the pit area blue.
2. Color the four turns red.
3. Color the two straightaways green.
4. Color the master control tower orange.
5. Color the garages yellow.
6. Color the hospital purple.
7. Locate and mark the start/finish line.

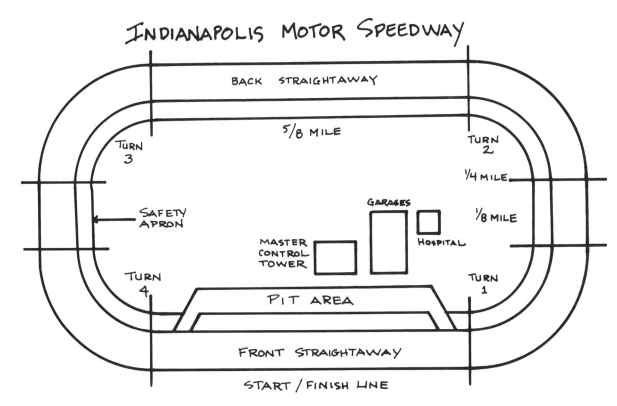

OPTIONAL ACTIVITY On the back of this sheet, design a racing car that you would like to own and drive. Explain or describe the abilities and unique characteristics of this car.

Meet Dorothy Hamill: World-Champion Figure Skater

Dorothy started skating on a pond behind her grandmother's house. She used a pair of too large, hand-me-down skates. Her ankles were weak, her legs wobbled, and she kept falling. But she kept skating.

Dorothy Hamill was born on July 26, 1956, in Chicago, Illinois, but grew up in Riverdale, Connecticut. After skating all winter with the old skates, Dorothy begged her parents to buy her a new pair. She loved skating and began group lessons. The more she learned, the more she wanted to learn. It was not easy for her parents to pay for private lessons and coaching, but Dorothy and her coaches convinced them that she had the talent and self-motivation to become a champion. She began competing in local events and quickly moved up to state and national competitions. It was not always easy. Her friends went on dates and to parties while Dorothy went to practice. However, the fleeting sorrow passed the moment she stepped onto the ice. Dorothy spent her high school years traveling, practicing, competing, and studying, whenever she was in one place long enough to enroll in a school. After winning several World Championships, Dorothy competed in the 1976 Winter Olympics at Innsbruck, Austria. On February 13th, Dorothy won the Gold Medal for women's figure skating.

Today, Dorothy is a professional skater for ice shows. She gave her gold medal to her grandmother. "Just think," her grandmother marveled, "it all started down there on our pond!"

READ MORE ABOUT DOROTHY HAMILL

- Gutman, *Modern Women Superstars.* Dodd, Mead, 1977.
- Hamill, *Dorothy Hamill: On and Off the Ice.* Knopf, 1983.
- Van Steenwyk, *Dorothy Hamill: Olympic Champion.* Harvey House, 1976.
- Also of interest: Faulkner, *I Skate!* Little, Brown, 1979.

DISCOVERY ACTIVITIES

- Dorothy Hamill became the fourth American woman skater to win all the national and international women's figure-skating titles. Using reference sources, discover the names of the other three American women skaters.
- Using reference sources, discover when and where American women won the gold medal in the Winter Olympic's figure-skating competition.
- In your opinion, what does a skater need to have to aspire to become a world champion?

Dorothy Hamill: World-Champion Figure Skater

DIRECTIONS Every sport has its own vocabulary. For anyone interested in a sport, knowledge of the vocabulary is necessary. Using reference sources, locate the meaning of the figure-skating terms listed below. Write the meaning of each term on the lines provided.

1. Axel
2. Flip
3. Lay-back spin
4. Loop jump
5. Lutz
6. Salchow
7. Spiral
8. Spread eagle
9. Sit spin
10. Toe loop jump

1. _____

2. _____

3. _____

4. _____

5. _____

6. _____

7. _____

8. _____

9. _____

10. _____

Meet Billie Jean King: Seventeen Wimbledon Wins

Billie Jean had a problem. She was an exceptional athlete. She could easily beat the boys in team sports, and they could not accept that fact. Billie Jean wanted them to accept her but did not want to downplay her ability. Her father suggested playing an individual sport. Billie Jean agreed and chose tennis.

Billie Jean Moffitt King was born November 22, 1943, in Long Beach, California. A chunky, brown-haired girl with glasses, Billie Jean excelled in team sports, as did her younger brother, Randy. But whereas Randy was encouraged to be a star, Billie Jean was encouraged to be a good team player. Billie Jean worked at odd jobs, bought a tennis racket, and took free lessons at the city park. She played in her first tournament at age eleven. She plays an aggressive game of tennis, charging the net rather than waiting at the base line to return the ball. Billie Jean has won seventeen Wimbledon championships. She has never been a popular player; the fans don't like her aggressive attitude or strong language. Billie Jean feels that being the fans' favorite is no substitute for winning. After marrying Larry King in 1965, Billie Jean continued winning matches and titles. Her most publicized match was against Bobby Riggs in 1973. Riggs belittled women's tennis and bragged how easy it would be to beat a woman. She defeated him 6-4, 6-3, 6-3. Billie Jean led the fight for equal tennis opportunities, financial rewards, and sports scholarships for women.

Today, Billie Jean's days of record-breaking, exciting matches are over. She plays team tennis, coaches at free tennis clinics, and is active in the Women's Tennis Association.

READ MORE ABOUT BILLIE JEAN KING

- Baker, *Billie Jean King.* Grosset and Dunlap, 1974.
- Gemme, *King on the Court: Billie Jean King.* Raintree Editions, 1976.
- Hahn, *King! The Sports Career of Billie Jean King.* Crestwood House, 1981.

DISCOVERY ACTIVITIES

- Using reference sources, discover how the rewards of championship tennis for women compares today with the rewards for championship tennis for men.
- Using reference sources, discover the differences between an amateur athlete and a professional athlete. What is occurring today between the two designations?
- What are the similarities and differences between being a star in an individual sport and being a star in a team sport? Would you prefer to be a star in an individual sport or a team sport? Why?

Billie Jean King: Seventeen Wimbledon Wins

Billie Jean King was discouraged from being the star in team sports. She turned to an individual sport, tennis, so she could be the star.

DIRECTIONS Below is a list of both individual and team sports. Circle the individual sports.

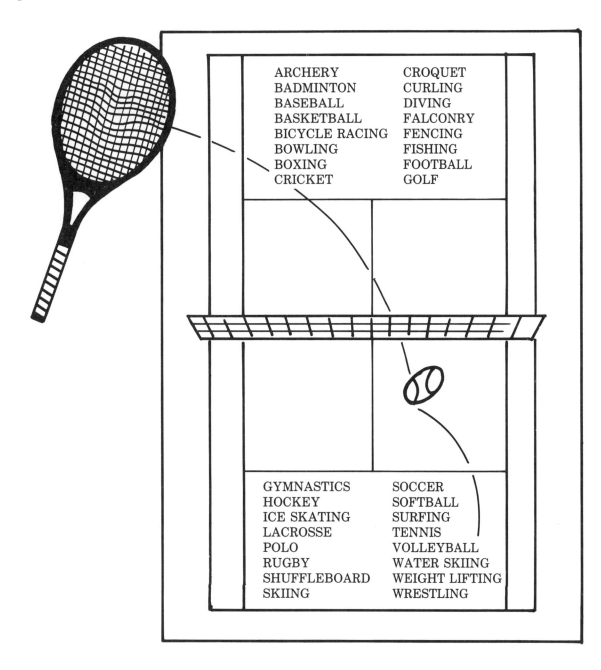

ARCHERY
BADMINTON
BASEBALL
BASKETBALL
BICYCLE RACING
BOWLING
BOXING
CRICKET

CROQUET
CURLING
DIVING
FALCONRY
FENCING
FISHING
FOOTBALL
GOLF

GYMNASTICS
HOCKEY
ICE SKATING
LACROSSE
POLO
RUGBY
SHUFFLEBOARD
SKIING

SOCCER
SOFTBALL
SURFING
TENNIS
VOLLEYBALL
WATER SKIING
WEIGHT LIFTING
WRESTLING

Meet Jack Nicklaus: Golfer of the Century

When Jack was ten years old, his father injured his ankle. After an operation his ankle mended, but not well enough to allow him to play golf with his usual partners. He asked Jack to play with him.

Jack Nicklaus was born January 21, 1940, in Columbus, Ohio. Jack enjoyed all sports, but after playing golf with his father, he developed a special interest in the game. He took lessons with Jack Grout, the pro at the Scioto Country Club. Jack played golf all through high school. He won local, state, and national championships. He was offered several college golf scholarships but turned them down. Golf was his love, but he planned to become a pharmacist in his father's drug store. During his years at Ohio State, Jack continued to win tournaments. Sportswriters were calling him the greatest amateur ever. Jack loved the challenge of golf and enjoyed the study and daily practice of the game. In 1961, at the age of twenty-one, Jack turned professional. His husky, burly build and blonde hair earned him the nickname "Golden Bear." Jack has won more tournaments than any other player. He is also a very successful businessman, owning a company called the Golden Bear, Inc., and for which he designs golf courses.

Now that Jack has turned fifty, he is eligible to play in the Seniors' tournaments as well as in the regular tournaments. He has no plans to retire and will continue a schedule of rigorous practice. He will enter the tournaments that he feels will be to his benefit and that he feels he will have an excellent chance of winning.

READ MORE ABOUT JACK NICKLAUS

- Deegan, *Jack Nicklaus: The Golden Bear.* Creative Education, 1974.
- Miller, *Johnny Miller's Golf for Juniors.* Doubleday, 1987.
- Van Riper, *Golfing Greats: Two Top Pros.* Garrard, 1975.

DISCOVERY ACTIVITIES

- Using reference sources, discover the history of golf, including where the game was invented, how it developed and grew in popularity in the United States, and the status of golf today in the United States.

- Using reference sources, discover the difference between the amateur and the professional player. Can a player take part in both amateur and professional tournaments?

- Using reference sources, discover the major professional golf tournaments held each year. How does a player win a professional tournament? Is golf a growing sport in the United States, or is it declining?

Jack Nicklaus: Golfer of the Century

Golf is an outdoor sport. The challenge of the game is for the player to drive a small, hard ball into a hole, with as few long and short drives as possible.

DIRECTIONS Complete the following activities.

1. Using the word bank, label the parts of the golf club pictured below.

Face	Grip	Hosel	Sole
Ferrule	Heel	Shaft	Toe

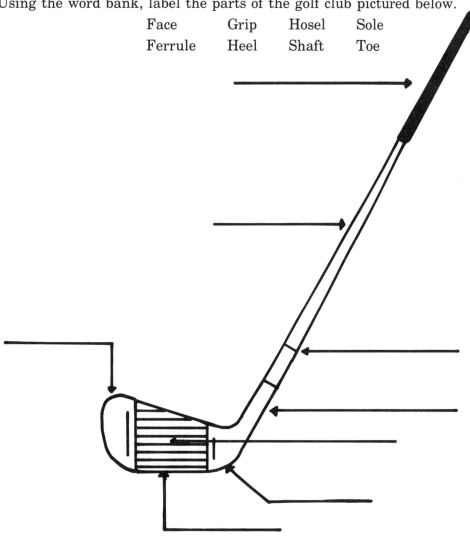

2. The basic set of golf clubs consists of _____ clubs.

3. The two types of clubs are _____ and _____.

4. The parts of a golf course usually consist of:

   a. _____   c. _____

   b. _____   d. _____

Meet Bobby Orr: Spark Plug of the Bruins

When Bobby started skating at age four, his ankles were so weak that the shoes of his skates scraped the ice and everyone laughed. When he began playing in the Minor Squirt League a year later, everyone laughed and said he was too small to play hockey. When he won Ontario's Most Valuable Pee Wee award at age nine, everyone stopped laughing and began applauding.

Robert Gordon Orr was born in Parry Sound, Ontario, Canada, on March 20, 1948. His father loved hockey and at one time had a bid to try out for the Boston Bruins, but World War II intervened and he joined the Navy. When Bobby showed an early promise of talent, his father helped and encouraged him. At age twelve, Bobby dreamed of becoming a pro. The Bruins became interested in Bobby and dreamed of Bobby's saving the team. As Bobby began winning award after award, the Bruin fans eagerly awaited March 20, 1966, when Bobby would turn eighteen and could sign a contract with the Bruins. Bobby proved to be an inspiration to the team. He never provoked an argument or a fight, but would defend himself and the team. Bobby set new standards of excellence in the position of defenseman. Bobby played with the Bruins from 1966 through 1976. He signed with the Chicago Black Hawks in 1976 but played very little due to knee injuries. Bobby retired from professional hockey in 1978.

Bobby was the first defenseman to score one hundred points during a season. He holds the career record for the most points ever scored by a defenseman. Bobby is considered one of the greatest defensemen in the history of the National Hockey League.

READ MORE ABOUT BOBBY ORR

- Devaney, *The Bobby Orr Story*. Random House, 1973.
- Liss, *Bobby Orr: Lightning on Ice*. Garrard, 1975.
- May, *Bobby Orr: Star on Ice*. Crestwood House, 1973.

DISCOVERY ACTIVITIES

- Using reference sources, discover the history of hockey. Where and when is hockey thought to have started and how did it evolve to the game of today?
- Using reference sources, discover the history of the National Hockey League. Where and when was it organized? What teams are included in the league?
- Bobby Orr won an impressive number of honors and trophies. Using reference sources, discover all these honors and trophies. Include the name of the award and the year.

Bobby Orr: Spark Plug of the Bruins

Ice hockey is a very fast game. The object of the game is to advance a hard rubber disk down the ice and shoot it into the opponent's goal. The team that scores the highest number of goals during three periods of fifteen minutes each wins the game. Standard procedures set the number of players on a team and the rules and regulations the players must follow.

DIRECTIONS   Below is a diagram of a hockey rink. Below the rink is a list of the official divisions or parts of the rink. The divisions are indicated on the rink by a small circle. Using reference sources, identify each part of the rink and place the number of each part within the small circle. The same number may need to be placed in more than one circle.

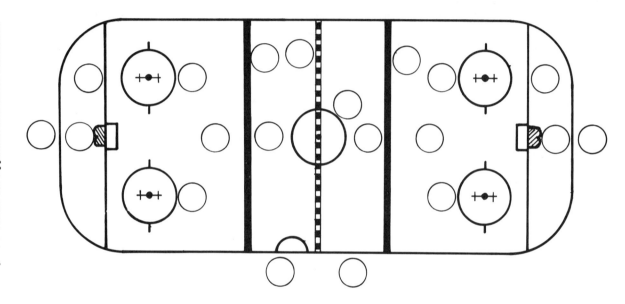

1. Attacking/defending zones
2. Blue lines
3. Center red line
4. Face-off circle
5. Goals

6. Goal judges
7. Goal lines
8. Neutral zones
9. Penalty bench
10. Penalty timekeeper

Meet Jesse Owens: Ambassador of Sports

When J.C. entered St. Clair Grammar School in Cleveland, Ohio, a teacher asked him his name. "J.C. Owens," he replied. The teacher misunderstood and wrote down Jesse Owens. "After that, everyone, except my mother, called me Jesse," he recalls. "Jesse became my name."

James Cleveland Owens was born near Oakville, Alabama, on September 12, 1913. His father was a sharecropper who worked long, hard hours but was the Sunday afternoon champion runner of the county. In 1921, the family moved to Cleveland, Ohio. Jesse loved to run and easily beat everyone in school races. While in high school, Jesse broke records for the 100-yard dash, the 200-yard dash, and the broad jump. He qualified for the 1936 Olympics in Berlin, Germany. He won four gold medals, but Adolf Hitler refused to shake his hand or acknowledge his honors. He was given a ticker-tape parade in New York City, but no job offers. He finally earned the money to finish college through racing a horse before each game in a black baseball league. When Jesse entered into partnership in a dry-cleaning business, his partners skipped town, leaving him with huge debts. In 1955, the U.S. Government appointed Jesse a Good Will Ambassador. He toured everywhere, talking with schoolchildren and young athletes. Jesse continued a career in public relations until his death in Tucson, Arizona, on March 30, 1980.

Jesse Owens never received the honors and rewards usually enjoyed by great athletes. However, he never outwardly showed bitterness. He believed that all men are created equal. His goal was that all athletes shall be given opportunity and recognition based on their talents.

READ MORE ABOUT JESSE OWENS

- Kaufman, *Jesse Owens*. Thomas Y. Crowell, 1973.
- Owens and Neimark, *The Jesse Owens Story*. Putnam, 1970.

DISCOVERY ACTIVITIES

- Jesse Owens won four gold medals at the 1936 Olympics. Using reference sources, discover the events for which Jesse won gold medals.
- Adolf Hitler refused to acknowledge Jesse Owens. Using reference sources, discover the reasons why Hitler treated Jesse in this manner.
- Using reference sources, discover when each of Jesse Owens's individual records was broken. Include the year, the name of the person, the country, and the new record.

Jesse Owens: Ambassador of Sports

The track-and-field section of the Olympics is divided into a variety of events.

DIRECTIONS Using reference sources, discover the events included in the track-and-field section of the Summer Olympics. List the name of each event on the lines given below.

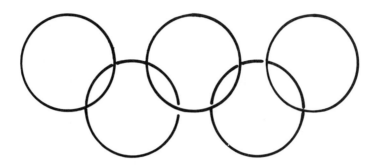

MEN   **WOMEN**

_____ _____   _____ _____

_____ _____   _____ _____

_____ _____   _____ _____

_____ _____   _____ _____

_____ _____   _____ _____

_____ _____   _____ _____

_____ _____   _____ _____

_____ _____   _____ _____

_____ _____   _____ _____

_____ _____

Meet Pelé: Brazil's "National Treasure"

Whenever Pelé came home with his uniform covered with dirt, his mother knew he had not been to school. She put him over her knee and spanked him. "Playing hookey again to play soccer," she scolded. "I'll teach you!"

Edson Arantes Do Nacimento, called Pelé, was born on October 23, 1940, in Trés Coracōes, Brazil. His father had been a local soccer star. His father began teaching Pelé soccer as soon as the boy could walk. Pelé loved soccer, and lived to play soccer. He organized a local boys team. Valdemar de Brito, a former international soccer star, noticed Pelé's talent and began coaching him. At age fifteen, Pelé signed with the junior Santos team. In 1957, he was chosen to be a member of Brazil's national soccer team. That year, Brazil won its first World Cup title. Pelé played with the Santos until 1974. The team won international fame. Brazil declared Pelé "a national treasure." Pelé was a great team player. Not only could he score, he was always ready to "set up" another team member to score. In 1975, Pelé signed with the New York Cosmos soccer team. His superior ability and dynamic presence drew enormous crowds and tripled the popularity of soccer in the United States. On October 1, 1977, after playing 1,363 games and scoring 1,281 goals, Pelé retired. He was proclaimed "The greatest soccer player that ever lived."

Pelé believes soccer has one real goal: to create world friendship. He says he does not think of all the goals he scored or the games he played. He remembers all the people he met and the friends he made through playing soccer.

READ MORE ABOUT PELÉ

- Gault, *Pelé: King of Soccer.* Walker, 1975.
- Hahn, *Pelé! The Sports Career of Edson Do Nacimento.* Crestwood House, 1981.
- Machin, *Pelé: King of Soccer.* Longman, 1984.

DISCOVERY ACTIVITIES

- Using reference sources, discover the history of soccer from the earliest days through today. What is the status of soccer today in the United States?

- The highest honor in soccer is to win the World Cup title. Using reference sources, discover all you can about World Cup soccer.

- Pelé said, "I believe soccer can unite all the peoples of the world. Soccer can fill the world with peace and love. Through soccer we can all be brothers." What do you believe are the pros and cons of these statements?

Pelé: Brazil's "National Treasure"

Pelé's family was very poor. They could not afford to buy a soccer ball. Pelé learned to play soccer using a homemade ball. Until Pelé began playing in competition, he played soccer barefoot.

DIRECTIONS Below you will find directions for making Pelé's first soccer ball. Complete the directions and try practicing with the ball. Practice with or without shoes. Remember to dribble, move the ball forward, with the inner side of your foot, not the toe.

PELÉ'S FIRST
SOCCER BALL

MATERIALS

1. An old, discarded man's sock
2. A quantity of newspapers
3. A length of string

DIRECTIONS

1. Crumple the newspapers and stuff the sock as hard and full as possible.
2. Lace the hole shut with the string.

NOTE

Pelé's soccer ball was about the size of an orange and was not perfectly round.

Meet Mary Lou Retton: "Hard Work Pays Off"

Mary Lou was a bundle of perpetual, physical motion. Her mother enrolled her in ballet and gymnastics classes at the age of seven to channel her energy away from using the furniture as playground equipment.

Mary Lou Retton was born in Fairmont, Virginia, on January 24, 1968. She is the youngest of five children in a very athletic family. Mary Lou's stocky, muscular frame was not suited to ballet, but she excelled in gymnastics. She began competing, winning her first statewide meet at age eight and her first international meet at age fourteen. Mary Lou is responsible for changing gymnastics from graceful ballet movements to a style of power, speed, and agility. She studied with Bella Karolyi, a Hungarian coach of several former Olympic champion gymnasts. Mary Lou's number-one goal was to be an Olympic gold medalist. She began by winning in the McDonald's American Cup, the World Championships, and the Chunichi Invitational in 1983, and the McDonald's American Cup again in 1984. At the 1984 Olympics at Los Angeles, the four-foot, nine-inch, one-hundred-and-five pound, sixteen-year-old Mary Lou, flashing a pixie grin, scored perfect "10s" to become the first United States woman ever to win an Olympic Gold Medal.

Mary Lou retired in 1986. She completed high school and enrolled at the University of Texas. She returned to gymnastics again in 1989 to participate in a successful eight-city United States tour with Olga Korbut. Mary Lou has thought about making a comeback at the 1992 Olympics but feels she no longer has the discipline and dedication necessary for success. She will continue her studies and is planning to be married soon.

READ MORE ABOUT MARY LOU RETTON

- Retton, *Mary Lou: Creating an Olympic Champion*. McGraw-Hill, 1986.
- Silverstein, *Mary Lou Retton and the New Gymnasts*. Franklin Watts, 1985.
- Washington, *Mary Lou Retton: Power Gymnast*. Lerner Publications, 1985.

DISCOVERY ACTIVITIES

- What do you believe are the qualifications necessary for a woman to have a chance at becoming an Olympic medalist in gymnastics?
- Using reference sources, discover Bella Karolyi. How was Mary Lou able to be coached by him?
- Using reference sources, discover the symbol, the motto, the creed, the oath, and the flame of the Olympic Games. Make a copy or a drawing of each.

Mary Lou Retton: "Hard Work Pays Off"

DIRECTIONS There is a great deal of interest in gymnastics by young people today. What three books found in your library's collection would you recommend to aspiring gymnasts? On the back of this sheet, write why you chose each of these three titles.

Author _____

Title _____

Publisher _____ Copyright Date _____

Author _____

Title _____

Publisher _____ Copyright Date _____

Author _____

Title _____

Publisher _____ Copyright Date _____

Meet Jackie Robinson: Courage Not to Strike Back

When Jackie was two and one half years old, his sister entered kindergarten. There was no one at home to take care of Jackie, so he went with her. He played in the sandbox in the schoolyard until the school day ended, then went home with her.

Jackie Robinson was born in Cairo, Georgia, on January 31, 1919. When his father deserted them, Jackie's mother took the family to Pasadena, California, to begin a new life. Jackie's mother instilled love, cooperation, and togetherness into her five children. Each Robinson child had total support for the others. Jackie was a natural athlete and excelled in all sports. He earned a high school letter in basketball, baseball, football, and track. He often played two sports simultaneously in college. After serving as an officer in the Army during World War II, Jackie joined a black baseball league. In 1945, Branch Rickey, boss of the Brooklyn Dodgers, asked him to consider joining their farm organization. Jackie signed the contract and became the first black player in major league baseball. Reaction was swift—both positive and negative. The boiling problems affected Jackie's playing, but slowly he began to build confidence. Baseball was his love, not people, and soon he was able to separate playing baseball from public reaction. In 1947, he began playing for the Brooklyn Dodgers. He had to battle prejudice and bigotry throughout his career. He played with the Dodgers until his retirement in 1956. In 1962, Jackie was inducted into Baseball's Hall of Fame in Cooperstown, New York. Jackie became a businessman and worked for civil rights legislation until his death on August 24, 1972.

Branch Rickey said, "This young man came through with courage beyond what I ever could have asked. He buried the burning inside him, and turned the other cheek to shape the future."

READ MORE ABOUT JACKIE ROBINSON

- Davidson, *The Story of Jackie Robinson, the Bravest Man in Baseball.* Yearling Books, 1988.
- Robinson, *Breakthrough to the Big League: The Story of Jackie Robinson.* Harper and Row, 1965.
- Scott, *Jackie Robinson.* Chelsea House, 1987.

DISCOVERY ACTIVITIES

- Using reference sources, discover the Baseball Hall of Fame. What was unusual about Jackie Robinson's being elected to it?
- Using reference sources, trace the history of the Brooklyn Dodgers from when Jackie Robinson played for them until today.
- In your opinion, what might have happened had Jackie Robinson been offered a contract to play major league basketball or football rather than baseball?

Jackie Robinson: Courage Not to Strike Back

In 1962, Jackie Robinson became the first black player to be inducted into the Baseball Hall of Fame.

DIRECTIONS Using reference sources, research the Baseball Hall of Fame. On the lines below, write a report about it.

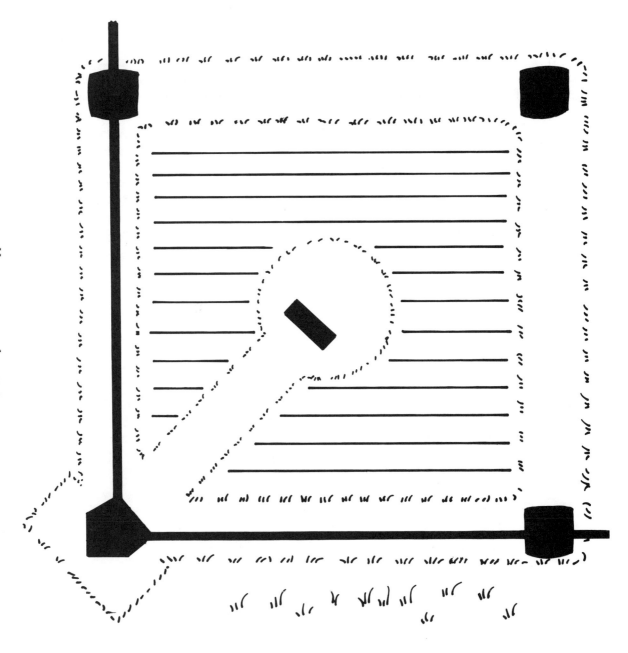

Meet Babe Ruth: Baseball's Immortal Giant

George's mother was too ill to take care of him. His father was too busy to look after him. Until the age of seven, George ran wild on the streets of Baltimore.

George Herman Ruth was born in Baltimore, Maryland, on February 6, 1895. At age seven, he was sent to St. Mary's Industrial School for Boys. George loved the afternoons, when the eight-hundred boys, divided into teams and leagues, played baseball. George was a natural ball player. He had excellent eyesight, strength, coordination, timing, and a burning desire to play. At age fifteen, George caught the interest of Jack Dunn, owner of the Baltimore Orioles, who offered him a contract. At spring training, the team teased the new rookies. They were told to lay off George, he was one of Dunn's "babes." The team picked up on that and George forever after was called "Babe." Babe was traded to the Boston Red Sox and in 1920 his contract was sold to the New York Yankees. Babe began building his famous career. He was flamboyant, and often overweight and out of training. But he was a great player and the fans loved him. His skills on the field could not be matched. No other player in history so completely dominated his competition. Babe played with the Yankees until 1934. On July 13, 1934, Babe hit his 700th home run and continued until his career home-run record was 714. After a season with the Boston Braves, Babe retired from baseball in 1935. Babe died on August 16, 1948.

Babe Ruth is still considered one of the world's greatest players. He set dozens of records, many of which still stand. There was always that extra excitement on the field, in the stands, and even in the air, at every game Babe played.

READ MORE ABOUT BABE RUTH

- Bains, *Babe Ruth.* Troll Associates, 1985.
- Berke, *Babe Ruth: The Best There Ever Was.* Franklin Watts, 1988.
- Van Riper, *Babe Ruth: One of Baseball's Greatest.* Macmillan, 1983.

DISCOVERY ACTIVITIES

- Babe Ruth hit 714 home runs during his career. Using reference sources, discover whether this record still stands. If not, when and by whom was it broken?
- Using reference sources, discover when the major league teams began issuing numbers to the members of the team. What were the reasons for issuing a number to each player? What was Babe Ruth's number?
- Using reference sources, discover the number of times the New York Yankees won the World Series. Include the team defeated, the score, and the date.

Babe Ruth: Baseball's Immortal Giant

Babe Ruth is considered one of the world's greatest baseball players. Since his death on August 16, 1948, there have been players that have also become real superstars of baseball.

DIRECTIONS   In your opinion, which players have become baseball greats? Choose four. On the lines below, write why you chose these four.

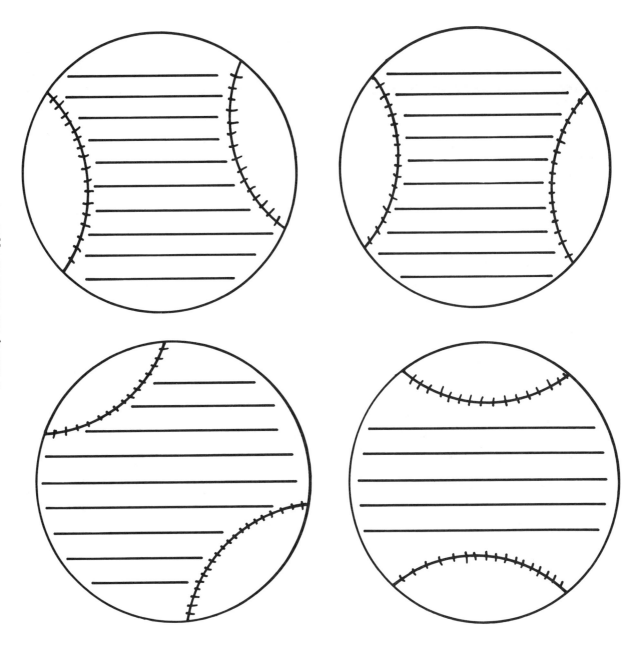

Meet Jim Thorpe: The Wonder of Sports

"Can one be considered a great chief by being a famous athlete?" Chief Black Hawk's great grandson wondered.

James Francis Thorpe was born on May 28, 1888, in Oklahoma territory. Jimmy and his twin brother Charlie loved hunting, fishing, physical games, and listening to Father tell stories about their great grandfather, Chief Black Hawk of the Black and Fox tribe. Jimmy was determined to prove himself worthy to be the great grandson of a chief. At boarding school on the reservation, Jimmy excelled in all sports. He learned by watching the best players, then practicing. At Carlisle Institute in Pennsylvania, he trained with "Pop" Warner and won outstanding recognition in football. At the 1912 Olympics in Stockholm, Sweden, Jim won the pentathlon and decathlon by a wide margin. A year later, he was stripped of all honors. The Olympic Committee ruled that the small salary he had been paid the summer before for playing baseball made him a professional and disqualified him. Jim turned professional and played major league baseball and football. In 1950, Jim was named the greatest all-around athlete of the half century, 1900 to 1950. In 1951, Jim was one of the first players to be named to the National Football Foundation's Hall of Fame.

Jim was always the leader of the team. He died on March 28, 1953, knowing he had proved himself worthy to be called a great chief through his involvement in sports, and he was honored by all people as a great chief. Today, Jim is considered one of the greatest all-around athletes in history.

READ MORE ABOUT JIM THORPE

- Hahn, *Thorpe! The Sports Career of Jim Thorpe.* Crestwood House, 1981.
- Richards, *Jim Thorpe: World's Greatest Athlete.* Crestwood House, 1984.
- Van Riper, *Jim Thorpe: Olympic Champion.* MacMillan, 1986.

DISCOVERY ACTIVITIES

- Using reference sources, discover how many and what events are included in the pentathlon and decathlon competitions in the Olympics.
- Jim Thorpe's medals and honors were restored to him. Using reference sources, discover when the medals and honors were restored to him.
- Using reference sources, discover Jim Thorpe's association with major league baseball and football. What teams did he play with? What were his contributions to professional football?

Jim Thorpe: The Wonder of Sports

Jim Thorpe excelled in both professional baseball and professional football.

DIRECTIONS   Below is a bank of words describing skills needed for baseball or football, or for both. Check each word:

1. If the word is a baseball skill, write it in the baseball.
2. If the word is a football skill, write it in the football.
3. If the word is a skill for both games, write it in both balls.

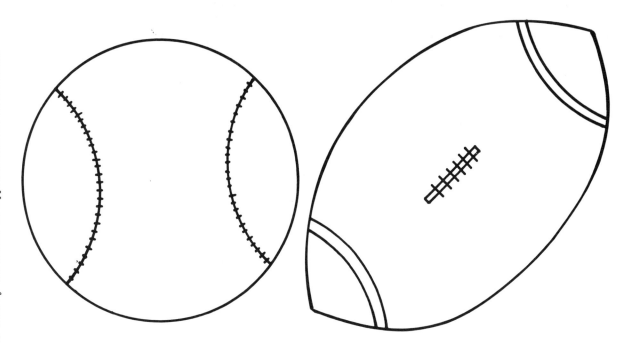

BANK OF SKILLS

Batting	Passing
Bunting	Running
Catching	Sliding
Jumping	Tackling
Kicking	Throwing

Meet Mildred Didrikson Zaharias:
All-Time Champion Athlete

Millie began playing baseball in fifth grade. "Wow," yelled a classmate. "Millie hits a ball just like Babe Ruth." That did it! From that day forward, Millie was called Babe, at her insistence.

Mildred Ella Didrikson was born on June 26, 1913, in Port Arthur, Texas. Babe was the youngest of seven children. Her parents believed in fresh air and exercise. They built an exercise gym in the backyard and had the children sleep on an open porch. Babe was a bundle of constant physical energy. She loved all sports. Before she was old enough to participate, she read the sports pages daily. She discussed the games and current sports heroes with her father. Babe was very competitive; whether it was schoolwork or athletics, she had to be the very best. She had no time for friends or social events. She was going to win a gold medal in the Olympics. She just had to decide in which sport it would be. Babe played basketball through high school, then switched to track and field to prepare for the 1932 Olympics in Los Angeles. She won two gold medals and broke many world records. To earn money to support herself and help her family, Babe switched to golf. She met George Zaharias, a pro golfer. They were married December 23, 1938.

After winning a string of tournaments in the United States, Babe won the British Women's Amateur in Scotland. A bout with cancer stopped Babe for a while, but she regained her health and went on to win more championships. During June of 1955, her doctors found that the cancer had spread. Babe fought valiantly. She even had her golf clubs in her hospital room. But it was not to be. Babe died June 22, 1955. She is considered the greatest woman athlete of all time.

READ MORE ABOUT MILDRED DIDRIKSON ZAHARIAS

- Hahn, *Zaharias! The Sports Career of Mildred Zaharias.* Crestwood House, 1981.
- Knudson, *Babe Didrikson: Athlete of the Century.* Viking Kestral, 1985.
- Smith, *The Babe: Mildred Didrikson Zaharias.* Raintree Editions, 1976.

DISCOVERY ACTIVITIES

- The summer Olympic Games were held in Los Angeles in 1932. Using reference sources, discover when the Olympic Games returned to Los Angeles.
- Babe competed in three events in track and field in the 1932 Olympics. Using reference sources, discover how many events are included in track and field.
- Babe won two gold medals, one for the javelin throw, one for the 80-meter hurdle. Using reference sources, discover whether anyone else has won two or more medals for events in track and field at one Olympic meeting.

© 1991 by The Center for Applied Research in Education

Name _____ Date _____

Mildred Didrikson Zaharias: All-Time Champion Athlete

DIRECTIONS Babe competed in basketball, a team sport; and track and field, an individual sport. In the columns below, list as many team and individual sports as possible.

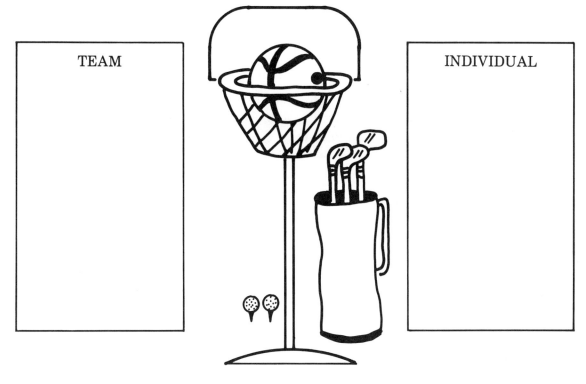

TEAM

INDIVIDUAL

What qualifications are needed for team sports versus individual sports?

Team Sports _____

_____

_____

Individual Sports _____

_____

_____

World
Leaders

You cannot shake hands with a clenched fist.

—*Indira Gandhi*

I have never seen difficulties that prevented
leading politicians of great maturity and strong
personalities from getting together when they felt
it made sense.

—*Dag Hammarskjöld*

Meet Corazon Aquino: The Hope of the Philippines

The rising yellow sun holds the promise of a bright, new day. Cory wore a yellow dress when she was sworn in as president to signify a bright, new day for the Republic of the Philippines. At the same time, on the same day, Ferdinand Marcos was also sworn in as president. Two presidents, one country—which one would govern?

Corazon Cojuangco Aquino was born January 25, 1933, in Tarlac Province. Cory attended schools in Manila and in the United States. Her classmates remember her as an independent student with a humorous sparkle or an angry snap in her dark eyes. She married Benigno S. Aquino, or Ninoy as he was called, on October 11, 1953. Cory acted as hostess at Ninoy's political meetings while he was mayor of Concepcion and Tarmac, and later governor of Tarmac. In 1976, Ninoy planned to run for president against Marcos. Marcos declared martial law and canceled elections. Ninoy was arrested and suffered a heart attack in prison. Marcos released him, and the family went to Texas, where Ninoy underwent successful heart surgery. The family moved to Boston.

In 1983, Ninoy returned to the Philippines to run for president. He was shot and killed on arrival. When Marcos announced elections to be held in 1986, the people urged Cory to run. Both Cory and Marcos claimed victory. Both had themselves sworn in. Marcos, however, lost the support of the military forces. He fled with his family to Hawaii, leaving Cory victorious.

Cory began to build a democracy. She freed political prisoners. She restored human rights and a free press. A new constitution was passed in 1987. Today, Corazon Aquino is president of the Philippines by the choice of the people. She has been called the people's hope of the future.

READ MORE ABOUT CORAZON AQUINO

- Haskins, *Corazon Aquino: Leader of the Philippines.* Enslow Press, 1988.
- Nadel, *Corazon Aquino: Journey to Power.* Messner, 1987.
- Scariano, *The Picture Life of Corazon Aquino.* Franklin Watts, 1987.

DISCOVERY ACTIVITIES

- On September 22, 1972, Marcos declared martial law. Using reference sources, discover what powers are enacted under martial law.
- Using reference sources, discover the Republic of the Philippines. Where is it located, what is its geography, and what is its history?
- Using reference sources, discover how the Republic of the Philippines is faring today.

Corazon Aquino: The Hope of the Philippines

DIRECTIONS Complete the crossword puzzle below. The answers can be found in the cameo on Corazon Aquino on the preceding page.

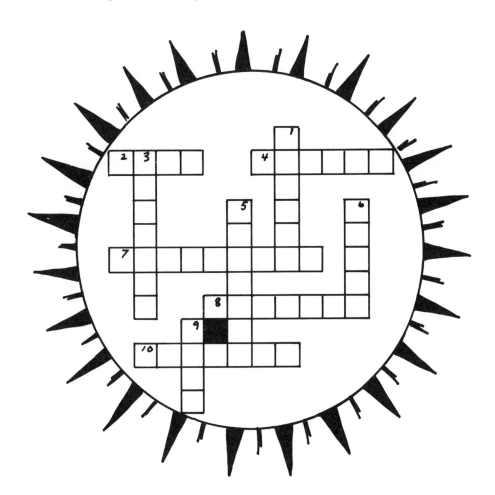

ACROSS

2. Corazon's husband was ____ when he returned to Manila.
4. Marcos fled to ____ after losing support of the army.
7. Corazon is trying to build a ____.
8. Both Corazon and Marcos claimed ____ in 1986.
10. Corzaon has been called the ____ hope of the future.

DOWN

1. Corazon was born in ____ Province.
3. Corazon acted as ____ for her husband's political meetings.
5. Marcos declared ____ law, in 1972, and cancelled elections.
6. Corazon's husband was called ____.
9. Corazon Aquino is called ____.

Meet Robert Baden-Powell: World Scout

B-P enjoyed vacation days more than school days. He and his three older brothers went on long canoe trips. They camped, caught and cooked their own food, and carried the canoe from one waterway to another all across England.

Robert Stevenson Smyth Baden-Powell, called B-P, was born on February 22, 1857, in London, England. B-P spent more time in the woods "reading" animal signs and tracks than reading books. He was expected to follow his brothers to Oxford University but failed the entrance exam twice. He took and passed the exam for the British Army and became an officer. He moved up the ranks and became a full colonel at age fifty, in charge of his own regiment. B-P was a natural leader and became a hero to his men. He took a group of boys, from all walks of life, on a long camping trip to test his theories of instilling skills and self-reliance into boys at an early age. The trip was so successful that B-P retired from the army; rewrote *Aids to Scouting,* a book he had written for his troops, into a book for boys; and devoted himself to organizing scout troops. He set up a headquarters; wrote the scout laws, rules, and regulations; designed a uniform, and recruited leaders. By 1910, troops were established throughout Europe and the United States. With the help of his sister, Agnes, the Girl Guides were organized. B-P continued traveling to visit troops, organizing jamborees, writing articles on scouting, answering letters from scouts, and setting up new troops until his death on January 8, 1941.

B-P introduced a new way of life to millions of boys and girls, a way of life that he felt would help make them more alert and self-reliant, which would help them grow into better adults, which would make their nation stronger.

READ MORE ABOUT ROBERT BADEN-POWELL

- Blassingame, *Baden-Powell: Chief Scout of the World.* Garrard, 1966.
- Catherall, *The Young Baden-Powell.* Roy Publishers, 1961.
- Freedman, *Scouting with Baden-Powell.* Holiday House, 1967.

DISCOVERY ACTIVITIES

- The Boy Scouts of America today is divided into age-group sections. Using reference sources, discover the different groups.
- Using reference sources, discover when the first Boy Scout troop was organized in the United States.
- Robert Baden-Powell dreamed of a "brotherhood among the young, in every nation, on the basis of their common membership in the human family." Using reference sources, discover the number of scouts in the world today.

Robert Baden-Powell: World Scout

Robert Baden-Powell wrote the Scout Oath, the Scout Law, and the Scout Motto. To become a Scout, a boy must promise to obey the Oath, the Law, and the Motto.

DIRECTIONS Within the Scout emblems below, write the Scout Oath, the Scout Law, and the Scout Motto.

Meet David Ben-Gurion: Mandate for Peace

David grew up in a family that believed the dream of the Jewish people, to have a Jewish state again in the land of their ancestors, could come true.

David Green was born on December 16, 1886, in Russian-controlled Plonsk, Poland. He always took himself and his studies very seriously. His father was a Zionist and believed his people would someday return to Zion, the land of their ancestors. In 1896, an international Zionist meeting was held in Switzerland. The goal was to begin planning a Jewish nation in Palestine. Every Jew in the world was invited to become a member of this nation. David moved to Palestine in 1906 to work toward this goal. He began publishing articles in the *Unity*, a newspaper published in Palestine. He signed his articles Ben-Gurion (son of young lion). Shortly after, he changed his name to David Ben-Gurion. David became a Zionist leader and founded the United Labor Party. He became chairman of the Jewish Agency for Palestine. David was in charge of all Jewish affairs in the country. He traveled everywhere, raising money and inviting Jews to return to live in Palestine. During the Second World War, he directed underground activities from England and the United States. In May of 1948, the country of Israel was born. David served as Israel's first prime minister from 1948 through 1953. He retired to join a kibbutz, but returned to serve as prime minister again from 1955 through 1963. David continued to work for peace and stability for Israel until his death on December 1, 1973.

David was a journalist, farmer, statesman, scholar, and fighter who relentlessly pursued his dream to fruition.

READ MORE ABOUT DAVID BEN-GURION

- Bar-Zohar, *Ben-Gurion: A Biography*. Delacorte, 1979.
- Kurzman, *Ben-Gurion: Prophet of Fire*. Simon and Schuster, 1983.
- St. John, *Builder of Israel: The Story of Ben-Gurion*. Doubleday, 1961.

DISCOVERY ACTIVITIES

- Using reference sources, discover the people who have served Israel as prime minister. Include names and dates of service.
- Using reference sources, discover the kibbutz. Write a short report on the aims and objectives of the kibbutz.
- Using reference sources, discover the form of government of Israel. Describe the divisions of the government.

David Ben-Gurion: Mandate for Peace

The country of Israel was born in May of 1948. Israel, part of the Middle East, is a long, narrow country bounded by the Mediterranean Sea, Egypt, Jordan, and Lebanon.

DIRECTIONS Below is a map of the Middle East. Using reference sources, complete the following activities:

1. Locate the country of Israel. Color it blue.
2. Locate the Dead Sea. Color it red.
3. Locate the city of Tel Aviv. Mark it with a red dot.
4. Locate the city of Jerusalem. Mark it with a green dot.

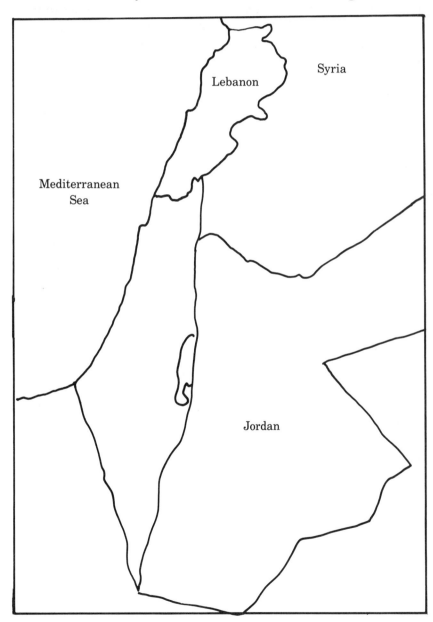

Meet Elizabeth Blackwell: The First Woman M.D.

Babies died so often in the Blackwell family that Elizabeth was filled with despair. "When I grow up, I shall be a doctor. I shall help babies to live and stay healthy."

Elizabeth Blackwell was born on February 3, 1821, in Bristol, England. Although there were nine living children in the family, her mother as well as her aunts had many more babies who died in infancy. Elizabeth's father believed in equal educational opportunities for all his children. They were tutored at home in the academic subjects. In 1832, the Blackwells moved to the United States. Upon completion of high school, Elizabeth taught school and studied at night. She applied to twenty-nine medical schools but was rejected as none would accept women. She was finally accepted at the Geneva Medical College of Western New York. In 1849, she graduated with high honors and became the first woman M.D. in the United States. When Elizabeth began practicing medicine, male doctors ridiculed her and hospitals barred her from the wards. As a result, she started the New York Infirmary for Women and Children. She went on to establish a medical school for women, trained nurses during the Civil War, and wrote books on the importance of cleanliness and diet. Elizabeth returned to England where she fought for equal rights for women doctors. She became a professor at the new London School of Medicine for Women. Elizabeth died May 31, 1910, as the result of injuries suffered in an accident at her summer home in Scotland.

Elizabeth Blackwell was the first doctor to practice preventive medicine. As well as curing the disease, she sought to prevent it from occurring.

READ MORE ABOUT ELIZABETH BLACKWELL

- Baker, *The First Woman Doctor.* Scholastic, 1987.
- Brown, *Elizabeth Blackwell.* Chelsea House, 1989.
- Sabin, *Elizabeth Blackwell: The First Woman Doctor.* Troll Associates, 1982.

DISCOVERY ACTIVITIES

- Using reference sources, discover the American Medical Association. When was it established and what is its purpose?
- Using reference sources, discover the Elizabeth Blackwell Medal. When was it established and to whom is it awarded?
- Using reference sources, discover how applicants are accepted to medical schools today.

Elizabeth Blackwell: The First Woman M.D.

DIRECTIONS Locate three books in your school or public library that you would recommend to a classmate interested in becoming a doctor. Read the books and write on the lines below why you recommend these particular titles.

1. Author _____

   Title _____

   Publisher _____ Copyright Date _____

   I recommend this title because _____

   _____

   _____

2. Author _____

   Title _____

   Publisher _____ Copyright Date _____

   I recommend this title because _____

   _____

   _____

3. Author _____

   Title _____

   Publisher _____ Copyright Date _____

   I recommend this title because _____

   _____

   _____

Meet Winston Churchill: Statesman of the Hour

Winston's school reports always contained the same phrases: no ambition, poor academic work, and disruptive behavior.

Winston Churchill was born at Bleinheim Palace in Oxfordshire, England, on November 30, 1874. The combination of lack of affection from his parents, a fear of the physical punishments at school, and the frustration of having to study hated subjects caused Winston's school years to be a total failure. He prepared for a career in the army. While on assignment in India, he found he had a talent for writing and began publishing in English newspapers, accounts of battles. Winston held a variety of political appointments. He served as Prime Minister during World War II. His leadership, extraordinary courage, inspirational words, and complete faith in freedom helped carry England to victory. After World War II, Winston retired to complete writing, *A History of the English-Speaking Peoples* for which he won a Nobel Prize for Literature. Winston continued to make and write history until his death on January 24, 1965.

Winston, a stubborn, high-spirited man, became a soldier, journalist, artist, speaker, author, leader, and hero. The reports written about his adult life differ vastly from those written about a schoolboy. Winston Churchill is considered one of the greatest statesmen in world history.

READ MORE ABOUT WINSTON CHURCHILL

- Gilbert, *Churchill.* Doubleday, 1980.
- Keller, *Winston Churchill.* Franklin Watts, 1984.
- Wibberley, *The Life of Winston Churchill.* Farrar, Straus and Giroux, 1965.

DISCOVERY ACTIVITIES

- Winston Churchill created symbols that became his trademarks. Using reference sources, discover these symbols.
- Winston Churchill's career spanned the years of 1895 to 1964. Using reference sources, prepare a time line of the most important events of his life.
- Using reference sources, discover World War II. When did the war begin and end? Which countries fought against which other countries?

Winston Churchill: Statesman of the Hour

World War II has often been called "The Great War." It was supposed to have been the war to end all wars. However, that has not happened. There have been wars since, but World War III has not yet occurred. Some people, however, believe that World War III is possible.

DIRECTIONS Within the V for victory, one of Winston Churchill's symbols during World War II, write your feelings about the possibilities of a World War III and why you feel that way.

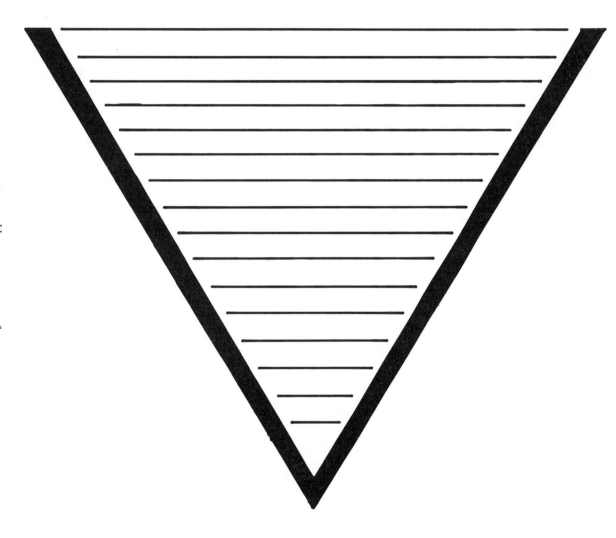

Meet Indira Gandhi: Star of India

When Indira was twelve, she organized a branch of the "Monkey Brigade" in her home town. These junior members of the Indian National Congress ran errands, posted notices, and carried messages. The police paid little attention to children and never realized what they were doing.

Indira Priyadarshini Nehru Gandhi was born on November 19, 1917, in Allahabad, India. She was the only child in a well-educated, politically active family. Her father and grandfather were leaders in the Indian National Congress, a group striving for independence for India. She attended Oxford University and lived in London during World War II. After returning home, she married Feroze Gandhi. In 1947, when India gained its independence, Indira's father became prime minister. Because her mother had died years before, Indira became her father's official hostess and was present at all meetings. In 1966, Indira was elected prime minister. Her natural ability, toughness, and political experience combined with a great determination that India be strong and united made her a strong leader. It was because of these characteristics, however, that she was also accused of being a dictator. After being defeated in 1972, Indira was reelected in 1980. In June of 1984, Indira sent the army into Punjab, where the Sikhs were revolting. The army invaded the Golden Temple and placed Punjab under military law. The Sikhs vowed revenge. On October 31, 1984, Indira was assassinated by two Sikhs, part of her personal guard, as she walked through her garden to a meeting.

Indira Gandhi was a person of great courage and purpose. When asked in 1966, how it felt to be a woman and to be prime minister, she replied, "I do not regard myself as a woman. I am a person with a job to do."

READ MORE ABOUT INDIRA GANDHI

- Fishlock, *Indira Gandhi.* Hamish Hamilton Children's Books, 1986.
- Greene, *Indira Nehru Gandhi: Ruler of India.* Childrens Press, 1985.
- Raju, *Indira Gandhi: A Short Biography for Children.* Coronet Books, 1980.

DISCOVERY ACTIVITIES

- Using reference sources, discover the history of the Indian National Congress. What is the status of the party today?
- Using reference sources, discover the caste system in India. What are the pros and cons of the caste system?
- Using reference sources, discover the main political, economic, and social problems facing India today.

Indira Gandhi: Star of India

India is a federal union with twenty-two states. The chief executive is the prime minister, who is elected by the majority party in Parliament. The members of the cabinet are members of Parliament. The chief minister in each state is chosen by the majority party in the state legislature.

DIRECTIONS Listed below are the names of the twenty-two states of India. Using reference sources, locate each state on the map by placing the number of the state in its correct location.

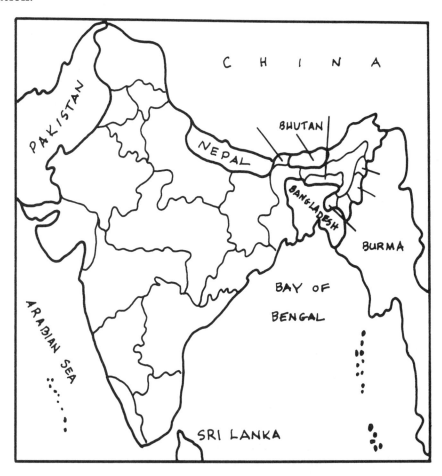

1. Andhra Pradesh
2. Assam
3. Bihar
4. Gujarat
5. Haryana
6. Himachal Pradesch
7. Jammu and Kashmir
8. Karnataka (Mysore)
9. Kerala
10. Madhya Pradesh
11. Maharashtra
12. Manipur
13. Meghalaya
14. Nagaland
15. Orissa
16. Punjab
17. Rajasthan
18. Sikkim
19. Tamil Nadu (Madras)
20. Tripura
21. Uttar Pradesh
22. West Bengal

Meet Mahatma Gandhi: "The Great Soul"

Mohandas was so deeply revered by the Indian people that he was given the title Mahatma, meaning "The Great Soul."

Mohandas Karamchand Gandhi was born on October 2, 1869, in Porbandar, India. After graduating from high school, he studied law at London University in England. In 1893, Mohandas went to South Africa to represent a Muslim firm. After a year, he left the firm and spent the next twenty years working for rights for Indian immigrants as British subjects in South Africa. After his return to India, Mohandas became the leader of the Indian National Congress. From 1918 to 1945, he worked for independence for India. He preached nonviolent civil disobedience. Mohandas was arrested many times. He used personal fasting as a means to bring about change. Mohandas believed behavior was more important than achievement. He set an example through living a very simple life. In 1947, Britain granted independence to India, but divided the country into two nations, India and Pakistan. Fights and riots occurred all over the land. Mohandas traveled everywhere, leading daily prayers of unity and acceptance. Everyone was welcome to attend. On January 3, 1948, on the outskirts of Delhi, just before the start of prayers, Mohandas was assassinated by a young Hindu radical.

Albert Einstein said of Mahatma Gandhi, "Generations to come, it may be, will scarce believe that such a one as this ever in flesh and blood walked upon this earth."

READ MORE ABOUT MAHATMA GANDHI

- Faber, *Mahatma Gandhi.* Julian Messner, 1986.
- Hunter, *Gandhi.* Watts, 1987.
- Nicholson, *Mahatma Gandhi: The Man Who Freed India and Led the World in Nonviolent Change.* Gareth Stevens, 1988.

DISCOVERY ACTIVITIES

- Mahatma Gandhi urged his followers to practice nonviolent civil disobedience. Using reference sources, discover how this action works.
- Using reference sources, discover the factors that led to India being divided into two separate states, India and Pakistan.
- It has been more than forty-two years since India's Independence Day of August 15, 1947. Using reference sources, discover the status of India and Pakistan today and their relationship toward one another.

Mahatma Ghandi: "The Great Soul"

DIRECTIONS Using reference sources, locate, label, and color the following countries on the map below.

India – blue   Pakistan – yellow
Nepal – green   Bhutan – red
Bangladesh – orange

209

Meet Dag Hammarskjöld: A Man For Peace

When Dag was named secretary general of the United Nations, Trygve Lie, the former secretary general told him, "You are taking on the world's most impossible job." Dag's father told him, "Your whole life has been pointed towards this day."

Dag Hammarskjöld was born July 29, 1905, in Jönköping, Sweden. He grew up in a four-hundred-year-old castle. Dag was a shy, reserved child. He had an astonishing memory and soaked up information like a sponge. He loved hiking and camping.

After receiving a doctorate in economics, Dag began a career in government service. A tall, slim man, Dag possessed remarkable intelligence, along with fine judgment, a cool, calm manner, and the ability to compel people to work together to make decisions and solve problems. Dag seemed to be a happy man, and he was respected and admired. But he was a very lonely man. He did not marry, as he felt government service took all his time. He kept a secret journal, in which he wrote his innermost thoughts and feelings, which he had no one to share with.

On April 7, 1953, Dag was named secretary general of the United Nations. The United Nations was failing in dignity, direction, and mission. Dag restored all three. As crisis after crisis developed, he dealt with each, always thoroughly prepared, ready to travel anywhere to discuss and negotiate peaceful solutions.

On September 13, 1961, Dag and several aides flew from Leopoldville (Kinshasa), Zaire to Ndola, on the Rhodesian border. The plane mysteriously crashed and all aboard were killed. Dag Hammarskjöld was mourned by the entire world. He has been called, "the world's greatest natural asset."

READ MORE ABOUT DAG HAMMARSKJÖLD

- Montgomery, *Dag Hammarskjöld: Peacemaker for the UN*. Garrard, 1973.
- Seldon, *Dag Hammarskjöld*. Chelsea House, 1987.
- Soderberg, *Hammarskjöld: A Pictorial Biography*. Viking, 1962.

DISCOVERY ACTIVITIES

- Using reference sources, discover the purpose of the United Nations.
- Using reference sources, discover the responsibilities of the secretary general of the United Nations.
- Using reference sources, make a list of the countries that belong to the United Nations. What countries do not belong?

Dag Hammarskjöld: A Man for Peace

Dag Hammarskjöld kept a journal, which was published after his death. This was not a diary of events, but writings concerning his thoughts, feelings, and beliefs about his life and what he must do with his life. He wrote in both prose and poetry.

DIRECTIONS   Below are printed some of the entries from Dag Hammarskjöld's journal. Read them thoughtfully. Keep a journal for a week. Write your thoughts and feelings about your life, and your hopes and dreams for the future. Share your journal with someone close to you.

Life yields only to the conqueror
Never accept what can be gained
by giving in. You will be living
off stolen goods and your muscles
will atrophy.

Work as an anesthetic against
loneliness, books as a substitute
for people-!

If only I may grow: firmer,
simpler–quiet, warmer.

–Night is drawing nigh–
For all that has been–Thanks!
To all that shall be–Yes!

What I ask for is absurd:
That life shall have a meaning.
What I strive for is impossible:
That my life shall acquire a meaning.

God sometimes allows us to take the
credit–for his work.

He wasn't wanted
When, nonetheless, he came,
He could only watch them play.

School was over.
The yard was empty.
The ones he sought
Had found new friends.

The road, you shall follow it.
The fun, you shall forget it.
The cup, you shall empty it.
The pain, you shall conceal it.
The truth, you shall be told it.
The end, you shall endure it.

What you have to attempt—
to be yourself.

Without our being aware of it,
our fingers are so guided that
a pattern is created when the
thread gets caught in the web.

Meet Winnie Mandela: "The Struggle Is My Life"

Winnie grew up happily, running barefoot, playing ball, and modeling clay toys and animals. She never dreamed of the role that fate would thrust upon her.

Winnie Madikizela was born on September 26, 1936, in Bazana, Pondoland. She was a quiet, reserved child, with a warm, wide smile. Although poor economically, Winnie grew up rich in the love and affection of her family. At the age of sixteen, Winnie moved to Johannesburg to study to become a medical social worker. She began attending meetings of the Black National Congress, which was fighting apartheid where she met Nelson Mandela, a well-known political activist. They were married at her village in Pondoland in June of 1958.

Winnie saw little of her husband. He was traveling and fighting for rights for black South Africans. He was arrested and put in jail. Fearing his voice would not be heard, Winnie became a political activist and began to speak for him. The police harassed her and put her under house arrest. People were ordered not to associate with her or her daughters. She lost her job. She defied the ban against public speaking, although her voice was heard only by small gatherings. No newspaper, radio or TV station was allowed to carry her message. She continued to speak out when ever and where ever she could while Nelson was in prison.

After spending twenty-five years in prison, Nelson was finally released. Today, he is traveling around the world, speaking for black Africans. Winnie travels with him. Her voice, today, is heard through Nelson.

READ MORE ABOUT WINNIE MANDELA

- Harrison, *Winnie Mandela.* Braziller, 1987.
- Meltzer, *Winnie Mandela: The Soul of South Africa.* Viking Kestral, 1986.
- Vail, *Nelson and Winnie Mandela.* Chelsea House, 1989.

DISCOVERY ACTIVITIES

- Winnie Mandela is fighting against apartheid. Using reference sources, discover the meaning of the term. From where did the term come?
- Most of the problems in South Africa are centered within Johannesburg. Using reference sources, discover the history of Johannesburg.
- Using reference sources, discover the status of black Africans today. In your opinion, what do you feel the future holds for South Africa?

Winnie Mandela: The Struggle Is My Life

DIRECTIONS   Below is a map of the continent of Africa.

1. Color South Africa.
2. With a different color, color the countries that border South Africa.

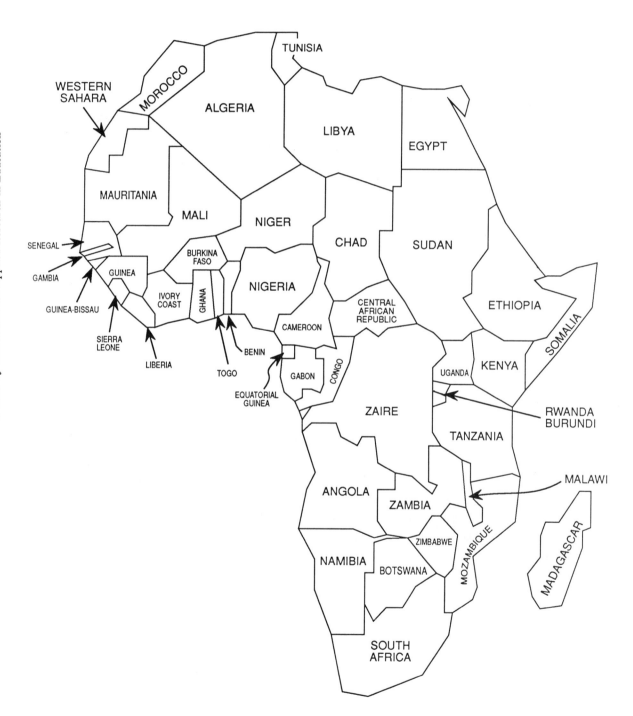

Meet Margaret Mead: World-Famous Anthropologist

Margaret lived in sixty different houses before she turned thirteen. With each move, she carefully watched the people around her to see how and where she would fit in.

Margaret Mead was born December 16, 1901, in Philadelphia, Pennsylvania. Her father was responsible for organizing branches of the University of Pennsylvania all over the state. Margaret was educated at home by her mother and grandmother until she attended high school. She was a sturdy, willful child. She always had to know everything about what was going on around her. She loved to read and to watch people. She wondered what made families so alike and yet so different.

After completing her studies in anthropology, the study of mankind, at Barnard College and Columbia University, Dr. Margaret Mead set out to study the peoples of the world. She was interested in every phase of human life. She believed that climate, animals, plants, and other materials limited what a people could do, but did not determine what a people would do. People solved the basic problems of living in ways that are not necessarily better, just different.

At the time of her death on November 15, 1978, Margaret had written thirty-nine books, more than one thousand articles, and received forty different awards. Her ideas and theories were not always accepted. She was a great thinker and often provoked arguments to make people think. She believed the world's people were becoming homogenized, that the individual culture of each people was becoming extinct. Too soon, she felt, the people of the world would all be the same and would put aside the value of their heritage. That, she believed, would be a great loss to mankind.

READ MORE ABOUT MARGARET MEAD

- Mead, *People and Places.* World, 1959.
- Saunders, *Margaret Mead: The World Was Her Home.* Viking Kestral, 1987.
- Ziest, *Margaret Mead.* Chelsea House, 1990.

DISCOVERY ACTIVITIES

- Margaret studied anthropology, the study of mankind. Using reference sources, what characteristics does a person need to be interested in selecting anthropology as a career?
- Margaret believed that the primary differences in men and women are based on the mother. She believed mothers pushed girls toward being similar and boys toward being different. How do you react to that statement?
- In 1950, Margaret said society "overvalues youth, undervalues the middle years, and merely tolerates old age." Using reference sources, discover whether you think that statement holds true today.

Margaret Mead: World-Famous Anthropologist

Margaret Mead believed the people of the world were all becoming the same. She believed they were putting aside their heritage and history to be just like everybody else.

DIRECTIONS   On the lines below, react to these statements. Do you believe this is true? Why or why not?

_____
_____
_____
_____
_____
_____
_____
_____
_____
_____
_____
_____
_____
_____
_____
_____
_____
_____
_____

Meet Golda Meir: Daughter of Israel

Golda spent her early years living in terror of the Russian Cossacks who constantly galloped through town, causing death and destruction.

Golda Marbowitz Meir was born in Kiev, Russia, on May 3, 1898. Her father emigrated to Milwaukee, Wisconsin, in 1903. Golda, her mother, and her two sisters joined him three years later. Golda was a pretty, slender girl with a strong, forceful personality. She was an activist and an organizer, always involved in causes. Golda became a member of the Zionists, a group who believed that the Jews must return to Palestine and rebuild their nation. Her whole mission in life was directed toward that goal. After World War I, Golda and her new husband, Morris Myerson, moved to Palestine. Golda worked tirelessly, traveling and raising money for the new state of Israel. She served as ambassador to Moscow, minister of labor, and foreign minister. After the Six-Day War, Golda became prime minister. She led Israel through a war with the Arabs. After the peace conference in Geneva, she retired on June 3, 1974. Until her death on December 8, 1978, Golda spent her time writing, traveling, and serving her country as a consultant advisor.

Golda Myerson, who changed the family name Myerson to the Hebrew form, Meir, in 1957, believed in peace and understanding. She believed the day would come when Israel and its neighbors would live together in a spirit of harmony and cooperation.

READ MORE ABOUT GOLDA MEIR

- Dobrin, *A Life for Israel: The Story of Golda Meir*. Dial Press, 1974.
- Keller, *Golda Meir*. Franklin Watts, 1983.
- Meir, *My Life*. Putnam, 1975.

DISCOVERY ACTIVITIES

- Using reference sources, discover Zionism. Who was its founder? What is its philosophy and its objectives? What is its status today?
- On November 29, 1947, the United Nations created the first Jewish state in two thousand years. Using reference sources, discover how this came about, and how Palestine was divided.
- Using reference sources, discover the Six-Day War. How did it come about, and how did it end?

Golda Meir: Daughter of Israel

DIRECTIONS Using reference sources, complete the following activities concerning Israel.

Mediterranean
Sea

Egypt

Jordan

Founded _____

Capital _____

Offical languages _____

_____

National Anthem _____

Monetary Unit _____

Locate the following places on the map. Write the name in the correct location.

1. Jerusalem   4. Golan Heights
2. Haifa   5. West Bank
3. Tel Aviv   6. Gaza Strip

Draw the flag of Isreal

Meet Dr. Maria Montessori: Champion of Children's Rights

When Maria decided she wanted to study medicine, she was told it was impossible, because she was a woman. However, Maria became the first woman to be admitted to a medical college in Italy. In 1896, Maria became the first woman in Italy to receive the degree of Doctor of Medicine.

Maria Montessori was born in Chiaravalle, Italy, on August 31, 1870. While Maria was practicing in clinics in Rome, she became interested in children. She felt that the public schools were too rigid and strict. She developed methods and materials that she felt would set free children's inner spirit and knowledge. She stated that her methods would be successful with every child. The Montessori method is based on two main points: (1) The duty of the teacher is to help, not to judge. (2) True mental work gives nourishment to the inner spirit. Maria believed that children up to the age of six should be taught completely through the use of the senses. They could then easily learn abstract ideas and concepts. She practiced her methods on all types of children. News of her successful results spread throughout the world.

In 1909, Maria began lecturing and training teachers. It was her belief that only teachers trained by her personally could properly teach her methods. Her lectures were always crowded, and teachers returned again and again to learn about new and different methods and materials. Maria wrote many books on her methods, which she continuously revised and updated. She continued to train teachers and to set up Montessori schools all over the world until her death in Noordwijk, Holland, on May 6, 1952.

READ MORE ABOUT DR. MARIA MONTESSORI

- Kramer, *Maria Montessori: A Biography.* Putnam, 1976. (for older readers)
- Lillard, *Montessori: A Modern Method.* Schocken, 1971. (for older readers)
- Standing, *Montessori: Her Life and Work.* Hollis and Carter, 1957. (for older readers)

DISCOVERY ACTIVITIES

- Using reference sources, discover how Montessori schools are set up today and how Montessori teachers are trained today.
- If there is a Montessori School in your community, try to have a visit arranged for you. Compare the school with a school in your community.
- Dr. Maria Montessori believed that groups of children of various ages should work together. What is your opinion of this arrangement? Why?

Maria Montessori: Champion of Children's Rights

Dr. Maria Montessori believed that children under the age of six should be taught entirely through their senses. This is called sensory education.

DIRECTIONS Below are activities that might appear in a Montessori curriculum. Try the activities with a classmate. As you are both beyond the age of six, the partner doing the activity will need to be blindfolded for some of the activities.

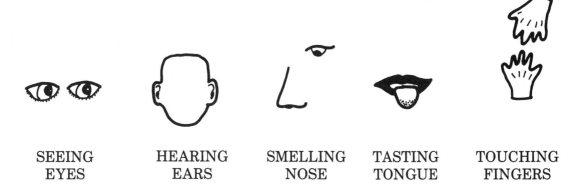

| SEEING EYES | HEARING EARS | SMELLING NOSE | TASTING TONGUE | TOUCHING FINGERS |

1. Gather six stones of various sizes. Blindfold your partner. Have your partner put them in a row according to size, from smallest to largest.
2. Collect a penny, a nickel, a dime, and a quarter. Blindfold your partner. Have your partner put them in a row according to size, smallest to largest.
3. Collect several different foods. Blindfold your partner. Have your partner identify the foods through the smell of each food.
4. Collect several different foods. Blindfold your partner. Have your partner identify the foods through tasting each food.
5. Collect several objects. Blindfold your partner. Have your partner identify the objects through touch and feel.
6. Tape-record sounds that interest you. Have your partner identify the sounds.
7. Obtain some plastic alphabet letters. Blindfold your partner. Have your partner identify the letters through touch and feel.
8. Think up more activities similar to these that involve the senses and try them out on your partner.

Meet Florence Nightingale: Mother of Nursing

Florence's friends loved teas, parties, and balls. Florence thought those things were a waste of time. She wanted to do something important with her life.

Florence Nightingale was born on May 12, 1820, in Florence, Italy, where her parents happened to be living at the time. She spent a happy childhood in England at her wealthy parents' country estates. When she played dolls, she pretended they were ill. She would bathe and bandage them and make them well. Florence grew into a beautiful and popular woman, but rejected all would-be suitors, much to the dismay of her mother. Florence wanted to be a nurse. Her mother and sister were horrified and refused to discuss the subject. Under the guise of traveling, Florence studied at a hospital in Germany. On her return, she became superintendent of a hospital for gentlewomen in London. When the Crimean War broke out, there were no facilities for the sick and wounded. More soldiers died of illness and infection than on the battlefield. At the request of the government, Florence and a band of nurses went to Turkey. She had to cope with male prejudice, filth, and a deplorable lack of supplies. Using tact and diplomacy, along with incredible energy, Florence established a routine of order, cleanliness, and efficiency, saving the lives of countless soldiers. After the war, Florence established a nursing school in London, marking the beginning of the professionally trained nurse. Florence wrote books on health and nursing and remained active until her death on August 13, 1910.

Florence was a pioneer and a guiding light in the field of nursing. Training schools based on her philosophy and principles were established throughout the world. Many of these were headed by graduates of Florence's school.

READ MORE ABOUT FLORENCE NIGHTINGALE

- Johnson, *The Value of Compassion: The Story of Florence Nightingale.* Oak Tree Publications, 1986.
- Shor, *Florence Nightingale.* Silver Burdett, 1987.
- Turner, *Florence Nightingale.* Franklin Watts, 1986.

DISCOVERY ACTIVITIES

- Why were Florence's mother and sister so opposed to even thinking about Florence's becoming a nurse?
- Using reference sources, discover the Crimean War. When, where, and why did this war occur?
- In 1907, Florence received the Order of Merit. Using reference sources, discover the founding, the purpose, and the recipients of this award.

Florence Nightingale: Mother of Nursing

Although Florence Nightingale is considered the most famous nurse of all time, other women have also made great contributions to the field of nursing and care of the peoples of the world.

DIRECTIONS   Below is a list of famous nurses. Choose three names from this list. Using reference sources, write a short report on the life of each.

Clara Barton

Mary Ann Bickerdyke

Mary Breckinridge

Edith Cavell

Genieve de Galard

Elizabeth Kenny

Rose Hawthorne Lathrop

Jeanne Mance

Janna Nienhuys

Sister Dulce Lopes Pontes

Princess Tsahai Haile Selasse

Meet Anwar el-Sadat: Negotiator for Peace

Anwar was a private man. Few people shared his thoughts. "I go it alone," he said. "My years in prison turned me into a very self-controlled, self-sufficient man."

Anwar el-Sadat was born in Mit-Abul-Kum, Egypt, on December 25, 1918. His parents were *fellahin,* or poor peasant, but managed to send him to school. Anwar's childhood heroes were Gandhi, leader of the Indian National Congress, and Ataturk, leader of the 1908 Turkish Revolution. Both men fought for freedom for their country. Anwar wanted to free Egypt from British rule.

Anwar graduated from the Egyptian Military Academy in 1938. Later he was court martialed for working against the British. He spent two years in prison. After World War II, Anwar worked with Gamel Abdel Nasser, leader of the Free Officers' Association, who was plotting to overthrow the British. On July 23, 1952, the Free Officers Association seized control of Egypt. Anwar was the spokesperson who announced the take-over to the world.

Nasser became president of Egypt in 1954. He named Anwar vice-president in 1969. After Nasser's death in 1970, Anwar was elected president of Egypt. He worked to end the long-standing, bitter conflict between Egypt and Israel. In 1978, Anwar and Israeli Prime Minister Begin met with President Carter at Camp David. They came to an agreement and the treaty known as the Camp David Accords was signed. Anwar and Begin shared the 1978 Nobel Peace Prize for this agreement. Arab leaders denounced the treaty and began terrorist acts to protest. On October 6, 1981, Anwar was assassinated in Cairo by Egyptian religious militants who were opposed to his policies.

Anwar worked hard to bring peace and stability to Egypt. He believed, "To have stability, a country must have peace. Peace opens the door to stability."

READ MORE ABOUT ANWAR EL-SADAT

- Carroll, *Anwar Sadat.* Franklin Watts, 1982.
- Sadat, *In Search of Identity: An Autobiography.* Harper and Row, 1978.
- Sullivan, *Sadat: The Man Who Changed Mid-East History.* Walker, 1981.

DISCOVERY ACTIVITIES

- Using reference sources, discover the Six-Day War between Egypt and Israel. How did Egypt retaliate?
- Using reference sources, discover the relationship between Israel and Egypt today.
- Using reference sources, discover the importance of the Suez Canal to Egypt and to the world.

Anwar el-Sadat: Negotiator for Peace

DIRECTIONS Egypt is a land of contrast between the ancient and the modern. Below is a list of words associated with ancient Egypt, modern Egypt, or both. Think about each word carefully. Place a check in the proper column.

	HISTORICAL	MODERN	BOTH
Aswan Dam			
Bazaars			
Camels			
Citadel			
Desert			
Hieroglyphics			
High-rise buildings			
Irrigation			
Lake Nasser			
Oasis			
Oil wells			
Pharaohs			
Pyramids			
Sphinxes			
Suez Canal			

Meet Levi Strauss: The King of Blue Jeans

Levi came to America in 1847 with his mother and two sisters. They came in the cheap, crowded hold of a ship, hoping for a better life.

Lob Strauss (whose name was changed to Levi) was born in Bavaria, Germany, on January 26, 1829. After the death of his father, the family joined Levi's two older brothers in New York City. Levi quickly adapted to American ways. He became a peddler, selling goods and hardware for his brothers. Levi enjoyed traveling, and his customers liked his friendly, honest personality. When gold was discovered at Sutter's Mill in 1849, Levi sailed to California to sell dry goods and hardware to the miners. He quickly sold everything but the rolls of canvas. He discovered that men's pants were scarce, so he began sewing canvas pants. Soon everyone wanted the waist-high overalls, which they called "Levi's pants." The canvas pants, although tough and durable, were uncomfortable. Levi switched to denim, which was cheap, strong, and soft, but white. He dyed the denim with blue indigo dye and produced the first blue jeans. The name "jeans" was adapted from the name Genoa, Italy, where the dye was made. A tailor, Jacob Davis, began adding rivets to pants pockets for strength. He took the idea to Levi. They became partners, patented the process, and added rivets to all their jeans. Levi named the company Levi Strauss & Company. Soon everybody was wearing Levi's. Levi continued expanding the company until his death on September 26, 1902.

Levi Strauss & Company has continued to grow. In addition to jeans, they make jackets, shirts, and other types of clothing. Today, Levi Strauss & Company is the largest clothing manufacturer in the world.

READ MORE ABOUT LEVI STRAUSS

- Dru, *The First Blue Jeans.* Contemporary Perspectives, 1978.
- *Small Inventions That Make a Big Difference.* National Geographic Society, 1984.
- Van Steenwyk, *Levi Strauss: The Blue Jeans Man.* Walker, 1988.

DISCOVERY ACTIVITIES

- Using reference sources, discover how the styles and fabrics of jeans have changed over the years.
- Levi made his first pants only for men. Who wears jeans today and where are they worn?
- Using reference sources, discover the logo or trademark for Levi's jeans. What is the meaning behind the logo or trademark?

Levi Strauss: The King of Blue Jeans

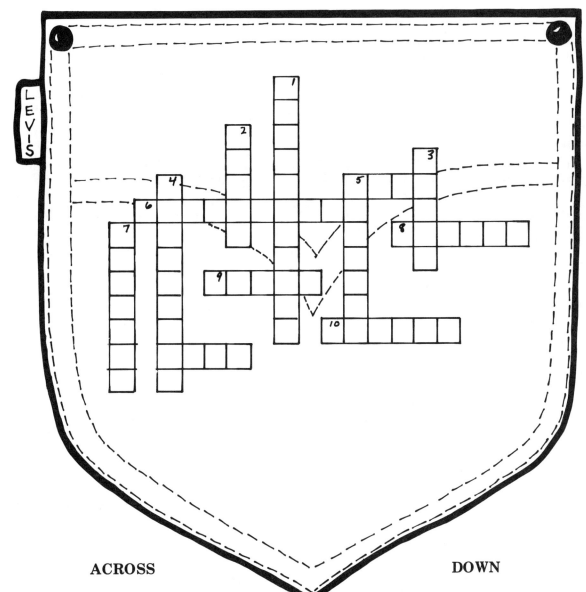

ACROSS

5. Levi dyed his pants ——.
6. Levi went to —— to sell dry goods and hardware.
8. To make the pockets stronger, Levi and Jacob added ——.
9. Today, Levi Strauss's pants are known as ——.
10. Levi made his first pants out of ——.
11. People rushed to California to search for ——.

DOWN

1. Gold was discoved in 1849 at ——.
2. Levi's first pants were —— and uncomfortable.
3. Levi changed the fabric of his pants to ——.
4. Levi's overalls were ——.
5. Levi Strauss was born in ——, Germany.
7. Levi's first job in America was that of a ——.

Meet Mother Teresa: Sister to Those in Need

Mother Teresa goes about her work calmly, totally committed to her belief. "I am called to love and to help each poor person."

Agnes Gonxha Bojaxhui was born August 26, 1910, in what is today Skopje, Yugoslavia. Growing up, she lived happily with family, friends, and the Church. In 1920, when her father died, her mother held the family together through deep faith in the Roman Catholic Church. Agnes Gonxha loved the Church and helping people. She joined the Sisters of Loreto. When she took her final vows in 1931, she chose the name Teresa. Mother Teresa believes she is to help those who no one else helps. She formed the Sodality of Mary. This small group helped the sick to die in peace and rescued abandoned children from the streets of Calcutta, India. In 1936, Mother Teresa left the Sisters of Loreto. She put on the white with blue stripe sari of the poor. She formed the Sisters of Charity, and the Missionary Brothers of Charity. In 1979, Mother Teresa won the Nobel Peace Prize.

Today, her group is called the Missionaries of Charity. The group numbers more than eight hundred and is still growing. They work all over the world. Each sister and brother lives a life dedicated to helping others. Each is committed to helping a fiery-eyed, outspoken, tiny woman with a good sense of humor, and an absolute belief in the road she has chosen to follow: to help the poorest of the poor, one by one.

READ MORE ABOUT MOTHER TERESA

- Giff, *Mother Teresa: Sister to the Poor.* Viking Kestral, 1986.
- Greene, *Mother Teresa: Friend of the Friendless.* Childrens Press, 1983.
- Leigh, *Mother Teresa.* Franklin Watts, 1986.

DISCOVERY ACTIVITIES

- Using reference sources, discover why Mother Teresa began her work in Calcutta, India.
- Mother Teresa has no source of income. Using reference sources, discover how Mother Teresa is able to obtain the funds needed to carry on her work.
- Using reference sources, discover how the Missionaries of Charity help people today.

Mother Teresa: Sister to Those in Need

Mother Teresa has dedicated her life to helping others. There are many ways that each person can help other people.

DIRECTIONS

1. Within the "helping hands" below, list the ways that you could help others at home and in school.
2. Choose two from each list and actually do them for a week. Helping others can become a good habit. Perhaps when the week is up you will wish to continue.

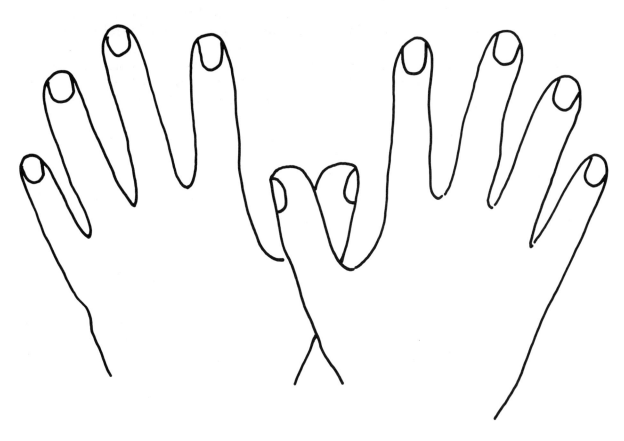

My "helping hands" will help others in the following ways:

At home   1. _____

              2. _____

At school   1. _____

              2. _____

Meet Margaret Thatcher: "Iron Lady" Prime Minister

When Margaret was nine, she won a poetry-reading contest at school. "You were lucky," her teacher said. "I wasn't lucky," Margaret replied. "I worked hard; I deserved to win."

Margaret Roberts Thatcher was born in Grantham, Lincolnshire, England, on October 13, 1925. She was fascinated by politics. She worked in her father's grocery store so she could listen to the men talk politics. She had a great ambition to be a political leader. After graduating from Oxford University, Margaret ran twice for Parliament as a member of the Conservative party. She was defeated both times. She married Denis Thatcher and began studying law. She passed the law exams two months before giving birth to twins.

In 1959, Margaret ran for Parliament again and won. Her sharp voice and stern manner reminded many of her colleagues of past school teachers. She was not very popular but earned respect by always being ready with the facts.

When the Conservative party gained control from the Labour party in 1970, Margaret was named Secretary of Education but the Labour party won the next election and Margaret lost that post. In 1975, when Edward Heath resigned, Margaret became leader of the Conservative party. She worked long and hard to prove a woman could handle the job. When the Conservatives won the election in 1979, Margaret, as leader of the party, became Britain's first woman prime minister. She remained Prime Minister for more than ten years, resigning in 1990. She is strong willed and has been called the "Iron Lady." Margaret does not think of herself as a woman politician but a politician who happens to be a woman. She believes she succeeded because she deserved to, as in the poetry-reading contest.

READ MORE ABOUT MARGARET THATCHER

- Faber, *Margaret Thatcher: Britain's "Iron Lady."* Viking Kestral, 1985.
- Garfinkel, *Margaret Thatcher.* Chelsea House, 1985.
- Harris, *Margaret Thatcher.* Little, Brown, 1988.

DISCOVERY ACTIVITIES

- Using reference sources, discover how often national elections are held in Britain. What are the names of the two major parties?
- A candidate for election in the United States must live in the district in which he or she is running. Using reference sources, discover if this is also true in Britain.
- Using reference sources, discover which countries are included in Great Britain.

Margaret Thatcher: "Iron Lady" Prime Minister

The British Isles are situated off the western coast of the European mainland. They consist of two large islands, Great Britain and Ireland, and thousands of smaller islands. Great Britain is divided into three parts, England, Scotland, and Wales. The United Kingdom is made up of these countries along with Northern Ireland.

DIRECTIONS Below is a map of the British Isles.
Color the countries that make up Great Britain red.
Color Northern Ireland red to make up the United Kingdom.
Color the Republic of Ireland blue.

Meet Bishop Desmond Tutu: The Conscience of His Nation

One day, young Desmond witnessed Father Trevor Huddleston, a white man, tip his hat to Desmond's mother, a black woman, as a natural courtesy to another person. Desmond never forgot that!

Desmond Mpilo Tutu was born in Klerksdorp, South Africa, on October 7, 1931. It was the custom to give children European and native names. Desmond was such a frail baby that he was given the name "Mpilo," meaning life. His parents were strict, but warm and loving. Desmond was serious about his studies. He loved learning and increasing his knowledge. He was also lively and fun loving, bubbling with good humor and laughter. Desmond studied to be a teacher, then became an Anglican priest. After serving many parishes, he served as Dean of Johannesburg. He became active in politics, attending meetings and speaking whenever and wherever possible for solutions to the racial conflicts splitting South Africa. He dedicated himself to "the struggle for the liberation of our beloved land, South Africa." When Desmond was elected the first black bishop of Johannesburg, he angered many by using the pulpit as a platform for political pressure. In 1986, Desmond was elected archbishop of Cape Town. He is an internationally renowned figure who has received many awards, including the Nobel Peace Prize in 1984. He travels constantly to work for peace for his homeland and throughout the world.

Apartheid still continues in South Africa. Bishop Tutu is aware of the dangers he faces daily but will not cease his work. "Freedom will come," he believes. "Because all of us, blacks and whites together, are made for freedom."

READ MORE ABOUT BISHOP DESMOND TUTU

- Bentley, *Archbishop Tutu of South Africa.* Enslow Publications, 1989.
- Davis, *Apartheid's Rebels: Inside South Africa's Hidden War.* Yale University Press, 1987.
- Wepman, *Desmond Tutu.* Franklin Watts, 1989.

DISCOVERY ACTIVITIES

- Using reference sources, discover the meaning of apartheid and how it affects South Africa.
- From the time Bishop Tutu became dean of Johannesburg, he could live where he wished. Why did he continue to live in Soweto?
- Bishop Tutu is quoted as saying, "Freedom will come. Because all of us, blacks and whites together, are made for freedom." In your opinion, what does the future hold for South Africa?

Bishop Desmond Tutu: The Conscience of His Nation

Bishop Tutu travels all over the world speaking for freedom for the black people of South Africa.

DIRECTIONS In your opinion, how can or how should the countries of the world help the black people of South Africa attain their freedom?

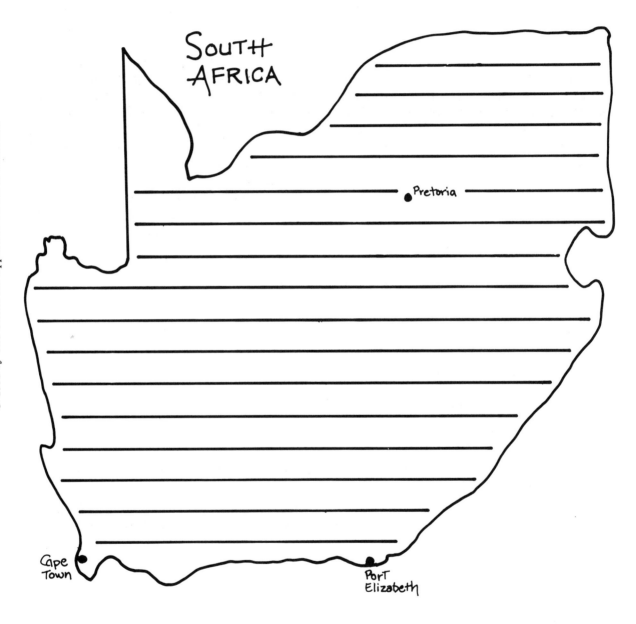

Answer Key

page 9, Benjamin Banneker: Self-Taught Genius

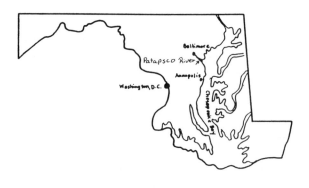

page 17, Amelia Earhart: The Pilot Who Disappeared

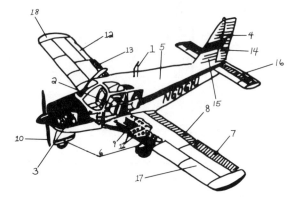

page 11, Clara Barton: "The Angel of the Battlefield"

- Train and certify life guards and life savers
- Train and certify instructors for swimming skills programs
- Provide swimming skills programs certifying swimmers from beginners through advanced swimmers
- Regulate swimming programs
- Train, certify, and provide instructors for programs in:
  - Personal swimming safety and self-rescue
  - Bathing places
  - Small aquatics craft operation
  - Elementary swimming and small craft rescue
  - Resuscitation
  - General water safety

page 23, Rebecca Gratz: Founder of the First Jewish Sunday School in America

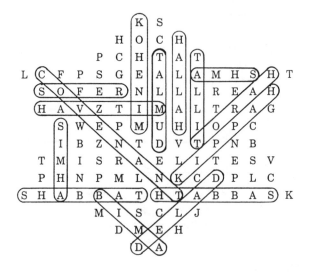

232

page 43, Alice Freeman Palmer: College President

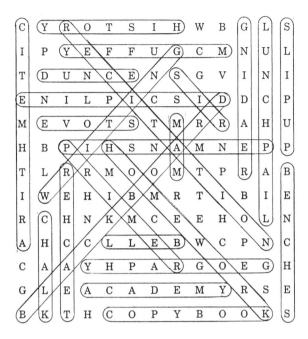

page 47, Frances Perkins: The First Madame Secretary

Secretary of State
Secretary of Treasury
Secretary of Defense
Attorney General
Secretary of Interior
Secretary of Agriculture
Secretary of Commerce
Secretary of Labor

Secretary of Health and Human Services
Secretary of Housing and Urban Development
Secretary of Transportation
Secretary of Energy
Secretary of Education

page 57, Harriet Tubman: A Woman Called "Moses"

Confederate States were: Alabama, Arkansas, Florida, Georgia, Louisiana, Mississippi, North Carolina, South Carolina, Tennessee, Texas, Virginia

Other states that had been admitted to the Union by 1861 were: California, Connecticut, Delaware, Illinois, Indiana, Iowa, Kansas, Kentucky, Maine, Maryland, Massachusetts, Michigan, Minnesota, Missouri, New Hampshire, New Jersey, New York, Ohio, Oregon, Pennsylvania, Rhode Island, Vermont. West Virginia had been part of Virginia until 1861, when Virginia seceded. West Virginia was admitted as a new state in 1863. The remaining areas on the map were territories.

You may wish to tell your students that some states, notably Kentucky, Missouri, and West Virginia, were represented by regiments in both sides of the conflict.

page 65, Marian Anderson: World-Renowned Contralto

- February 29, 1902–Marian Anderson was born.
- December 30, 1935–Marian debuted in New York City.
- April 9, 1939–Marian sang at the Lincoln Memorial.
- January 30, 1955–Marian sang with the Metropolitan Opera.

page 87, Johannes Gutenberg: The Father of Printing

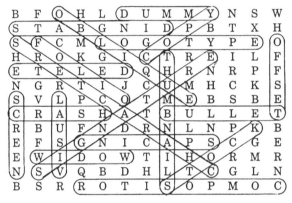

page 105, Maria Tallchief: First Internationally Recognized American Indian Ballerina

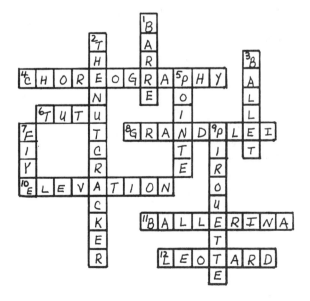

**page 113, Frederick Banting: The Mysterious
    Hormone X**

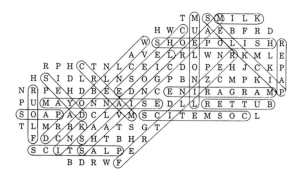

**page 121, George Washington Carver:
    Agricultural Scientist**

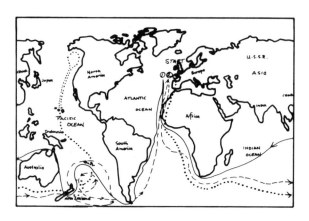

**page 122, Captain James Cook: Explorer of
    the Pacific Ocean**

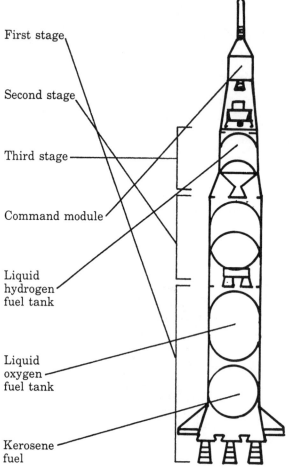

Key to Captain Cook map: solid line—first voyage;
dashed line—second voyage; dotted line—third voyage

page 135, Robert Goddard: Rocket Pioneer

First stage

Second stage

Third stage

Command module

Liquid
hydrogen
fuel tank

Liquid
oxygen
fuel tank

Kerosene
fuel

**page 137, Samuel F. B. Morse: Instant
    Communication**

WHAT HATH GOD WROUGHT

page 149, Eli Whitney: Mechanical Genius

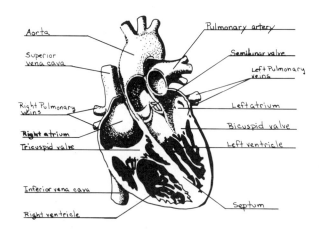

page 165, Rod Carew: A Dream and a Goal

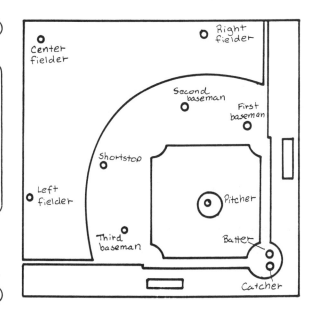

page 151, Daniel Hale Williams: Pioneer of Heart Surgery

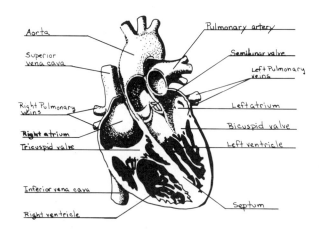

page 169, Mary Decker: Fast and Feminine

100-meter run

1928—Elizabeth Robinson
1936—Helen Stephens
1960—Wilma Rudolph

1968—Wyomia Tyus
1984—Evelyn Ashford
1988—Florence Griffith-Joyner

200-meter run

1960—Wilma Rudolph
1964—Edith McGuire
1984—Valerie Brisco-Hooks

1988—Florence Griffith-Joyner

400-meter run

1984—Valerie Brisco-Hooks

800-meter run

1968—Madeline Manning

page 173, Dorothy Hamill: World-Champion Figure Skater

1. A one-and-one-half revolution jump from forward outside edge of skate
2. A single rotation in the air
3. A spin on one foot with free leg in arched position
4. A jump with single rotation in the air, landing on same foot
5. A long glide to a jump with single rotation, landing on same foot
6. A jump from backward inside edge of skate with single rotation, landing on backward outside edge of skate
7. Forward glide on one leg, body parallel to ice, free leg extended
8. Glide on both feet, heels turned inward
9. Spin on one foot in sitting position, free leg extended
10. Jump from backward outside edge, single rotation, landing on backward outside edge

page 176, Jack Nicklaus: Golfer of the Century

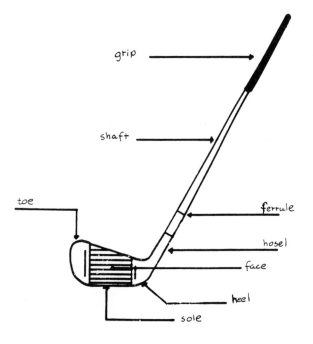

page 179, Bobby Orr: Spark Plug of the Bruins

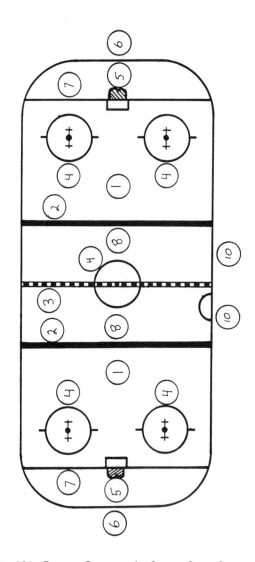

page 181, Jessee Owens: Ambassador of Sports

men

100 meter run	400 meter hurdles
200 meter run	high jump
400 meter run	long jump
800 meter run	400 meter relay
1,500 meter run	1,600 meter relay
3,000 meter steeple	pole vault
5,000 meter run	hammer throw
10,000 meter run	discus throw
marathon	triple jump
20 kilometer walk	16 lb. shotput
50 kilometer walk	javelin
110 meter hurdles	decathlon

women

100 meter run	100 meter hurdles
200 meter run	400 meter hurdles
400 meter run	10,000 meter hurdles
800 meter run	heptathlon
1,500 meter run	high jump
3,000 meter run	discus throw
10,000 meter run	javelin throw
400 meter relay	shotput
1,600 meter relay	long jump
80 meter hurdles	marathon

page 197, Corazon Aquino: The Hope of the Philippines

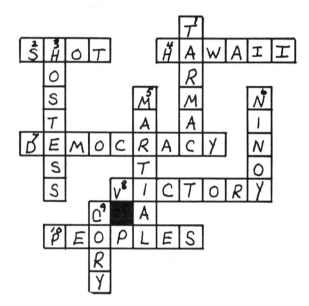

page 199, Robert Baden-Powell: World Scout

Scout Oath

On my honor, I will do my best to do my duty to God and my country, and to obey the Scout Law; to help other people at all times; to keep myself physically strong, mentally awake, and morally straight.

Scout Law

A scout is: trustworthy, loyal, helpful, friendly, courteous, kind, obedient, cheerful, thrifty, brave, clean, and reverent.

Scout Motto

Be prepared.

page 201, David Ben-Gurion: Mandate for Peace

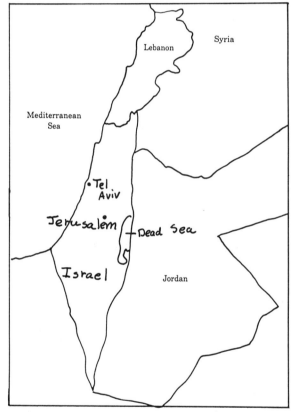

page 207, Indira Gandhi: Star of India

page 209, Mahatma Gandhi: "The Great Soul"

page 217, Golda Meir: Daughter of Israel

page 225, Levi Strauss: The King of Blue Jeans

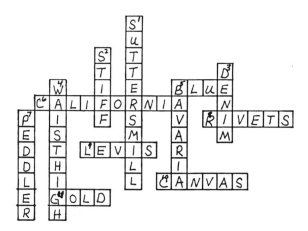

Alphabetical Index

A

Aaron, Henry, 156-157
Abdul-Jabbar, Kareem, 158-159
Adams, Abigail, 2-3
Addams, Jane, 4-5
Ali, Muhammad, 160-161
Anderson, Marian, 64-65
Anthony, Susan B., 6-7
Aquino, Corazon, 196-197
Audubon, John James, 66-67

B

Baden-Powell, Robert, 198-199
Banneker, Benjamin, 8-9
Banting, Frederick, 112-113
Barton, Clara, 10-11
Baryshnikov, Mikhail, 68-69
Bell, Alexander Graham, 114-115
Ben-Gurion, David, 200-201
Bernstein, Leonard, 70-71
Bethune, Mary McLeod, 12-13
Blackwell, Elizabeth, 202-203
Blume, Judy, 72-73
Braille, Louis, 116-117
Bryant, Paul "Bear," 162-163

C

Carew, Rod, 164-165
Carson, Rachel, 118-119
Carver, George Washington, 120-121
Catlin, George, 74-75
Chavez, Cesar, 14-15
Churchill, Winston, 204-205
Clemente, Roberto, 166-167
Cook, James, 122-123
Cosby, William Henry, Jr., 76-77
Cousteau, Jacques Yves, 124-125
Curie, Marie, 126-127

D

Decker, Mary, 168-169
Dickinson, Emily, 78-79
Disney, Walt, 80-81

E

Earhart, Amelia, 16-17
Edison, Thomas Alva, 128-129
Einstein, Albert, 130-131

F

Frank, Anne, 82-83
Franklin, Benjamin, 18-19
Freud, Sigmund, 132-133

G

Gallaudet, Thomas, 20-21
Gandhi, Indira, 206-207
Gandhi, Mahatma, 208-209
Geisel, Theodor Seuss, 84-85
Goddard, Robert, 134-135
Gratz, Rebecca, 22-23
Gutenberg, Johannes, 86-87
Guthrie, Janet, 170-171

H

Hamill, Dorothy, 172-173
Hammarskjöld, Dag, 210-211
Homer, Winslow, 88-89
Hughes, Langston, 90-91

J

Jordan, Barbara, 24-25

K

Kamekeha, Lydia, 26-27
Keller, Helen, 28-29
Kipling, Joseph Rudyard, 92-93
King, Billie Jean, 174-175
King, Martin Luther, Jr., 30-31
Kroc, Ray, 32-33

L

Lazarus, Emma, 94-95

Low, Juliette, 34–35
Lyon, Mary, 36–37

M

Mandela, Winnie, 212–213
Mann, Horace, 38–39
Mead, Margaret, 214–215
Meir, Golda, 216–217
Montessori, Maria, 218–219
Morse, Samuel F. B., 136–137
Moses, Anna Mary Robertson, 96–97
Muir, John, 138–139

N

Nicklaus, Jack, 176–177
Nightingale, Florence, 220–221
Nobel, Alfred, 140–141

O

O'Connor, Sandra Day, 40–41
O'Keeffe, Georgia, 98–99
Orr, Bobby, 178–179
Owens, Jesse, 180–181

P

Palmer, Alice Freeman, 42–43
Parks, Rosa, 44–45
Pasteur, Louis, 142–143
Pelé, 182–183
Perkins, Frances, 46–47

R

Retton, Mary Lou, 184–185
Ringling Brothers, 48–49

Robinson, Jackie, 186–187
Roosevelt, Eleanor, 50–51
Ruth, Babe, 188–189

S

Sacagawea, 144–145
el-Sadat, Anwar, 222–223
Schweitzer, Albert, 146–147
Sequoyah, 52–53
Spielberg, Steven, 100–101
Stevenson, Robert Louis, 102–103
Strauss, Levi, 224–225

T

Tallchief, Maria, 104–105
Teresa, Mother, 226–227
Thatcher, Margaret, 228–229
Thorpe, Jim, 190–191
Truth, Sojourner, 54–55
Tubman, Harriet, 56–57
Tutu, Bishop Desmond, 230–231

W

Washington, Booker T., 58–59
Webster, Noah, 60–61
Whitney, Eli, 148–149
Wilder, Laura Ingalls, 106–107
Williams, Daniel Hale, 150–151
Wright, Frank Lloyd, 108–109
Wright, Orville, 152–153
Wright, Wilbur, 152–153

Z

Zaharias, Mildred Didrikson, 192–193